N | **NAS**
R | **NAE**
C | **IOM**

National Academy Press

The National Academy Press was created by the National Academy of
Sciences to publish the reports issued by the Academy and by the
National Academy of Engineering, the Institute of Medicine, and the
National Research Council, all operating under the charter granted to
the National Academy of Sciences by the Congress of the United States.

Biographical Memoirs

NATIONAL ACADEMY OF SCIENCES

NATIONAL ACADEMY OF SCIENCES

OF THE UNITED STATES OF AMERICA

Biographical Memoirs

VOLUME 60

NATIONAL ACADEMY PRESS

WASHINGTON, D.C. 1991

The National Academy of Sciences was established in 1863 by Act of Congress as a private, nonprofit, self-governing membership corporation for the furtherance of science and technology, required to advise the federal government upon request within its fields of competence. Under its corporate charter the Academy established the National Research Council in 1916, the National Academy of Engineering in 1964, and the Institute of Medicine in 1970.

INTERNATIONAL STANDARD BOOK NUMBER 0-309-04442-1

LIBRARY OF CONGRESS CATALOG CARD NUMBER 5-26629

Available from

NATIONAL ACADEMY PRESS

2101 CONSTITUTION AVENUE, N.W.

WASHINGTON, D.C. 20418

PRINTED IN THE UNITED STATES OF AMERICA

CONTENTS

PREFACE

On March 3, 1863, Abraham Lincoln signed the Act of Incorporation that brought the National Academy of Sciences into being. In accordance with that original charter, the Academy is a private, honorary organization of scientists, elected for outstanding contributions to knowledge, who can be called upon to advise the federal government. As an institution the Academy's goal is to work toward increasing scientific knowledge and to further the use of that knowledge for the general good.

The *Biographical Memoirs,* begun in 1877, are a series of volumes containing the life histories and selected bibliographies of deceased members of the Academy. Colleagues familiar with the discipline and the subjects' work prepare the essays. These volumes, then, contain a record of the life and work of our most distinguished leaders in the sciences, as witnessed and interpreted by their colleagues and peers. They form a biographical history of science in America—an important part of our nation's contribution to the intellectual heritage of the world.

PETER H. RAVEN
Home Secretary

ELIZABETH J. SHERMAN
Editor

Biographical Memoirs

VOLUME 60

JOSEPH HALL BODINE

September 19, 1895–July 23, 1954

BY E. J. BOELL

JOSEPH HALL BODINE spent most of his scientific life investigating a single organism—the embryo of the grasshopper *Melanoplus differentialis,* and a single process or event—the diapause (or developmental block) that intervenes between two periods of active growth and development. His research work and publications, spanning the period from 1918 to 1953, have made notable contributions to the physiology and biochemistry of embryonic development.

EARLY LIFE

Joseph Bodine, son of Gilbert and Annie Hall Bodine, was born in Lake Hopatcong, New Jersey, on September 19, 1895. He died in Iowa City on July 23, 1954. Ironically, although he did not smoke and indeed disapproved of the habit, his death was due to lung cancer.

After preparing for college in the schools in Lake Hopatcong, Bodine entered the University of Pennsylvania. He was awarded the B.A. degree in 1915 and enrolled in the graduate school at the University of Pennsylvania immediately thereafter, but his work toward the Ph.D. degree was interrupted by his service in the American Expeditionary Forces. During World War I he served as a captain in the Medical Corps, and he did not receive his graduate degree until 1925.

3

In his last predoctoral year, Bodine held an appointment as instructor in zoology and, on receiving his degree, was advanced to assistant professor. His promotion to a full professorship occurred in 1928.

Bodine and Sarah Heimach were married in 1919 and had one son, Joseph Hall, Jr. After Sarah's death, Bodine married Eunice Beardsley in Iowa City.

DEPARTMENT OF ZOOLOGY, THE UNIVERSITY OF IOWA

In 1929, Bodine accepted an appointment as professor and chairman of the Department of Zoology at the State University of Iowa. He served in this position until his death. When he came to Iowa, the undergraduate curriculum in the Department of Zoology was oriented largely toward students intending to continue professional training in dentistry, medicine, or nursing. Graduate work in the Department, except for a vigorous program of teaching and research under the direction of Professor Emil Witschi, was also narrowly focused.

When Bodine accepted the chairmanship at Iowa he received a mandate from the University administration to infuse new life into the Department. What was more, he was given the fiscal support necessary to do so. Accordingly, with budgetary provisions for several new faculty positions over the next few years, appointments were made in protozoology, general physiology, genetics, parasitology, cytology, and embryology, greatly broadening and strengthening the teaching and research activities of the Department.

At about the same time, the Department of Zoology gathered under its wing a struggling biological laboratory on Lake Okoboji in northwest Iowa. With Bodine as director, the Iowa Lakeside Laboratory provided significant new opportunities for graduate teaching and research in the areas of aquatic biology, comparative physiology, and limnology for students at Iowa's Department of Zoology and from other institutions throughout the Midwest.

During Bodine's first years at Iowa, the nation was in the depths of the Depression that followed the 1929 stock market crash. Farm states in the Midwest were particularly hard hit, for this was the time of mortgage foreclosures and bank failures. Tax-supported universities suffered a great deal, for each year there was worry—and not without cause—that already low budgets would be further reduced. In 1930, graduate student teaching-and-research assistantships provided tuition and a stipend of fifty-seven dollars a month. In 1932 the stipend was cut to forty-five dollars. At that time, furthermore, there were no agencies like the National Science Foundation or the National Institutes of Health to supply funds in support of research and graduate fellowships. In spite of this, Bodine always managed to allocate a part of his Department's meager budget to support the research activities of the faculty and their students.

He was, however, a frugal man and insisted that his students construct the apparatus and equipment needed for research from laboratory odds and ends whenever possible, so that being a gadgeteer proved both an asset and a necessity. In 1934 Bodine received a substantial grant from the Rockefeller Foundation to support his research program. Though this ushered in an era of relative opulence, he used most of the funds to make additions to his research staff rather than for equipment, and the habit, developed during the Depression years, of "making what you need for your work" persisted. If, by then, being a gadgeteer was no longer a necessity, it was still an asset.

Melanoplus differentialis

The major part of Bodine's research (and, therefore, that of his students) was devoted to investigating the process of embryonic development within the egg of a grasshopper, *Melanoplus differentialis*. In his publications he emphasized the unique features that make the eggs of this grasshopper ideal for investigating a number of physiological and biochemical aspects of development. One of the most important is a developmental block, occurring naturally without experimental intervention, that interrupts the process of embryogenesis in the egg. This type of block is called "diapause" to differentiate it from the temporary suspensions of growth brought about by adverse environmental conditions.

In the temperate zone, *Melanoplus* females lay eggs throughout late spring and most of the summer. Within the eggs the embryos undergo development for approximately three weeks when diapause intervenes, and growth and differentiation are completely suspended for a prolonged period. In nature, eggs enter diapause in late summer or early fall and remain in the blocked state during the winter months. Thus in the grasshopper, diapause may serve as an intrinsic protective mechanism, insuring that—after an initial short period of growth and differentiation—development will not proceed again until environmental conditions have become favorable for the completion of the process and the survival of the newly hatched nymph.

Grasshopper eggs reared in the laboratory at a constant temperature of 25°C will develop for three weeks and then, even though developmental conditions remain favorable, will enter diapause just as they do in nature. Under such circumstances, the length of diapause in different batches of eggs varies from a number of weeks to several months, but at any time after its onset, diapause can be broken by subjecting the eggs for several weeks to temperatures between zero and 5°C. If the eggs are then returned to a temperature of 25°C, development is resumed and hatching occurs about two and a half weeks later.

Bodine showed that just before and during diapause, and

immediately after it is broken (either naturally or by subjecting eggs to low temperatures for an appropriate time), embryos are morphologically indistinguishable. Yet they have strikingly different physiological properties. Whereas the cells of embryos in diapause do not divide, mitotic activity in developing embryos can be observed both before and after diapause. Although the eggs consume oxygen and release carbon dioxide throughout development, these processes occur at greatly diminished rates during diapause. Finally, the respiratory inhibitor, potassium cyanide, has no effect on the oxygen consumption of eggs in diapause but will strongly depress the respiration of developing eggs.

The Diapause Factor Theory

From these data, Bodine developed the theory that, during early development in the egg, diapause is caused by the gradual synthesis of a diapause factor. At a certain stage this factor becomes operative, blocking further growth and differentiation and reducing metabolic activity. He further hypothesized that "a slow, gradual destruction or loss of potency of the diapause factor occurs at constant, high temperatures above developmental zero," and that "diapause factors are extremely sensitive to low temperatures (above developmental zero) and can be completely destroyed or inhibited by appropriate exposure to these temperatures." Because he was unable to determine the nature of the hypothetical diapause factor, how it is formed, and its mode of action, the theory has limited value in elucidating the nature of diapause. It does, however, provide a useful summary of grasshopper development.

Oxygen Consumption of Developing Eggs

Later work showed that the oxygen consumption of developing eggs exposed to a mixture of carbon monoxide and oxygen was reversibly depressed in proportion to the partial pressure of carbon monoxide. By contrast, the oxygen consumption of eggs in diapause was unaffected by carbon monoxide and under certain conditions was actually accelerated. The increased utilization of oxygen proved to be due to the ability of the embryonic cells to oxidize CO to CO_2—a property possessed also by the eggs of several other invertebrates and the tissues of various animals.

The depression of oxygen consumption in living cells by carbon monoxide is generally interpreted as due to the inhibition of an integrated system of respiratory enzymes collectively known as the cytochrome-cytochrome oxidase system. The failure of such agents as carbon monoxide and cyanide to depress respiration could mean that either the enzyme system is absent or that, if present, it is not functioning. Quantitative determinations of enzymatic activity and other experimental data point to the latter possibility. The enzyme system is present in diapause as well as in developing stages, but it functions only in the latter. The results thus indicate that during diapause the cytochrome-cytochrome oxidase system is thrown out of gear, so to speak. The enzymes that make up the system are present but not operative. How this occurs is not known, but it is clear that the decrease in the rate of respiration, characteristic of the diapause state, is a consequence rather than a cause of the developmental block.

Between 1934 and 1954, several generations of Bodine's students published the results of a series of quantitative assays of the activity of oxidative and other enzymes throughout development under the general title, *Enzymes in Ontogenesis*. Some of the earliest papers in the series indicated that the level of cytochrome oxidase activity (indophenol oxidase) of diapause embryos was identical to that of developing embryos of the same morphological stage. Only in developing embryos, however, was it evident that the enzyme functions in the process of cellular respiration. During development, owing to the synthesis of new enzyme, the activity of cyto-chrome oxidase increases. Since this process parallels the transformation of raw materials into the living substance of the embryo, it serves as an indirect measure of embryonic growth. Such enzymes as tyrosinase and cholinesterase, by contrast, reflect the functional differentiation of specific groups of cells or tissues, rather than growth of the embryo as a whole.

These studies, as Florence Moog put it, provided a great deal of information on enzymes as *objects* rather than *agents* of differentiation.

The eggs produced by some animals contain all of the raw materials required for the growth and maintenance of the developing embryos within them. The prime example is the avian egg, which contains within its shell and membranes not only the genetic blueprint and all of the organic and inor-ganic materials that become elaborated into cells, tissues, and organs of the new individual, but all of the required water as well. An egg of this type has been designated by Joseph Needham as "*cleidoic*" (closed box) to distinguish it from the type of egg that depends upon the environment for every-thing needed for development except organic materials.

In most respects the grasshopper egg may be regarded as *cleidoic*, though it depends upon the environment for much of the water required for development. In some of his earliest work, Bodine showed that the shell and membranes sur-rounding the grasshopper egg are permeable, the egg taking up water from the environment by osmotic forces and losing it through evaporation. But with the onset of diapause, water uptake ceases and does not begin again until after diapause has been broken.

In a series of experiments carried out over the course of several years, Eleanor Slifer, one of Bodine's graduate students at Pennsylvania and subsequently a research associate at the University of Iowa, found that water was taken up through only a restricted part of the total egg surface, the micropyle.[1] By covering the micropyles of eggs in which diapause had been broken with an impermeable coating, both water uptake and further development were prevented. In addition, Slifer found that the waxy layer was reduced during the course of diapause and that, when development had resumed after diapause, no trace of the waxy layer could be seen. Slifer then made the exciting discovery that by immersing eggs for a brief period in a fat solvent such as xylol, the waxy layer was dissolved and diapause broken.

This investigation has never been continued, but the available evidence points to the likelihood that diapause is induced by a mechanism—probably genetic in nature—preventing imbibition of water, and that diapause is broken by the destruction of the waxy barrier, thus permitting water uptake and the resumption of development.

HONORS AND SERVICE TO SCIENCE

At various times in his career Bodine served on a number of important local, state, and national committees: the University of Iowa School of Religion's Board of Control; Iowa Basic Science Board; National Research Council Fellowship Board; Atomic Energy Commission Fellowship Board; chairman, Scientific Advisory Committee, Cold Spring Harbor Biological Laboratory; and Executive Committee, Division of Biology and Agriculture, National Research Council. He was associate editor of the *Journal of Morphology* and, at the time

---

[1] E. H. Slifer, "Formation and Structure of a Special Water-Absorbing Area in the Membranes Covering the Grasshopper Egg," *Quarterly Journal of Microscopic Science* 80(1938):437; and "A Simplified Procedure for Breaking Diapause in Grasshopper Eggs," *Science* 107(1948):152.

of his death, was a member of the editorial board of *Physio-logical Zoology*.

Bodine was a member of various scientific societies in-cluding the Iowa Academy of Science, American Physiolog-ical Society, American Association of Zoologists (president, 1947), American Microscopical Society, and the Society for Experimental Biology and Medicine. He was a fellow of the American Association for the Advancement of Science and, from 1953, a member of the National Academy of Sciences.

Bodine's research activities covered a span of almost four decades during which the publications from his laboratory enriched the literature of both comparative physiology and developmental biology. As new insights and new techniques became available he returned to old subjects, tackling par-tially solved problems again and again. As the testimony of his publications shows, Bodine's scientific life could have served as the model for Sir Michael Foster's image of the growth of knowledge, which he likened to "the ascent of a spiral stair from which the observer periodically surveys the same landscape, but each time from a higher level than the last."[2]

I AM INDEBTED to Professor Harold W. Beams of the University of Iowa for providing some of the biographical data and other mate-rial included in this memoir.

[2] This quotation heads the chapter on nutrition in Meyer Bodansky's *Introduction to Physiological Chemistry*, 3rd ed. (New York: J. Wiley & Sons, 1934).

SELECTED BIBLIOGRAPHY

1923

Physiological changes during hibernation in certain Orthoptera. *J. Exp. Zool.* 37:457.

1929

Factors influencing the rate of respiratory metabolism of a developing egg. *Physiol. Zool.* 2:459.

1932

Hibernation and diapause in certain Orthoptera. III. Diapause—theory of its mechanism. *Physiol. Zool.* 5:549.

1933

The effect of hypertonic solutions on oxygen consumption of a developing egg. *Physiol. Zool.* 6:150.

1934

The effect of cyanide on the oxygen consumption of normal and blocked embryonic cells (Orthoptera). *J. Cell. Comp. Physiol.* 4:397.

With E. J. Boell. Action of carbon monoxide on respiration of normal and blocked embryonic cells (Orthoptera). *J. Cell. Comp. Physiol.* 4:475.

With E. J. Boell. Respiratory mechanisms of normally developing and blocked embryonic cells (Orthoptera). *J. Cell. Comp. Physiol.* 5:97.

1935

With E. J. Boell. Enzymes in ontogenesis (Orthoptera). I. Tyrosinase. *J. Cell. Comp. Physiol.* 6:263.

1936

With E. J. Boell. Enzymes in ontogenesis (Orthoptera). II. The indophenol oxidase. *J. Cell. Comp. Physiol.* 8:213.

With E. J. Boell. Respiration of embryo versus egg (Orthoptera). *J. Cell. Comp. Physiol.* 8:357.

1937

With T. H. Allen and E. J. Boell. Enzymes in ontogenesis (Orthoptera). III. Activation of naturally occurring enzymes (tyrosinase). *Proc. Soc. Exp. Biol. Med.* 37:450.

With E. J. Boell. The action of certain stimulating and inhibiting substances on the respiration of active and blocked eggs and isolated embryos. *Physiol. Zool.* 10:245.

1938

With T. H. Allen. Enzymes in ontogenesis (Orthoptera). IV. Natural and artificial conditions governing the action of tyrosinase. *J. Cell. Comp. Physiol.* 11:409.

With T. H. Allen. Enzymes in ontogenesis (Orthoptera). V. Further studies on the activation of the enzyme, tyrosinase. *J. Cell. Comp. Physiol.* 12:71.

With E. J. Boell and W. A. Robbie. A study of the mechanism of cyanide inhibition. I. Effect of concentration on the egg of *Melanoplus differentialis*. *Physiol. Zool.* 11:54.

1939

With T. H. Allen, L. D. Carlson, and O. M. Ray. Enzymes in ontogenesis (Orthoptera). VIII. Changes in the properties of the natural activator of protyrosinase during the course of embryonic development. *J. Cell. Comp. Physiol.* 14:173.

With T. H. Allen. Enzymes in orthopteran ontogenesis. IX. The influence of various solutes on the activity of tyrosinase. *J. Cell. Comp. Physiol.* 14:183.

1940

With T. H. Allen. Enzymes in ontogenesis (Orthoptera). XIII. Activation of protyrosinase in the oxidation of ascorbic acid. *J. Gen. Physiol.* 24:99.

1941

With T. H. Allen. Enzymes in ontogenesis (Orthoptera). XX. The site of origin and the distribution of protyrosinase in the developing egg of a grasshopper. *J. Exp. Zool.* 88:343.

1945

With D. L. Hill. The action of synthetic detergents on protyrosinase. *Arch. Biochem.* 7:21.

1947

With L. Fitzgerald. A spectrophotometric study of a developing egg (Orthoptera) with special reference to riboflavin and its derivatives. *J. Exp. Zool.* 104:353.

1948

The copper content of an egg and its distribution during the development of the embryo (Orthoptera). *J. Exp. Zool.* 109:187.

1950

With K. Lu. Oxygen uptake of intact embryos, their homogenates and intracellular constituents. *Physiol. Zool.* 23:301.

The action of sodium azide upon the oxygen uptake of mitotically active and blocked embryos. *J. Cell. Comp. Physiol.* 35:461.

1952

Succinic dehydrogenase in mitotically active and blocked embryonic cells. *Physiol. Zool.* 25:109.

ARTHUR CLAY COPE

June 27, 1909–June 4, 1966

BY JOHN D. ROBERTS AND JOHN C. SHEEHAN

ARTHUR CLAY COPE, an extraordinarily influential and imaginative organic chemist, was born on June 27, 1909, and died on June 4, 1966. He was the son of Everett Claire Cope and Jennie (Compton) Cope, who lived in Dunreith, Indiana, but later moved to Indianapolis to enhance their son's educational possibilities. Everett Cope was in the grain storage business and his wife worked for some time at the local YWCA office.

In 1929 Arthur received the bachelor's degree in chemistry from Butler University in Indianapolis, then, with the support of a teaching assistantship, moved to the University of Wisconsin for graduate work.

His thesis advisor at Wisconsin was S. M. McElvain, whose research program included the synthesis of organic compounds with possible pharmaceutical uses—especially local anesthetics and barbiturates. Cope's thesis work, completed in 1932, was along these lines. It led to the discovery of a useful local anesthetic and provided the major theme of his research for many years.

Cope clearly made a strong impression at Wisconsin during his graduate career. He completed his thesis work and three independent publications in three years and was recommended by the Wisconsin organic chemistry faculty (then

17

headed by the redoubtable Homer Adkins) for one of the highly sought-after National Research Council Fellowships at Harvard. In 1933, he moved to Harvard to work under one of the leading organic chemists of the day, E. P. Kohler.

At the end of his first year of graduate work Cope married intelligent, articulate, and forceful Bernice Mead Abbott, who had also attended Butler University and had met Cope as the teaching assistant in her freshman chemistry course. Bernice, known as "B," exerted a strong influence over his early career. The Harvard period was a productive one for Cope, and the papers he published on diverse subjects reflect a general Kohler influence.

BRYN MAWR (1934–1940)

In 1934, Cope accepted his first academic position, associate in chemistry at Bryn Mawr College. Bryn Mawr was to some degree isolated from the mainstream of organic research of the period, but Cope—looking for a position in the depth of the Great Depression—could hope to follow in the footsteps of the famous Louis Frederick Fieser, who had made it in one jump from Bryn Mawr to Harvard. Bryn Mawr, in any case, had a Ph.D. program, and Cope had many friends in the field with whom he kept in contact through attending meetings and symposia. After spending a summer at the University of Illinois as an assistant professor in 1935, he was promoted to the same position at Bryn Mawr and to associate professor in 1938.

While at Bryn Mawr, Cope spent some time trying to determine the structure of Grignard reagents by precipitation procedures. Comparable approaches had been tried by a number of highly competent organic chemists with little success. Realizing the intractability of this approach, he began to concentrate on the theme of his thesis work—the synthesis of substances with potential pharmaceutical interest.

For many, this would be pedestrian chemistry—using existing procedures to synthesize easy-to-prepare compounds. But Cope directed his attention to developing new synthetic reactions for substituted barbiturates and novel amino-alcohol local anesthetics.

Bryn Mawr supplied Cope with two outstanding graduate students: Evelyn Hancock and Elizabeth Hardy, who coauthored almost half the papers arising from his stay there. He also received substantial interest and support from the Sharpe and Dohme Laboratories in Philadelphia, where he eventually accepted a consultantship.

One result of Cope's Bryn Mawr period was the development of a commercial barbiturate known as Delvinyl Sodium. More important for organic chemistry as a whole was his discovery of a facile thermal rearrangement from one carbon to another in a three-carbon system of an allyl group. The well-known "Claisen allyl-ether rearrangement" involves an analogous shift of an allyl group, but the unique carbon-to-carbon feature—and the clarity with which Cope detailed the process—caused this kind of reaction to become generally known as the "Cope rearrangement." In recent years, variations on it have become extremely important, and thoroughly investigated, key steps in the synthesis of complex natural products.

In 1939, Cope's career was given a boost through his election as secretary of the Organic Division of the American Chemical Society. Though his wife, B, helped him, it was tedious and in many ways a thankless job. Nonetheless, through it he developed many contacts and friends.

In 1940–41, Cope received a Guggenheim Fellowship but was not able to visit Europe because of the war. He spent part of the year doing research at Bryn Mawr and the rest visiting organic chemistry research groups at universities throughout the United States.

In 1941 he moved to Columbia University as associate professor, and when World War II started, joined the Office of Scientific Research and Development as technical aide and section chief of Division 9 of the National Research Council. He was responsible for projects ranging from chemical warfare agents and insect repellents to antimalarial drugs and, in 1946, received the Certificate of Merit for his contributions to the war effort.

MASSACHUSETTS INSTITUTE OF TECHNOLOGY
(1945–1966)

Cope's stay at Columbia was relatively brief. The Massachusetts Institute of Technology had been an early leader in American chemistry but had become heavily inbred. It needed a fresh approach, particularly in organic chemistry, and Karl Compton, then president of MIT, followed the strong recommendation of the University of Illinois' Roger Adams and offered Arthur Cope the job. In 1945 he came to MIT to head the Department of Chemistry.

By that time Cope had an outstanding research record and in 1944 had received the coveted American Chemical Society Award in Pure Chemistry for his discovery of the "Cope rearrangement." He was elected to the National Academy of Sciences in 1947.

Although eager to continue on into new fields of research, he was thoroughly cognizant of the need to revitalize the department at MIT, world-class at that time only in physical chemistry. As head of the department, he had substantial powers, particularly in the area of new appointments, and some felt he used those powers ruthlessly.

When Cope later became president of the American Chemical Society, he was described as "mild-mannered"; "outwardly mild-mannered" would have been more accurate. He was easy to underestimate: of average height, long-faced, usually with a pallor bespeaking an indoor life (although he was an avid skier at one point and—with Adkins, Marvel, and a few others—participated in an annual muskellunge fishing expedition), he was outwardly courteous and almost effetely affable. Yet this even façade covered a strong and hot-blooded temperament. In meetings where things were not going his way, he tended to speak more softly and slump deeper into his chair, and those who knew him soon learned these danger signals. His graduate students called him the "iron fist in the velvet glove."

Cope was given strong support by the MIT administration during the early years. The teaching laboratories were completely rebuilt to a very high standard, and the research facilities for organic, inorganic, and analytical chemistry became as good as, or better than, any other in the world. Among the new professorial faculty in 1945–46 were Charles D. Coryell from Caltech via UCLA and Oak Ridge, John C. Sheehan from Michigan via Merck, John D. Roberts from UCLA via Harvard, Gardner C. Swain from Harvard via Caltech, David N. Hume from Minnesota via Kansas and Oak Ridge, Lockhart B. Rogers from Princeton via Stanford, Richard C. Lord from Johns Hopkins, and David Shoemaker from Caltech.

This influx of first-rank new professors produced almost inevitable and long-lasting strains for many of the pre-existing faculty in the MIT Chemistry Department. But— along with new facilities and Cope's untiring efforts to get research support and the highest quality of graduate students and postdoctoral fellows—the effect on the Department's research productivity was both immediate and awe-inspiring.

SCIENTIFIC WORK

Cyclooctatetraene

During his war work, Cope had encountered an intriguing intelligence report from Germany regarding the use of cyclooctatetraene to treat mustard-gas poisoning. In 1911, the German chemist Richard Willstätter had published an arduous, multistep synthesis for this highly interesting cyclic polyolefin derived from a rare alkaloid occurring in small amounts in the bark of the pomegranate tree. Though the structure of cyclooctatetraene was seemingly well-documented, the resemblance of one of its transformation products to a derivative of styrene, the well-known isomeric substance, brought it into question in later years.

With fragmentary reports trickling in from Germany on the extraordinary properties of cyclooctatetraene (which Walter Reppe's group had prepared in one step by the tetramerization of acetylene), Cope determined to repeat the Willstätter synthesis. Having very little pomegranate bark, he developed an efficient synthesis of the alkaloid it contains, then proceeded to substantiate Willstätter's synthesis in all respects. Extending the Reppe process with mixtures of substituted acetylenes, he also devised alternative syntheses of both cyclooctatetraene and its derivatives. This massive effort led Cope and his coworkers into studies of the chemistry of medium-sized ring compounds.

Transannular Hydrogen Migration and Valence Tautomerism

One hallmark of Cope's research was meticulousness born of an almost morbid fear that some erroneous experimental result would be published under his name. At least once, this fear cost him priority for an important scientific discovery.

Cope and his students detected a most unusual rearrangement reaction, wherein a hydrogen on one side of a cyclooctane ring migrated directly across the ring to the other side through a carbocationic intermediate. Because one of his physical-organic colleagues was skeptical of the evidence for the initial observation, Cope spent another year verifying every detail while others, having heard of the results, exploited them in related systems. Investigation of transannu-

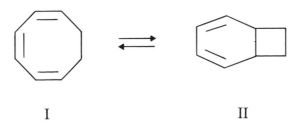

I   II

lar hydrogen migration, in fact, became an important theme in Cope's later research.

Much of Cope's work lapped over into physical organic chemistry, in which he repeatedly disavowed interest or competence while, at the same time, publishing perceptive observations that led to whole new areas of physical organic endeavor. One significant example is "valence tautomerism," where a compound isomerizes reversibly without intervention of external agents (except heat) by processes in which bonds are broken and made, usually simultaneously. What Cope and his coworkers discovered was the change of 1,3,5-cyclooctatriene (I) into bicyclo[4.2.0]-2,4-octadiene (II) at temperatures of 80–100°C.

Many chemists working intensively on processes of this type led eventually to the discovery and understanding of many other extraordinary examples. In 1981, R. Hoffmann received the Nobel Prize for the "Woodward-Hoffmann rules" predicting the ease and stereochemical consequences of such rearrangements. Valence tautomerism turned out to be a most important concept in understanding the chemistry of cyclooctatetraene and its derivatives.

Optical Isomers

One of the last important achievements of Cope's research program was his ingenious resolution of the optical isomers of *trans*-cyclooctene and *trans*-cyclononene. Using *trans*-cyclo-

III   IV

öctene as an example, there are two chiral forms (III and IV) that are nonidentical, mirror-image isomers. It turns out that if the cyclo̎octene double bond can turn over with its attached hydrogens through the loop of connected carbon atoms, then III will be converted into IV. The loop of carbons, however, is too tight for this to happen easily with III and IV. With the larger cyclononene ring, the interconversion is more easily possible, and the forms that correspond to III and IV are not very stable. With the still larger ring of *trans*-cyclodecene, interconversion is very easy and resolution extremely difficult, even at low temperatures. The possibility of stable chiral forms such as III and IV had been recognized long before, but it took imagination and enormous skill to demonstrate their existence.

SERVICE TO THE SCIENTIFIC COMMUNITY

After the war, Cope began to expand his service to chemistry on the national scene. In 1945, he was appointed to the editorial board of *Organic Syntheses*, a highly influential annual publication of tested laboratory procedures for the preparation of important organic compounds not yet available from commercial sources.

Through this group Cope became closely associated with Roger Adams, then the "Pope" of American organic chemistry. For many years head of chemistry at the University of Illinois and a consultant to the Du Pont Company, Adams had founded *Organic Syntheses*. He also had strong ties to the American Chemical Society, of which he would become president and chairman of the Board. In Cope, Adams recognized a comer, and Cope was in many ways Adams' successor. In 1947, Cope, also a consultant to Du Pont, joined the group that Adams had initiated to edit reviews in the influential series, *Organic Reactions*. He was the series' editor-in-chief from 1960 to 1966.

Cope served the American Chemical Society with great distinction. The posts he held after the war included chairman of the Division of Organic Chemistry (1946–1947); councillor (1950–1951); Northeastern Section chairman (1955–1956); Board of Directors (1951–1966); president-elect and president (1960–1961); chairman of the Board (1959–1960, 1962–1966); and a plethora of Board committees, including nine years on the important Committee on Professional Training.

Among other accomplishments as an American Chemical Society leader, Arthur Cope had much to do with averting collapse of *Chemical Abstracts* around 1960, a time when chemical abstracting services were failing. He served, in addition, as chairman of the National Academy of Sciences' Chemistry Section and was a member of the Academy's Committee on Science and Public Policy. A colleague described him during this period as the "busiest organic chemist in the world."

The cumulative strain of these widespread activities proved too much for Cope's marriage, and he and B (no children) were divorced in 1963. He later married Harriet Thomas Packard, née Osgood, who had been his secretary at MIT, and in the process acquired a stepson, Gregory.

Single-minded about the importance of chemistry education, Arthur Cope was not one to compromise his principles concerning thoroughness and breadth—principles only reinforced by his service on the ACS Committee on Professional Training. He resisted strongly MIT's decision to reduce the chemistry requirement in the undergraduate curriculum. This, along with a certain perception among the faculty that many of his decisions were arbitrary, led to the end of his almost twenty-year tenure as head of the Chemistry Department, but he remained active in research and in service to the American Chemical Society.

HONORS AND AWARDS

Arthur Cope received many honors and awards for his achievements in research. In addition to those already mentioned, he was elected to the American Academy of Arts and Sciences and the American Philosophical Society. He received the Chandler Medal of Columbia University, the W. H. Nichols Medal of the New York Section of the American Chemical Society, the Roger Adams Medal and Award of the American Chemical Society, and an honorary Sc.D. from his alma mater, Butler University.

With royalties from his pharmaceutical patents augmented by successful investments, Cope died a relatively wealthy man. He left half of his estate to the American Chemical Society to stimulate research in organic chemistry through the Cope Awards. The fund's current income of approximately $200,000 supports one major award and ten smaller Cope Scholar Awards. The principal Cope Award carries with it a medal, a substantial cash prize for the recipient, and a larger cash award in support of research at an institution of the recipient's choice.

The epitome of the workaholic, Arthur Cope was passionately and selflessly devoted to the public service of chemistry. In his own work, he was rigidly self-critical, adhering to the highest standards for scientific integrity. It is chemistry's tragic loss that he died suddenly at the age of fifty-six in Washington, D.C., where he had gone for American Chemical Society and National Academy of Sciences business. One could say of Arthur Cope what used to be said of Dodge automobiles—"They don't make 'em like that anymore."

WE WISH TO THANK Dr. Robert M. Joyce, Dr. Blaine C. McKusick, and Mrs. B. Abbott Cope, who provided valuable information and help with this memoir.

SELECTED BIBLIOGRAPHY[1]

1931

With S. M. McElvain. N-methyl-N-phenylalkyl-amino-alkyl benzoates and para-aminobenzoates. *J. Am. Chem. Soc.* 53:1587–94.

1932

The cleavage of disubstituted malonic esters by sodium ethoxide. *J. Am. Chem. Soc.* 54:4319–25.

1934

The mechanism of the reaction of dimethyl sulfate with arylmagnesium halides. *J. Am. Chem. Soc.* 56:1578–81.

1937

Condensation reactions. I. The condensation of ketones with cyanoacetic esters and the mechanism of the Knoevenagel reaction. *J. Am. Chem. Soc.* 59:2327–30.

1938

The precipitation of phenylmagnesium bromide by pyridine and by dioxane. *J. Am. Chem. Soc.* 60:2215–17.
With E. M. Hancock. The introduction of substituted vinyl groups. I. Isopropenyl alkyl malonic esters. *J. Am. Chem. Soc.* 60:2644–47.

1939

With E. M. Hancock. Substituted vinyl barbituric acids. I. Isopropenyl derivatives. *J. Am. Chem. Soc.* 61:96–98.

1940

With E. M. Hardy. The introduction of substituted vinyl groups. V. A rearrangement involving the migration of an allyl group in a three-carbon system. *J. Am. Chem. Soc.* 62:441–44.

---

[1] The twenty-five publications listed here were selected out of a total of 240, with a substantial degree of arbitrariness. Copies of the complete list of scientific publications by Arthur C. Cope are available in the NAS archives.

1941

With K. E. Hoyle and D. Heyl. The rearrangement of allyl groups in three-carbon systems. I. *J. Am. Chem. Soc.* 63:1843–52.

With C. M. Hoffman and E. M. Hardy. The rearrangement of allyl groups in three-carbon systems. II. *J. Am. Chem. Soc.* 63:1852–57.

1944

With E. M. Hancock. Benzoates, p-aminobenzoates and phenylurethans of 2-alkylaminoethanols. *J. Am. Chem. Soc.* 66:1448–53.

With R. Kleinschmidt. Rearrangement of allyl groups in dyad systems. Amine oxides. *J. Am. Chem. Soc.* 66:1929–33.

1948

With C. G. Overberger. Cyclic polyolefins. I. Synthesis of cyclooctatetraene from pseudopelletierine. *J. Am. Chem. Soc.* 70:1433–37.

With W. J. Bailey. Cyclic polyolefins. II. Synthesis of cyclooctatetraene from chloroprene. *J. Am. Chem. Soc.* 70:2305–9.

1950

With M. R. Kinter. Substituted cyclooctatetraenes. *J. Am. Chem. Soc.* 72:630–31.

1952

With M. Burg. Cyclic polyolefins. XIX. Chloro- and bromocyclooctatetraenes. *J. Am. Chem. Soc.* 74:168–72.

With A. C. Haven, Jr., F. L. Ramp, and E. R. Trumbull. Cyclic polyolefins. XXIII. Valence tautomerism of 1,3,5-cyclooctatriene and bicyclo[4.2.0]octa-2,4-diene. *J. Am. Chem. Soc.* 74:4867–71.

With S. W. Fenton and C. F. Spencer. Cyclic polyolefins. XXV. Cyclooctanediols. Molecular rearrangement of cyclooctene oxide on solvolysis. *J. Am. Chem. Soc.* 74:5884–88.

1957

With C. L. Baumgardner. Amine oxides. I. 1,4-pentadiene, 3-phenylpropene and 3-phenylcyclohexene by amine oxide pyrolysis. *J. Am. Chem. Soc.* 79:960–64.

With A. Fournier, Jr., and H. E. Simmons, Jr. Proximity effects. IX. Solvolysis of *trans*-cyclooctene oxide. *J. Am. Chem. Soc.* 79: 3905–9.

1960

With G. A. Berchtold, P. E. Peterson, and S. H. Sharman. Proximity effects. XXI. Establishment of 1,3- and 1,5-hydride shifts in the solvolysis of *cis*-cyclooctene oxide. *J. Am. Chem. Soc.* 82: 6366–69.

1963

With C. R. Ganellin, H. W. Johnson, Jr., T. V. Van Auken, and H. J. S. Winkler. Molecular asymmetry of olefins. I. Resolution of *trans*-cyclooctene. *J. Am. Chem. Soc.* 85:3276–79.

With D. M. Gale. Proximity effects. XXXVI. Solvolysis of deuterium-labeled cyclooctyl brosylate. *J. Am. Chem. Soc.* 85:3747–52.

1965

With K. Banholzer, H. Keller, B. A. Pauson, J. J. Whang and H. J. S. Winkler. Molecular asymmetry of olefins. III. Optical stability of *trans*-cyclononene and *trans*-cyclodecene. *J. Am. Chem. Soc.* 87:3644–49.

With B. A. Pauson. Molecular asymmetry of olefins. IV. Kinetics of racemization of (+ or −)-*trans*-cyclooctene. *J. Am. Chem. Soc.* 87:3649–51.

1966

With M. M. Martin and M. A. McKervey. Transannular reactions in medium-sized rings. *Q. Rev.* 20:119–52.

1968

With G. M. Whitesides and B. A. Pauson. Hindered rotation in substituted paracyclophenanes. *J. Am. Chem. Soc.* 90:639–44.

PHILIP JACKSON DARLINGTON, JR.

November 14, 1904–December 16, 1983

BY EDWARD O. WILSON

AMONG THE MOST ADMIRABLE of scientists are the naturalist explorers who return from arduous journeys to study their specimens, to reflect, and to build new theories of classification and evolution. Linnaeus, back from Lapland and Öland, was the eighteenth century exemplar. In the nineteenth century Darwin, Wallace, and Bates repeated the pattern on a more global scale. In our own time, Philip Jackson Darlington carried on the tradition. A tough explorer, he influenced the style and thinking of current field zoologists. An equally tough and original scientist, he transformed accepted wisdom regarding the way animals evolved and came to be distributed over the land.

EDUCATION AND EARLY LIFE

Like most major naturalists, Darlington grew up one. He was born in Philadelphia, Pennsylvania, on November 14, 1904, and spent most of his childhood in Hartford, Connecticut. With an inventive engineer for a father and a schoolteacher mother, his family environment was conducive to a life of the mind.

Everyone in his family was active in gardening and the study of local natural history, especially flowering plants and birds. Summers were spent at Penobscot Bay in Maine and

33

in various localities in New Hampshire, where Philip was able to collect and observe animals on a daily basis. Back in Hartford, he rode trolleys and bicycles to nearby natural environments to keep his hobby going. An Exeter physics teacher interested in natural history further influenced him, mentor and student often going out on field trips together. His housemaster once found snakes and turtles in his dresser drawer, and when Darlington graduated in 1922, his class yearbook appropriately designated him "a lover of the woods and fields."

As a teenager, Philip wanted to collect specimens for science but could not shoot birds because he was too young to obtain a gun license. He turned to beetles, saying, according to his brother Sidney, "No one cared if I collected bugs," and this became his ruling passion over the remainder of his life. (If beetles seem an odd choice for a future great zoologist, it should be remembered that Darwin's favorite group was also the Coleoptera.)

In 1922 Darlington entered Harvard College and took a wide range of courses in zoology and botany. He could hardly wait to get into the tropics (where the great bulk of insect diversity resides) and so postponed his graduate studies for a year to work for the United Fruit Company near Santa Marta, Colombia. Working extensively in the lowlands and in the surrounding mountains, he climbed up into the highest elevations nearby. Returning to Harvard in 1929, he brought with him a large collection of insects and vertebrates, including a surprising diversity of birds, and published his ornithological notes the following year.

Darlington completed his Ph.D. in 1931 with a thesis on the ground beetles (Carabidae) of New Hampshire. He then began an extraordinary series of field expeditions to Australia and the West Indies, bringing back to Harvard's Museum of Comparative Zoology massive collections of insects, reptiles, and other organisms, many of them new to science. Classifying the new beetles involved exacting techniques, such as counting the hairs on their eye margins and describing minutely the front foot of the male.

In 1940 he was appointed Fall Curator of Coleoptera at the Museum. Two years later he married Elizabeth Koch of Cambridge, who shared his love of natural history and accompanied him on many of his later excursions. (In 1956–57, the two of them and their son, Philip Frederick Darlington, spent eighteen months in the Australian wild living out of a truck.) In 1951 Darlington was appointed Curator of Insects and in 1962 Alexander Agassiz Professor of Zoology as well. He retired in 1971.

DARLINGTON IN THE FIELD

Darlington's collecting ability was legendary, as were his quiet toughness and determination in the field. Frank M. Carpenter, his colleague and friend of sixty years, recalled how, during an early field trip to the Smoky Mountains, Darlington insisted on sleeping under a tree at night and made an apple his breakfast and another his lunch so as not to waste time.

Before I departed on my own first tropical expedition to Cuba and Mexico in 1953, Darlington advised me that a good field biologist must be willing to endure discomfort. "Walk in a straight line across natural habitats," he told me. "It is a mistake to follow lazily along roads and trails, where you might miss some of the native fauna." And so he did himself, whether tracking through the forests of New Hampshire or proceeding directly up to the top of Pico Turquino, Cuba's highest mountain.

In 1933 he was one of the first to climb La Hotte, Haiti's highest and most hazardous mountain. Characteristically, he left his guides behind at 5,000 feet and cut and scrambled his way up the remaining 3,000 feet through unbroken forest. At the summit, however, he was disappointed to find the remains of a surveyor's camp; approaching from the other side, they had beaten him there by two years. But if not the first human being, he was at least the first biologist to reach the top, and on the slopes of La Hotte he collected many insects and other animals new to science, including a new genus of snakes, later named *Darlingtonia* in his honor.[1]

Shortly after Pearl Harbor, Darlington enlisted in the Army Sanitary Corps Malaria Survey as a first lieutenant. He served in the Sixth Army during the New Guinea, Bismarck Archipelago, Central Philippines, and Luzon Campaigns, retiring as a major in 1944. Before leaving New Guinea, he was able to collect great numbers of ground beetles and other insects in several regions of the country, including the Bismarck Range and even the summit of Mt. Wilhelm, the highest mountain in the range.

One Darlington exploit from that era became a standard of zoology lore. Alone in the jungle looking for specimens, he went out on a submerged log to sample water from the middle of a stagnant jungle pool, when a giant crocodile rose from the depths. As he edged back gingerly toward shore, he slipped into the water from the slimy log. The crocodile rushed him, mouth gaping, huge teeth bared. He tried to grasp its jaws, got one grip, then lost it.

"I can't describe the horror of that instant," he told reporters at the time, "but I was scared and I kept thinking: What a hell of a predicament for a naturalist to be in."

The thirty-nine-year-old Darlington was 6-foot 2-inches and 190 pounds; the crocodile several hundred pounds and in its element. It spun him over and over, finally carrying him to the bottom.

---

[1] This account of the La Hotte ascent is based on an unpublished manuscript by P. J. Darlington, "Through Rural Haiti," kindly provided me by Elizabeth Darlington.

"Those few seconds seemed hours," he said. "I kicked, but it was like trying to kick in a sea of molasses. My legs seemed heavy as lead and it was hard to force my muscles to respond." Whether because of a well-placed kick or some other reason, the animal suddenly opened its jaws and Darlington swam free. Despite torn arms, he made for the shore, scrambling frantically up the bank, since crocodiles sometimes pursue prey onto land. Slipping in the mud, he rolled back again into the ooze.

"It was a nightmare. That's the first time I've ever hollered for help," he said. "But there was no one to hear me." Finally reaching the jungle, he became aware of the pain in his arms and his weakness from loss of blood. "That hike to the hospital, which I knew was nearby, was the longest I've ever made." The muscles and ligaments of both arms were torn and the bones of his right arm were crushed, while the crocodile's teeth had pierced both his hands.

With characteristic understatement, Darlington wrote to his wife of "an episode with a crocodile" but supplied no further details.[2]

He was in a cast for several months, convalescing at Dobadura, Papua, where he perfected a left-handed technique for collecting insects: Have someone tie a vial to the end of a stick. Walk out into the forest, jam the stick into the ground, pull the cork out with the left hand, drop the specimens into the vial, replace the cork. He eventually regained full use of his hands and arms.

If a motion picture had been made of Darlington's life, Gary Cooper would have played him best. His direct, laconic approach to any problem was refreshing to all who knew him.

---

[2] The details of this encounter were reported by Sgt. Ward Walker, a Marine Corps combat correspondent, and distributed by the Associated Press. It appeared as "Harvard Scientist Fights Crocodile with Bare Hands," in the *Boston Globe*, evening edition, March 31, 1944; and "'Had Episode with Crocodile,' Wife Reads," in the same issue.

When Frank Carpenter was asked at Darlington's Harvard memorial service why Philip was so much fun to be with, he cited this quality and told the story—another old standby of zoology lore—of Darlington's debate during the late 1930s with Thomas Barbour, then director of the Museum of Comparative Zoology, regarding the long-distance dispersal of animals.

Barbour was an advocate of land bridges, while Darlington thought that animals might have been transported by winds for considerable distances before being dropped onto islands. Barbour doubted wind dispersal because he felt sure that larger animals, such as frogs, would be killed on striking the ground. To test his theory Darlington dropped several frogs from the fifth floor of the Museum to the grass below, where Barbour and a crowd of spectators were assembled. Carpenter recalls:

"As each frog landed . . . Dr. Barbour shouted to Philip, 'That one's dead!' When they had all been dropped, Philip called down to Dr. Barbour asking how they were, to which he replied, 'They're all dead.' But almost immediately the stunned frogs began to recover, and in a few minutes they began to hop about in all directions. I don't think that Dr. Barbour was convinced, but the discussions on the rear steps were on other subjects after that."[3]

CARABID BEETLES, MIMICRY, AND FLIGHTLESSNESS

The bulk of Darlington's research was on the systematics, distribution, and ecology of the carabid beetles, for which he was respected as one of the foremost insect taxonomists in the world. He went still further, using this expertise to make several contributions of general importance to biology.

In 1938 he published the results of a pioneering study he

[3] This account of the frog-falling experiment was published in the *Museum of Comparative Zoology Newsletter*, Harvard University, 13(Spring, 1984):4.

had conducted in Cuba on mimicry in beetles. This zoological classic describes how, when he modified the appearance of distasteful beetles and their mimics, both became acceptable to anole lizards that had previously rejected them. His experiment demonstrated the role of visual cues in mimicry and was the forerunner of many later studies that have brought us to our current firm understanding of the phenomenon.

From his thorough understanding of beetle distribution, Darlington successfully challenged Darwin's theory that flightlessness in island insects is due to winged forms being swept away by the wind. He did this partly by demonstrating that small, low oceanic islands, fully exposed to strong winds, have predominantly fully-winged faunas with very wide geographical ranges, whereas equally remote, high, forested islands tend to have a rich variety of flightless, endemic species. Darlington concluded that evolution proceeds by the arrival of winged carabids on mountainous islands, with subsequent specialization to the mountain habitats entailing reduction of dispersal ability and loss of wings.

THE ORIGIN OF DOMINANT VERTEBRATE GROUPS

Darlington's most important contribution to science was his theory of the Old World tropical origin of dominant vertebrate groups. He first sketched out this formulation—which would influence research in zoogeography for a generation—in *The Quarterly Review of Biology* of 1948, then presented it in full dress in his 1957 text, *Zoogeography: The Geographical Distribution of Animals.*

A theory of faunal dominance was first proposed by the American paleontologist William Diller Matthew in 1915. According to Matthew's scheme, new groups of vertebrates—such as the rhinoceros (Rhinocerotidae) and tapirs (Tapiridae)—had originated during the early Tertiary in the central

Eurasian-North American land mass. Hardened by the cold and fickle climate of the north, they became better fitted for competition and survival everywhere and accordingly spread south through the southern land masses and archipelagos, pushing out the previous inhabitants. Rhinos and tapirs, for example, gave way before the great herds of antelopes, bovids, and other artiodactyls that still prevail in both the northern and southern hemispheres.

Darlington realized, however, that Matthew had based his identification of the northern hemisphere as the key faunistic staging area on inadequate, and geographically biased, fossil data. Keeping Matthew's vision of dominance and cyclic replacement, he reconsidered the area of origin. With the aid of extensive new fossil evidence and close examination of the zoogeography of living cold-blooded vertebrates, he shifted the principal source area for dominant groups to the Old World tropics—more precisely, to central and northern Africa, southern Europe and the Middle East (tropical in climate during much of the Tertiary), and southern Asia.

Dominant terrestrial groups originated more frequently within this domain than elsewhere. Their species tended to spread to parts of the world that Darlington now conceived to be peripheral: across the Bering land bridge to North America, and thence to Central and South America; across the Indonesian archipelagos to Australia and the Pacific archipelagos; and straight north into temperate Asia and south into southern Africa.[4]

Since 1957 the demonstration of plate tectonics has complicated this picture greatly, requiring the superimposition of

[4] More detailed accounts of Darlington's research are given by W. L. Brown, "Philip Darlington's Contributions to Evolutionary Theory," in the memorial volume to Darlington edited by G. E. Ball, *Taxonomy, Phylogeny and Zoogeography of Beetles and Ants* (Dordrecht, Netherlands: W. Junk, 1985), pp. 11–16; and E. O. Wilson, "The Search for Faunal Dominance," ibid., pp. 489-93.

continental drift on theories of the distribution of terrestrial animal groups of Mesozoic (or earlier) origin. But the theory of Old World tropic dominance still holds, at least as a working model, for the many other groups of Tertiary origin.

IN CONCLUSION

Philip Darlington was a modest and reserved man with a strong sense of privacy. Though he did not seek fame or position, his contributions were widely recognized and honored. He was a Guggenheim fellow in 1947 and again in 1957, the year he also received the National Academy's Daniel Giraud Eliot Medal in zoology and paleontology. He was a fellow of the American Academy of Arts and Sciences and became a member of the National Academy of Sciences in 1964.

He allowed as little distraction from his family and science as he could manage. As his wife Elizabeth once put it, "Philip led an unfragmented life." The originality and independence of thought evident in all he did set high standards, both for the many who read his works and for the small group of entomologists and biogeographers privileged to work with him. In the tradition of Linnaeus and Darwin, he was a great naturalist.

SELECTED BIBLIOGRAPHY

1927

Auto-hemorrhage in *Tropidophis semi-cinctus*. *Bull. Antivenin Inst. Am.* 1:59.

1930

Notes on the senses of vultures. *Auk* 47:251–52.

1931

Notes on the birds of Rio Frio (near Santa Marta), Magdalena, Colombia. *Bull. Mus. Comp. Zool.* 71:349–421.

1933

A new tribe of Carabidae (Coleoptera) from western United States. *Pan-Pac. Entomol.* 9:110–14.

1934

Four new Bembidiini (Coleoptera: Carabidae) from Costa Rica and Colombia. *Occas. Pap. Boston Soc. Nat. Hist.* 8:157–62.

1936

The species of *Stenomorphus* (Coleoptera: Carabidae), with data on heterogony in *S. californicus* (Mén.). *Pan-Pac. Entomol.* 12:33–44.

Variation and atrophy of flying wings of some carabid beetles. *Ann. Entomol. Soc. Am.* 29:136–79.

A list of the West Indian Dryopidae (Coleoptera), with a new genus and eight new species, including one from Colombia. *Psyche* 43:65–83.

1938

The origin of the fauna of the Greater Antilles, with discussion of dispersal of animals over water and through the air. *Q. Rev. Biol.* 13:274–300.

Experiments on mimicry in Cuba, with suggestions for future study. *Trans. R. Entomol. Soc. London* 87:681–96.

1939

West Indian carabidae V: New forms from the Dominican Republic and Puerto Rico. *Mem. Soc. Cubana Hist. Nat. 'Felipe Poey'* 13:79–101.

1943

Carabidae of mountains and islands: Data on the evolution of isolated faunas and on atrophy of wings. *Ecol. Monogr.* 13:37–61.

1948

The geographical distribution of cold-blooded vertebrates. *Q. Rev. Biol.* 23:1–28, 105–23.

1950

Paussid beetles. *Trans. Am. Entomol. Soc.* 76:47–142.

1953

West Indian carabidae (IX): More about the Jamaican species. *Occas. Pap. Mus. Inst. Jamaica* 8:1–14.

1957

Zoogeography: The geographical distribution of animals. New York: John Wiley & Sons. 675 pp.

1959

The *Bembidion* and *Trechus* (Coleoptera, Carabidae) of the Malay Archipelago. *Pac. Insects* 1:331–45.

1960

The zoogeography of the southern cold temperate zone. *Proc. R. Soc. London* 152:659–68.

1964

Australian carabid beetles XIV: *Perigona. Psyche* 71:125–29.

1965

Biogeography of the southern end of the world: Distribution and history of far-southern life and land, with an assessment of continental drift. Cambridge: Harvard Univ. Press. 236 pp.

1969

Coleoptera: Carabidae, including Cicindelinae. *Insects Micronesia* 15:1–49.

1971

The carabid beetles of New Guinea, part IV: General considerations; analysis and history of fauna; taxonomic supplement. *Bull. Mus. Comp. Zool.* 142:129–337.

1980

Evolution for naturalists: The simple principles and complex reality. New York: John Wiley & Sons. 262 pp.

1983

Evolution: Questions for the modern theory. *Proc. Natl. Acad. Sci. USA* 80:1960–63.

JOHN FRANKLIN ENDERS

February 10, 1897–September 8, 1985

BY THOMAS H. WELLER
AND FREDERICK C. ROBBINS

THE INVESTIGATIVE CAREER of John Enders comprised three phases. For eight years he focused on pathogenic bacteria, in particular the pneumococcus. Switching in 1939 to the study of viruses, he refined tissue culture techniques for the study of viruses in vitro and made significant discoveries regarding mumps. This work prepared the way for the cultivation in 1949 of the polio viruses in non-nervous tissues, for which he was the corecipient of the 1954 Nobel Prize in Physiology or Medicine. Never one to rest on his laurels, Enders turned his focus to measles. This work led to the eventual production of a measles vaccine. By 1959, however, his research focus had shifted once again, this time to the problem of viral host-cell resistance and viral oncogenesis—the subject of the final segment of a magnificently productive investigative career.

EDUCATION AND EARLY CAREER

John Franklin Enders was born February 10, 1897, in West Hartford, Connecticut. His father headed the Hartford National Bank, and he was the first of four children in a family whose economic means were, as he once observed, "above average." Raised in a family whose business centered on finance and trade, he had little contact with science as a

47

boy. An uncle, a retired physician, who often visited the house, however, acquainted his nephew with certain aspects of science and medicine. The family also maintained contacts with luminaries in the field of literature, in particular handling the financial affairs of Mark Twain, whose spotless white suits impressed the young lad when the famous author visited.

Enders first attended the Noah Webster public grammar school in Hartford and in 1912 entered St. Paul's boarding school in Concord, New Hampshire, from which he graduated in 1915. Of the studies required, he wrote, "I preferred in the main certain of the so-called humanities—Latin, French, German, and English literature, although biological subjects always proved highly attractive. In mathematics and physics I encountered difficulties which were surmounted in a most mediocre fashion [and] only after great effort."[1]

In 1915, at the age of eighteen, he entered Yale University with no definite academic objectives. After two years there he enlisted in the Naval Reserve and learned to pilot aircraft. First as an ensign and then as a lieutenant, he served as a flight instructor at Pensacola, Florida, for three years. This experience influenced his mode of travel in later life which, if at all possible, was by train or boat—not by plane.

Free of economic pressures, Enders spent seven years after receiving his B.A. degree from Yale in 1920 seeking a suitable career. Starting with a real estate venture, he found business dull. He next considered a career as a teacher of English and moved from Yale to enroll in the Harvard Graduate School of Arts and Sciences. Receiving an M.A. degree in 1922, he spent the next three years exploring three different thesis topics in the field of philology, with little enthusiasm.

[1] Unpublished autobiographical note prepared in 1953 and now on file in the archives of the National Academy of Sciences.

MICROBIOLOGY AT HARVARD AND THE ZINSSER
INFLUENCE (1925–1946)

At this juncture Enders was living in a boarding house in Brookline, Massachusetts, where he shared lodgings with several young Harvard medical students and instructors. Among them was Dr. Hugh Ward, an instructor in Hans Zinsser's Department of Bacteriology and Immunology. "We soon became friends," Enders wrote, "and thus I fell into the habit of going to the laboratory with him in the evening and watching him work. I became increasingly fascinated by the subject—which manifestly gave him so much pleasure and about which he talked with such enthusiasm—and so eventually decided to change the direction of my studies."[2]

It was Ward who introduced Enders to microbiology and to Hans Zinsser, the magnetically attractive, charismatic man who was a major influence in determining John Enders's career. In 1927 he married Sarah Frances Bennett. That same notable year he began a doctoral program in bacteriology under Hans Zinsser at the Harvard Medical School—the move that initiated his illustrious scientific career. In 1930 he completed the requirements for the Ph.D. degree in biology under Zinsser, presenting as his doctoral thesis evidence that bacterial anaphylaxis and hypersensitivity of the tuberculin type are distinct phenomena.

In a memorial tribute to Zinsser, Enders wrote movingly of life in his department. During staff lunches the conversation, led by Zinsser, would become animated. "Literature, politics, history, and science—all he discussed with spontaneity and without self-consciousness. Everything was illuminated by an apt allusion drawn from the most diverse

[2] John F. Enders, "Personal recollections of Dr. Hugh Ward," *Austral. J. Exp. Biol.* 41:(1963):381–84.

sources, or by a witty tale. Voltaire seemed just around the corner, and Laurence Sterne upon the stair. . . . Under such influences, the laboratory became much more than a place just to work and teach; it became a way of life."[3]

In this congenial environment Enders slowly progressed up the academic ladder. He was an instructor from 1930 to 1935 and an assistant professor from 1935 to 1942.

Late in 1939, Dr. Alto E. Feller and Thomas H. Weller (then a senior medical student) undertook a research project under Enders cultivating vaccinia virus in roller cultures of chicken tissues. Even then Enders had developed characteristic and well established patterns in the laboratory. He would arrive in the middle of the morning carrying a simple lunch. His first priority was always to review any new observations. Although at the time he had no technician and only rarely participated actively in work at the bench, he delighted in looking at cultures and analyzing new data and knew exactly what was going on in his laboratory.

In those days, too, resources were limited and his entire research budget amounted to two hundred dollars a year. His junior associates spent much of their time, therefore, washing, plugging, and sterilizing glassware. Yet such menial tasks did not seem a chore, for as they worked Enders would lead wide-ranging discussions in the Zinsserian tradition—heady and stimulating interactions for a fourth-year medical student. (Parenthetically, the personal magnetism so evident in interactions with small groups was not evident when he lectured to large groups. Though he found them an unpleasant obligation, Enders always crafted his lectures to medical students with great care, then delivered them in a soft, uninflected, and almost apologetic tone.)

[3] "Hans Zinsser in the Laboratory: Address by John F. Enders at the Memorial Service for Hans Zinsser, Harvard Medical School, October 8, 1940," *Harvard Medical Alumni Bulletin* 15(1940):13–15.

BOSTON CHILDREN'S MEDICAL CENTER (1947–1972)

In 1940 Hans Zinsser died, initiating a difficult period for
Enders that was compounded by the unexpected death of his
wife, Sarah Frances, from acute myocarditis in 1943. From
1940 to 1942 he served as interim head of the Department
and in addition—with faculty departing during the war
years—augmented his own teaching duties. In 1942 he was
made associate professor and in 1943 his administrative duties, for which he had little liking, terminated with the appointment of his contemporary, Dr. J. Howard Mueller, as
permanent chairman of the Department.

Enders could then expand his own research on mumps,
and with additional funding from military sources, he was
able for the first time to employ a personal technician and a
succession of junior associates. Yet under Mueller, who began
work at six in the morning, the lifestyle of the Department
was not that of Enders.

In 1946 Dr. Charles A. Janeway and Dr. Sydney Farber
asked Enders to establish a laboratory for research on infectious diseases at the Boston Children's Hospital. He accepted
and in 1947 was allocated four rooms on the second floor of
the long-vacant Carnegie Building. Thus began his long and
productive association with the Children's Medical Center in
Boston, where, until 1972, he was chief of the Research Division of Infectious Diseases. Thereafter, though his contact
with Harvard Medical School was limited to one or two lectures a year, he was promoted to full professor in 1956 and
named University Professor in 1962—a title he held until
1967, when he became University Professor Emeritus.

Enders's unique personal magnetism in the laboratory
arose from the pleasure he took in discussions with his associates. Deeply interested in medical problems, he would
make astute observations regarding different diagnoses of a

puzzling case. He had a remarkable capacity to identify and exploit significant findings and, in a low-key manner, could stimulate junior associates to further productive endeavors.

Casual visitors viewed Enders as a quiet, somewhat reticent individual of great personal charm. Stoop-shouldered, he moved slowly about the laboratory, usually with a pipe in his mouth. He had a sly sense of humor and the occasional facetious remark was accompanied by a half-grin and a twinkle in his eyes. Though he lived comfortably his personal tastes were simple, and his frugality in the laboratory became legendary.

Most observers thought Enders impervious to honors, but his true intimates recognized a highly competitive spirit behind his humble façade. Once he had obtained fully convincing scientific data, therefore, there were no delays in publication.

As Enders's reputation spread his laboratory became increasingly attractive, and though the number of associates he accepted remained small, he was an influential force in the training of a generation of virologists. In 1967 when a symposium was arranged in honor of his seventieth birthday, more than a hundred associates and assistants from all over the world attended.

THE PRIVATE MAN

In 1951, eight years after the death of Enders's first wife, with whom he had two children—John Ostrom Enders II (deceased 1982) and Sarah Enders Steffian—he married Carolyn B. Keane. Known to a host of friends as "Carol," she proved a constant source of support, participating socially and scientifically in the subsequent events of her husband's life.

An autobiographical note written in 1953 lists carpentry,

photography, and gardening among Enders's avocations, but his major nonscientific interests were fishing and playing the piano.[4] The family spent summers in the Enders's compound at Waterford, Connecticut, from which they launched power-boat outings on Long Island Sound in search of striped bass. Enders himself made a pilgrimage each summer to his brother's fishing club in New Brunswick. If they were successful, salmon packed in ice would arrive at the laboratory.

Playing the piano was for the most part a private matter for Enders, and his interests ranged from Bach to Joplin. One exception, however, was the annual Christmas party he held at his home for his laboratory staff, and which regularly concluded with Enders at the piano, accompanying Christmas carols.

SCIENTIFIC CONTRIBUTIONS

Pathogenic Bacteria and the Pneumococcus (1929–1937)

During the first segment of Enders's long and prolific career he focused on pathogenic bacteria and, in particular, the pneumococcus. Throughout the thirties he published eighteen papers—both alone and with various collaborators—that demonstrated the relationship between virulence and the capacity of encapsulated Type III pneumococci to grow at elevated temperatures. He (and, concurrently, Oswald T. Avery and Walter F. Goebel) identified a new form of pneumococcal polysaccharide as an acetyl polysaccharide. He obtained evidence that serum complement expedited phagocytosis of pneumococci. His final paper of this period appeared in 1937 and recorded that inactive mixtures of pneumococci and homologous antisera regained virulence on dilution.

[4] Unpublished biographical note by Enders prepared in 1953.

Rickettsiae, Tissue Cultures, and Viruses (1937–1947)

The second phase of Enders's research—dealing with viruses—began in 1937 when he accepted the young epidemiologist, William McD. Hammon, as a doctoral degree candidate. When an epizoötic disease developed in their local stock of kittens, Hammon and Enders began an investigation. They published their findings in a series of papers describing malignant panleucopenia of cats, which established a viral etiology, and described procedures for the immunization of cats.

At the same time Enders was investigating the kinetics of inactivation of herpes simplex virus by specific antisera and with Dr. Morris F. Shaffer developed an indicator system using counts of foci on the chorio-allantoic membrane of the developing chick embryo.

As Zinsser's illness progressed, Enders also assumed responsibility for ongoing research on rickettsial diseases. Together with Zinsser and Harry Plotz he grew typhus rickettsiae in tissue culture in sufficient quantities to produce a vaccine. Resolving the laboratory problem posed by the lack of susceptible experimental animals, he, Dr. P. T. Liu, and Dr. John C. Snyder showed that European typhus rickettsiae produce a fatal infection in irradiated white mice.

During this period Enders utilized roller tissue cultures to propagate several viruses. With Dr. Feller and Thomas Weller he reported, in 1940, the prolonged growth of vaccinia virus, and with Dr. Harold E. Pearson in 1941, of influenza A virus. Enders and Dr. Alfred L. Florman then investigated the influence of antiserum and complement on the growth of vaccinia virus in roller cultures and the persistence of this virus in Maitland-type cultures. A leading proponent of cultural techniques in the study of viruses, Enders contributed the definitive chapter on the propagation of viruses and rickettsiae in tissue culture in the first (1948) edition of T. M. Rivers's classic *Viral and Rickettsial Infections of Man.*

Because mumps had been a major cause of days lost from duty in the armed forces during World War I, authorities in Washington at the beginning of World War II requested that Enders study the problem. Collaborating with Drs. Sydney Cohen and Lewis W. Kane, and with Mrs. Jeanette H. Levens, he began studying immunity in mumps.

At that time, although the viral etiology of mumps had been established using monkeys as the host, there were no diagnostic tests or techniques to assess susceptibility. Developing a complement fixation test that satisfied these deficiencies, Enders's group demonstrated that the intradermal injection of killed virus elicited a response in those previously infected. But their attempts to culture the virus and experiments directed at producing active or passive immunity proved less productive.

When, in 1945, Karl Habel reported the growth of mumps virus in embryonated hen's egg, Enders and Levens's confirmatory experiments showed the virus present in high titer in infected amniotic fluids, and that the infected fluids agglutinated erythrocytes. This meant that both infectivity and neutralizing antibody could be titrated.

In 1947 Enders's laboratory at the Children's Hospital became functional; Dr. Weller initiated virological studies; and in 1948 Dr. Frederick C. Robbins joined the group. Weller wanted to attempt growing varicella virus using cultures of human cells, but Enders suggested that he first try to develop a system to propagate a known agent: mumps virus. Slightly modifying the classical, Maitland-type culture, Weller maintained the tissue component for long periods by changing the nutrient fluids at three- to five-day intervals. In this way an egg-adapted strain of mumps virus was propagated in vitro for the first time and it was shown that viral replication could be assayed by hemagglutinins elaborated in vitro. Jeanette Levens, under Enders's direction, showed that Influenza A virus behaved in a similar fashion.

Poliomyelitis Virus (1948–1952)

In March 1948, Weller attempted to isolate varicella virus in a comparable system using human embryonic skin and muscle tissue as the tissue phase. A few unused cultures were inoculated with Lansing strain poliomyelitis virus. After twenty days in culture and three changes of medium, intracerebral inoculation of the fluids into mice resulted in paralysis of all inoculated. Serial passage in vitro was readily accomplished. At Enders's suggestion, Robbins—who was interested in using tissue cultures to identify a viral etiology of infantile diarrhea—used cultures of intestinal tissue obtained at the autopsy of a premature human infant and obtained similar results.

The potential significance of these observations was such that the laboratory directed its subsequent principal efforts to the study of poliomyelitis. First it was determined that Type I poliomyelitis virus could be similarly cultivated and supported in vitro by completely differentiated, nonnervous tissue (human foreskin). It was also noted early that the polio viruses, when propagated in cultures, induced degenerative changes in the cells in which they grew. The virus could be detected, therefore, by both metabolic and morphologic changes—a phenomenon Enders termed the "cytopathic effect."

Armed with these observations the researchers were able to assay virus in vitro and assess the neutralizing capacity of antisera. Thus a tissue culture could replace the experimental animal—usually a monkey. In June 1949 Robbins used the culture system successfully to isolate polio viruses from patients and a number of nonpolio enteroviruses from clinical cases of nonparalytic "polio." In the meantime Weller, concentrating on long-term propagation of the polio viruses, managed to obtain attenuated strains exhibiting decreased virulence. Dr. Arne Svedmyr and Ann Holloway, Enders's assistant, developed a complement fixation test for polio-myelitis using concentrated infected culture fluids as antigen.

In the decade following the war, Enders's spectacularly successful poliomyelitis team disbanded. In May 1952 Robbins left to accept a chair in pediatrics at Western Reserve University, while Weller departed in June 1954 to chair the Department of Tropical Public Health at Harvard.

The Measles Vaccine (1954–1960)

Though poliomyelitis was the primary focus of the re-search effort in Enders's laboratory between 1948 and 1952, the researchers also explored other illnesses of possible viral etiology. In 1950 Weller and Enders collaborated with Ms. M. Buckingham and Dr. J. J. Finn in a study that demonstrated that a Coxsackie virus was the etiologic agent of epidemic pleurodynia. With Dr. Franklin A. Neva, Enders described viruses isolated from patients with an unusual exanthema-tous illness—agents later classified as Echo 16 virus.

The measles segment of Enders's research began in 1954 when he suggested that Dr. Thomas C. Peebles, a research fellow, attempt to isolate the agent of this disease. In roller cultures of human kidney cells inoculated with acute-phase throat washings or blood from cases of rubeola, they ob-served unique changes with syncytial giant-cell formation. Se-rial passage was accomplished in cultures of human or mon-key kidney cells. This cytopathogenicity was neutralized by convalescent-phase measles sera. The researchers found a complement-fixing measles antigen in harvested culture fluids.

With Peebles and Dr. Kevin McCarthy, a research fellow

from Liverpool, Enders explained the irregular results achieved by earlier investigators attempting to infect monkeys. Monkeys held for a period in captivity often showed serologic evidence of a prior spontaneous infection, but monkeys first proven seronegative who were inoculated with measles virus inevitably developed the disease.

In collaboration with Drs. Milan V. Milovanovic and Anna Mitus, Enders showed that cultures of human amnion cells supported growth of measles virus and that the virus could be propagated in chick embryos. Working with Dr. Samuel L. Katz, he showed that the egg-adapted virus could be grown in cultures of chicken cells. By 1958 Enders, Katz, and Dr. Donald N. Medearis had sound evidence that a strain thus propagated became attenuated and that monkeys inoculated with the attenuated strain produced an antibody response with no viremia or recognizable disease.

Enders immediately turned all the resources of his laboratory to the task of developing a measles vaccine based on the attenuated, avianized strain, and the results of their labors were published in a series of papers in the *New England Journal of Medicine*'s July 28, 1960 issue. Three significant papers derived from the work of Enders's laboratory. Parallel clinical trials were carried out in Denver, New Haven, Cleveland, and New York. The combined findings involved 303 vaccinated children. A mild, modified infection resulted from these vaccinations. The vaccine virus did not spread, and protection was induced. This classic group of papers provided the basis for studies that led to the licensing of the measles vaccine in 1963 in the United States.

About this time, Kevin McCarthy recovered measles virus from the lungs of a patient diagnosed as having Hecht's giant-cell pneumonia, and it was shown that the measles virus was the etiologic agent. Enders—in collaborative studies with Anna Mitus, Dr. William Cheatham, and others—recovered rubeola virus from two other fatal cases of giant-cell pneumonia that had not exhibited clinical evidence of measles. The researchers subsequently observed that the rubeola virus persisted in the respiratory tracts of children with leukemia who had had measles to produce a giant-cell pneumonitis. They also obtained evidence that, in children with leukemia, measles vaccine might induce a chronic giant-cell pneumonia.

Though his cultivation of poliomyelitis viruses garnered Enders, Weller, and Robbins the 1954 Nobel Prize, Enders later wrote that this work on measles was more personally satisfying to him and more socially significant.

Virus and Host Cell: Interferon and Viral Oncogenesis (1959–1976)

By 1959 Enders's group had once again shifted the focus of their investigations, first to problems of viral host-cell resistance, then to viral oncogenesis—the subject of the final segment of Enders's investigative career.

Dr. Monto Ho observed that viral inhibitory substances were present in cultures infected with an avian-adapted Type II polio virus, substances later recognized as "interferon," as described by A. Issacs and J. Lindenmann in 1957. Enders, with Dr. Edward DeMaeyer, demonstrated that interferon was present in cultures infected with rubeola virus. He and Dr. Ion Gresser then showed that Sindbis virus also induced the production of interferon and that primary and established cultures of human amnion cells differed in their ability to produce interferon.

Although simian vacuolating viruses (SV_{40}) had been found in polio vaccines before Dr. Harvey M. Shein and Enders's 1962 report (*Proc. Soc. Exp. Biol. Med.* 109:495–500), evidence that SV_{40} would multiply in cultures of human cells was inconclusive. Enders obtained viral multiplication in cultures of several human tissues with both cell degeneration and apparent stimulation of cell proliferation occurring. In three related papers Enders described the appearance of chromosomal abnormalities in transformed cells and showed that immunofluorescence demonstrated persistent virus in some transformed cells. Hamster renal cells transformed by SV_{40}, furthermore, produced adenocarcinomatous tumors when introduced into the cheek pouch of hamsters. Enders and Dr. Albert Sabin then showed that cells so transformed exhibited new, specific, SV_{40}-tumor complement-fixing antigens.

Continuing these SV_{40} studies, Dr. George Diamandopoulos and Enders found that—in contrast to earlier results—an apparent *absence* of the viral genome in the transformed cells was associated with an increased oncogenic potential when hamster lung and liver cells were exposed to SV_{40}. Cultured transformed hamster cells, when X-irradiated or exposed to colchicine—showed polynucleate giant-cell formation.

Enders and his associates next examined the thesis that cellular resistance to viral infection in vitro might reflect a barrier at the cell surface. With Dr. John M. Neff he showed that, though naturally resistant, cultures of hamster and chick embryo cells would support growth of the poliovirus if they were fused in the presence of Sendai virus killed by irradiation or beta-propriolactone.

The relationships binding virus and host cell were explored with Dr. George Miller (1969). Using human placental cells as a feeder layer, the two had established continuous cell lines of human leukocytes, which they co-cultivated with X-irradiated cells of an EBV-infected line of leukocytes.

At the age of eighty Enders retired from laboratory work but continued to follow the literature avidly. Ever clear-minded, he enjoyed discussions with scientific visitors to his home to the end—as he had throughout the fifty years in his laboratory. On the evening of September 8, 1985, John Enders died quietly at his summer home in Waterford, Connecticut, as he sat reading T. S. Eliot aloud to his wife and daughter.

MATERIAL FOR THIS MEMOIR derived from several sources, including our personal files and autobiographical summaries prepared by Dr. Enders, one of which, a short summary prepared in 1953, is now on file in the Academy archives. Mrs. Carolyn Enders kindly provided additional material and access to bound volumes of Dr. Enders's publications.

MAJOR AWARDS AND DISTINCTIONS

1953 Election to National Academy of Sciences
1953 Passano Award
1954 Lasker Award
1954 Nobel Prize in Physiology or Medicine
1955 Charles V. Chapin Medal
1955 Gordon Wilson Medal
1961 *TIME* Man of the Year
1962 Robert Koch Médaille, Germany
1963 Presidential Medal of Freedom, United States
1967 Foreign Member, Royal Society of London
1981 Galen Medal of the Worshipful Society of Apothecaries, London.

Honorary doctoral degrees from thirteen universities.

SELECTED BIBLIOGRAPHY

1929

Anaphylactic shock with the partial antigen of the tubercle bacillus. *J. Exp. Med.* 50:777–86.

1933

With Hugh K. Ward. An analysis of the opsonic and tropic action of normal and immune sera based on experiments with the pneumococcus. *J. Exp. Med.* 57:527–47.

1935

With Arnold Branch. The immunization of guinea pigs with heat-killed and formol-killed tubercle bacilli. *Ann. Tuberc.* 32:595–600.

1939

With William McD. Hammon. A virus disease of cats, principally characterized by aleucocytosis, enteric lesions, and the presence of intranuclear inclusion bodies. *J. Exp. Med.* 69:327–52.
With Morris F. Shaffer. Quantitative studies on the infectivity of the virus of herpes simplex for the chorio-allantoic membrane of the chick embryo, together with observations on the inactivation of the virus by its specific antiserum. *J. Immunol.* 37:383–411.
With H. Zinsser and L. D. Fothergill. *Immunity. Principles and application in medicine and public health.* New York: Macmillan Co. 801 pp.

1940

With William McD. Hammon. Active and passive immunization against the virus of malignant panleucopenia of cats. *Proc. Soc. Exp. Biol. Med.* 43:194–200.
With A. E. Feller and T. H. Weller. The prolonged coexistence of vaccinia virus in high titre and living cells in roller tube cultures of chick embryonic tissues. *J. Exp. Med.* 72:367–88.

1945

A summary of studies on immunity in mumps. *Trans. Stud. Coll. Physicians Philadelphia* 13:23–36.

With J. H. Levens. The hemoagglutinative properties of amniotic fluids from embryonated eggs infected with mumps virus. *Science* 102:117–20.

1949

With T. H. Weller and F. C. Robbins. Cultivation of the Lansing strain of poliomyelitis virus in cultures of various human embryonic tissues. *Science* 109:85–87.

1950

With F. C. Robbins and T. H. Weller. Cytopathogenic effect of poliomyelitis viruses in vitro on human embryonic tissues. *Proc. Soc. Exp. Biol. Med.* 75:370–74.

1951

With F. C. Robbins, T. H. Weller, and G. L. Florentino. Studies on the cultivation of poliomyelitis viruses in tissue culture. V. The direct isolation and serologic identification of virus strains in tissue culture from patients with nonparalytic and paralytic poliomyelitis. *Am. J. Hyg.* 54:286–93.

1954

With T. C. Peebles. Propagation in tissue culture of cytopathogenic agents from patients with measles. *Proc. Soc. Exp. Biol. Med.* 86:277–86.

1957

With M. V. Milovanovic and A. Mitus. Cultivation of measles virus in human amnion cells and in the developing chick embryo. *Proc. Soc. Exp. Biol. Med.* 95:120–27.

1959

With S. L. Katz. Immunization of children with a live attenuated measles vaccine. *Am. J. Dis. Child.* 98:605.
With A. Mitus, J. M. Craig, and A. Holloway. Persistence of measles virus and depression of antibody formation in patients with giant-cell pneumonia after measles. *N. Engl. J. Med.* 261: 882–89.

1960

John F. Enders, S. L. Katz, et al. Studies on an attenuated measles-virus vaccine. VIII. General summary and evaluation of results of vaccination. *N. Engl. J. Med.* 263:180–84.

1962

With H. M. Shein. Multiplication and cytopathogenicity of simian vacuolating virus 40 in cultures of human tissues. *Proc. Soc. Exp. Biol. Med.* 109:495–500.

1965

Cell transformation by viruses as illustrated by the response of human and hamster renal cells to simian virus 40. *Harvey Lect.* 59:113–53.

John F. Enders, P. D. DeLay, et al. Clinical and immune response of alien hosts to inoculation with measles, rinderpest, and canine distemper virus. *Am. J. Vet. Res.* 26:1359–73.

With G. Th. Diamandopoulos. Studies on transformation of Syrian hamster cells by simian virus 40 (SV_{40}). Acquisition of oncogenicity by virus-exposed cells apparently unassociated with the viral genome. *Proc. Natl. Acad. Sci. USA* 54:1092–99.

1968

With J. M. Neff. Further observations on replication of Type I poliovirus in naturally resistant fused cell cultures. In: *Perspectives in virology*, ed. M. Pollard, vol. 6, pp. 39–53. New York: Academic Press.

1969

John F. Enders, M. J. Levin, et al. Virus-specific nucleic acids in SV_{40}-exposed hamster embryo cell lines: Correlation with S and T antigens. *Proc. Natl. Acad. Sci. USA* 62:589–96.

1970

John F. Enders, A. S. Levine, et al. Virus-specific deoxyribonucleic acid in simian virus 40 exposed cells: Correlation with S and T antigens. *J. Virol.* 6:199–207.

Edward C. Franklin

EDWARD CURTIS FRANKLIN

March 1, 1862–February 13, 1937

BY HOWARD M. ELSEY[1]

EDWARD CURTIS FRANKLIN, president of the American Chemical Society in 1923, was born on March 1, 1862 in Geary City, Kansas. He died at Stanford University on February 13, 1937, having become in the intervening seventy-five years one of America's most honored and best-loved scientists.

LOVE OF NATURE

As a boy Franklin was definitely not a scholar, though it is understandable that, when contrasted with the attractions to be found outdoors, the primitive educational facilities of frontier schools held but little appeal. Until 1854 Kansas had been in the hands of the Indians, so that the country Franklin grew up in was not yet spoiled by ruthless civilization. His brief autobiographical sketch—describing his boyhood pleasures of hunting, fishing, swimming in the Missouri (even then noted for being muddy), collecting fossils from the River's limestone banks, and the seemingly infinite variety of

---

[1] An earlier version of this article appeared in the *Journal of the American Chemical Society* 71(1949):1–5. The portrait of Edward Curtis Franklin that appears as this memoir's frontispiece was painted in 1928 by Rem Remsen, son of the noted chemist, Ira Remsen. It is reproduced here from a photograph furnished to the Academy by Franklin's daughter, Mrs. Anna Franklin Barnett, in 1937.

nuts, fruits, and berries for use and wildflowers to be admired—conveys something of his eagerness to avail himself
of his surroundings.

His delight in the beauties of the outdoor world, and particularly of the mountains, stayed with Franklin throughout
his life. As a youth he roamed the hills along the Missouri;
as a young man he climbed the mountains of Colorado and,
during a year as a student in Germany, he crossed the Alps
on foot. He was active in the Stanford Sierra Club until well
into his fifties, having by then climbed five peaks of over
fourteen thousand feet and many only slightly lower. Sight-
ing Kiliminjaro for the first time when he was sixty-seven and
attending a meeting as the guest of the British Association
for the Advancement of Science, he deeply regretted not
being able to climb the great peak that, even at a distance of
thirty or forty miles, towered majestically some nineteen
thousand feet above the clouds. In his later days, Franklin
climbed mountains by automobile; in 1933 he drove to the
fourteen-thousand-foot summit of Mount Evans.

In the last few years of his life Franklin managed to see
again most of the scenic wonders of our land. In 1936 he
drove to Kansas "by way of the Hoover Dam, Zion Canyon,
Bryce Canyon, the North Rim of the Grand Canyon, Albu-
querque, Santa Fe, and Boulder, Colorado," and thence on a
"wild tour of thirteen thousand miles, lecturing before
groups of defenseless chemists through the Middle West to
Philadelphia and Washington, and thence south to Florida
and home by way of the southern route." To Franklin, the
longest road was always the best if it offered even a slight
promise of more interesting views, new or old.

From 1914 to 1918 when I had the privilege of working
with him, it was always Franklin who first succumbed to
spring or fall fever and proposed that we play hookey on a
Saturday afternoon, running away on our bicycles into the

Stanford hills. We sought dove, quail, squirrels, and the ducks that could be hunted from a "sneak-boat" on nearby San Francisco Bay. Though we usually returned empty-handed, these too brief, back-to-nature jaunts were treasures that always ended with a vigorous and enthusiastic attack on the laboratory problem we had so rudely abandoned.

EDUCATION AND EARLY LIFE

In 1877, when Franklin was fifteen, he was sent away to a small sectarian college where he found himself both physically and spiritually starved. It was still possible fifty years later to find schools in that region whose dining hall rations might have kept a canary alive, but certainly not singing. Even as a youth, furthermore, Franklin was inclined to be a "free thinker" and agnostic. It is easy to understand that a man who, throughout his life, was blunt and honest could not be content in a rigid, fundamentalist environment. After two months, he ran away.

From 1880 to 1884 Franklin was a pharmacist's assistant in Severance, Kansas, where he also ran a small-job printing shop and played a cornet in the village band. In the fall of 1884, he visited his younger brother at the University of Kansas with no thought of making a new start on his own education. But once on campus, the congenial surroundings aroused his interest; then aged twenty-two, he decided to enroll as a special student in chemistry. He did odd jobs around the chemical laboratory during his first three undergraduate years and as a senior acted as an assistant in qualitative and quantitative analysis.

UNIVERSITY OF KANSAS (1888–1903)

Franklin apparently showed promise as a teacher, for he was retained on the faculty as an assistant in chemistry from 1888 to 1893, and as an associate professor from 1893 to

1899. He became professor of physical chemistry in 1899, which position he held until 1903. He was, however, still restless and footloose and felt uncertain about his future. Thus we find him from 1890 to 1891 as a student in Germany, and from 1893 to 1895 at Johns Hopkins, where he took his doctorate. These excursions might be regarded as part of an orderly preparation for a university career if one did not know that much of the year abroad was spent sight-seeing rather than in serious study, or had Franklin not taken leave again in 1896 for a one-year visit to Costa Rica to work as chemist and co-manager of a gold mine and mill.

The fact is (as he himself recorded), Franklin was still uncertain as to his fitness for the teaching profession. But there was no such doubt in the minds of his students. As E. E. Slosson, a Kansas alumnus, so succinctly put it, "all of his former students are his friends, and that is more than can be said of most teachers."

Others have written that Franklin relied little on books as a means of gaining knowledge, a conclusion not warranted by the evidence. For though, in the 1890s, two small cases in the department office contained the entire Kansas University chemistry library and the number of scientific journals received by the university as a whole was very small, each journal was watched for impatiently and devoured eagerly upon its arrival.

Barely finished reading of the discovery of argon, Franklin was already making plans to check the separation; the samples of both argon and helium he prepared were probably the first in America. The same could be said of his Dewar vessels and the X-ray tube he made for the use of Professor Blake of the Physics Department. Franklin needed the written word for information, but it was not sufficient for him. He had to do experiments and make equipment with his own hands; he had to see results with his own eyes.

Proud of his glass-blowing skill, Franklin prepared a considerable number of argon- and helium-containing Plücker tubes and sent them to friends and acquaintances in various universities. He was most satisfied to find, on his arrival at Stanford years later, his gifts to that school stored along with other valued items in an exhibit case on prominent display.

The diligence with which he trained himself in the laboratory arts, the eagerness with which he followed the chemical literature, and the pleasure he took in repeating for himself experiments that had led to the outstanding discoveries of the day show how diverse were Franklin's interests in the material world. By the 1890s, the sights and experiences within the walls of a laboratory had become fully as appealing to him as the outdoor attractions of his youth, for throughout his life, Franklin—like Kipling's elephant child of the *Just So Stories*—was filled with the most insatiable curiosity about all things around him.

Repeating others' work, while instructive and satisfying, did nothing to spark Franklin's creative gifts. That spark came rather from one of his students, H. P. Cady. In the autumn of 1896, Franklin records, he was teaching Cady (then an undergraduate) quantitative analysis:

"Observing after a time that the young man was becoming bored with his task . . . [Franklin], at the time giving instruction in analytical chemistry, proposed to him that he prepare several of the cobalt-ammine salts and confirm the composition of one or two of them by analysis. Some days later, with a beautifully crystallized specimen of one of these interesting salts in his hand, Cady stated that the ammonia in these and other salts containing ammonia must function in a manner very similar to that of water in salts with water of crystallization. He suggested furthermore that liquid ammonia would probably be found to resemble water in its physical and chemical properties. As a direct consequence of Cady's suggestion has followed all the work done in this country on liquid ammonia."

Franklin promptly ordered a cylinder of liquid ammonia, prepared the Dewar vessels, and obtained other apparatus needed for Cady's proposed study of ammonia as an electrolytic solvent. But the ammonia was slow in arriving and, before the experiments were started, he left for Costa Rica. On his return he learned that Cady had found many salts that dissolve in ammonia to form conducting solutions, even though the pure solvent further resembles water in being practically a nonconductor.

These results, obtained with simple apparatus designed and built with his own hands, aroused Franklin's research instincts for the first time. Ceasing to view research reported in the literature as a source of experiments to copy, he began instead to regard it as a source for devising new experiments he and his co-workers could conduct.

The years 1897 to 1903 were richly fruitful for the new research team, which was soon enlarged by the addition of C. A. Kraus, weaned from the Physics Department. There seemed to be no limits to the work Franklin's aroused imagination devised. Typical titles of papers from this productive period are: "Liquid ammonia as a solvent," "Determination of the molecular rise of the boiling point of liquid ammonia," "Metathetic reactions between certain salts in liquid ammonia," "Electrical conductivity of liquid ammonia solutions," and "Concentration cells in liquid ammonia."

But in the fall of 1903, this team of productive researchers, each outstanding in his own way, broke up. Kraus left for the Massachusetts Institute of Technology, Franklin went west to Stanford, and Cady remained at Kansas, where he would pass his entire professional career.

Franklin's evaluation of his two junior partners is of interest.

He said many times that Kraus was the most skilled glassblower and practitioner of all the laboratory arts whom he had ever known. I dare to question the first part of this opnion; Kraus might equal, but certainly could not surpass Franklin himself as an artist and artisan in the designing and working of the old German soft glass. Chemists of today who are accustomed to placing a piece of cold Pyrex tubing directly into the flame of an oxygen-gas blast lamp can have no appreciation of the difficulty of constructing the intricate cells used in the Franklin team's ammonia work. It required the patience of Job and the manipulative skills of a master, and these Franklin had. Kraus's later research record speaks for itself—an outstanding pupil graduated into an outstanding and productive research professor.

Franklin rated Cady his most brilliant student and co-worker, an evaluation I believe to be fair, though Cady's most productive and active research years were those spent under Franklin's stimulating guidance.

STANFORD YEARS (1903–1937)

In 1903 Franklin left Kansas for Stanford University to fill the chair of organic chemistry left vacant by Professor Richardson's death. Stanford was a rich school in those pre-earthquake days, and David Starr Jordan was adding outstanding research men (whenever he could find them) to his faculty.

For Franklin the change proved a happy one. Several Kansas friends had preceded him in this western journey, and one—Vernon Kellogg—was instrumental in persuading him to accept the Stanford offer. The university lay in a beautiful setting. Rolling foothills that began at the edge of the campus soon merged into the coastal mountains. Beyond these, only twenty miles from the university, lay the Pacific Ocean. While the Coast Ranges are comparatively low, the higher, much more rugged and scenic Sierras are only a hundred miles to the east. We can be sure that to Franklin, not the least of the attractions of this western wonderland were the mountains he loved so well.

While Franklin's work at Kansas had been spectacular because of its greater emphasis on physical-chemical measurements, the purely chemical work he did at Stanford was much the more important. To quote Alexander Findlay:

"From their earlier experiments . . . Franklin and his collaborators were led to an exhaustive examination of the parallelism between the chemical behavior of derivatives of ammonia dissolved in liquid ammonia and the behavior of derivatives of water, 'aquo-compounds' as Franklin called them, in aqueous solution. The investigation of the behavior of the former class of compounds, the 'ammono compounds' to use Franklin's nomenclature, constitutes the chief and most characteristic contribution of Franklin to chemistry."

The record of this contribution is embodied in his monograph, *The nitrogen system of compounds* (1935,1). His detailed classification of the organic compounds of nitrogen as belonging to the ammonia system make this book a classic and a most stimulating guide to further investigations.

Franklin wrote slowly and painstakingly; this monograph was rewritten many times and was over ten years in preparation. He also produced some eighty-seven papers, the step-by-step account of his forty years of research, though—due to his generosity toward his collaborators—less than half of these bear his name.

Franklin was a great experimentalist, and the few fortunate enough to have been accepted by him as collaborators insist he was also without peer as a teacher of graduate students. Every one of these men acquired a skill in laboratory technique far above the average; each learned to think independently, and, in addition, to view his own experimental results with that critical skepticism that is the true measure of a scientist.

Though Franklin never acquired the smooth and polished delivery characteristic of Julius Stieglitz, his lectures in organic chemistry were models of clear and orderly thinking. His experimental interests and belief in teaching by example made his lectures—illustrated by many elaborate and skillfully done demonstrations—unusually instructive.

He had an infinite capacity for making lifelong friends of all ages, from babes-in-arms to emeritus professors. He tailored the elaborate demonstrations in his Christmas lectures, which (like Faraday) he enjoyed giving to the children of his friends and colleagues, to fit the occasion and the audience. (I dare say that many a middle-aged matron of today[2] has in her jewel box a glass ring with a "red" stone made by Dr. Franklin just for her during one of these lectures.) To the end of his days he was a welcome and honored guest in the home of every former student and associate in this and other lands. He delighted in talking of his own work and pleasures and equally enjoyed listening to the exploits of others.

From the beginning of his professional career until the year of his death, he attended the meetings of the American Chemical Society and, of all the honors he received, valued his election to the presidency of that society the most.

His wife, Effie Scott Franklin, who was a student at Kansas at the time of their marriage in 1897, died in 1931. The older of two sons, Charles Scott Franklin, was killed in an airplane accident in 1928. Worthy of their parents, the two surviving children are: Dr. Anna Franklin Barnett, a happy wife, mother, and practicing physician; and John Curtis Franklin, an electrical engineer who [as of 1949 was] manager of Oak Ridge Directed Operations for the Atomic Energy Commission.

---

[2] Dr. Elsey was writing in 1949.

SELECTED BIBLIOGRAPHY

1894

With E. H. S. Bailey. Chemical examination of the waters of the Kaw river. *Kan. Univ. Q.* 3:1.

1898

On the decomposition of diazo compounds. *Am. Chem. J.* 20:455.

With C. A. Kraus. Liquid ammonia as a solvent. *Am. Chem. J.* 20:820.

With C. A. Kraus. Determination of the molecular rise of the boiling point of liquid ammonia. *Am. Chem. J.* 20:836.

1899

With C. A. Kraus. Metathetic reactions between certain salts in liquid ammonia. *Am. Chem. J.* 21:1; also in *Chem. News* 79:293.

With C. A. Kraus. Some properties of liquid ammonia. *Am. Chem. J.* 21:8; also in *Chem. News* 79:308; and in *Ice Refrig.* 16:439.

1900

With C. A. Kraus. The electrical conductivity of liquid ammonia solutions. *Am. Chem. J.* 23:277.

With C. A. Kraus. The conductivity temperature coefficient of some liquid ammonia solutions. *Am. Chem. J.* 24:83.

1902

With O. F. Stafford. Reactions between acid and basic amides. *Am. Chem. J.* 28:38.

1904

With H. P. Cady. On the velocities of the ions in liquid ammonia solutions. *J. Am. Chem. Soc.* 26:499.

1905

With C. A. Kraus. The electrical conductivity of liquid ammonia solutions. II. *J. Am. Chem. Soc.* 27:191.

1906

Reactions in liquid ammonia. *J. Am. Chem. Soc.* 27:820; also in *Z. Anorg. Chem.* 46:1.

1907

On the mercury nitrogen compounds (the mercuri-ammonium salts and bases). *J. Am. Chem. Soc.* 29:35.

Potassium ammonozincate (a representative of a new class of compounds). *J. Am. Chem. Soc.* 29:1274; also in *Z. anorg. Chem.* 45:195.

With H. D. Gibbs. Electrical conductivity of methylamine solutions. *J. Am. Chem. Soc.* 29:1389.

With C. A. Kraus. Experimental determination of the heat of volatilization of liquid ammonia at its boiling point at atmospheric pressure. *J. Phys. Chem.* 11:553.

Über den Siedepunkt des flüssigen Ammoniaks. *Ann. Phys.* 24:367.

1909

The electrical conductivity of liquid ammonia solutions. III. *Z. phys. Chem.* 69:272. (Arrhenius Jubelband).

1910

The instability of alloxan. *J. Am. Chem. Soc.* 32:1362.

1911

Potassium ammonoplumbite. *J. Phys. Chem.* 15:509.

The electrical conductivity of liquid sulfur dioxide solutions at $-33.3°$, $-20°$, $-10°$, $0°$, and $+10°$. *J. Phys. Chem.* 15:675.

1912

The ammonia system of acids, bases and salts. *Am. Chem. J.* 47:285.

A theory of the mercuri-ammonium compounds. *Am. Chem. J.* 47:361.

The ammonia system of acids, bases and salts. *J. Wash. Acad. Sci.* 2:215.

A theory of the mercury ammonia compounds. *J. Wash. Acad. Sci.* 2:290.

The organic acid amides and their metallic derivatives as acids and salts of the ammonia system of acids, bases and salts. *8th Int. Congr. Pure Appl. Chem.* 6:119.

The action of potassium amide on thallium nitrate in liquid ammonia solution. *J. Phys. Chem.* 16:682; also in *8th Int. Cong. Appl. Chem. Orig. Communication* 2:103.

With T. B. Hine. Potassium ammonotitanate. *J. Am. Chem. Soc.* 34:1497.

The action of potassium amide on cupric nitrate in liquid ammonia solution. *J. Am. Chem. Soc.* 34:1501.

1913

Potassium ammonomagnesiate, $Mg(NHK)_2 2NH_3$. *J. Am. Chem. Soc.* 35:1455.

1915

Potassium ammonoargentate, bariate, strontiate, calciate and sodiate. *Proc. Natl. Acad. Sci. USA* 1:65.

Metallic salts of ammono acids. *Proc. Natl. Acad. Sci. USA* 1:68.

Ammonobasic iodides of aluminium. *Proc. Natl. Acad. Sci. USA* 1:70.

Ammonobasic aluminium iodides. *J. Am. Chem. Soc.* 37:847.

Reactions in liquid ammonia. II. *J. Am. Chem. Soc.* 37:2279.

Potassium ammonobariate, ammonostrontiate, and ammonocalciate. *J. Am. Chem. Soc.* 37:2295.

1919

Potassium ammonosodiate, potassium ammonolithiate, rubidium ammonosodiate and rubidium ammonolithiate. *J. Phys. Chem.* 23:36.

1920

Metallic salts of pyrrole, indole and carbazole. *J. Phys. Chem.* 24:81.

1922

The ammono carbonic acids. *J. Am. Chem. Soc.* 44:486.

1923

Hydrocyanic acid, an ammono carbonous acid and a formic anammonide. *J. Phys. Chem.* 27:167.

1924

Systems of acids, bases and salts. *J. Am. Chem. Soc.* 46:2137.

1926

Reactions in liquid ammonia. New York: Columbia University Press.

1933

Some ammonolytic reactions. *J. Am. Chem. Soc.* 55:4912.
Metallic salts of carboxazylic acids. *J. Am. Chem. Soc.* 55:4915.

1934

Hydrazoic acid. *J. Am. Chem. Soc.* 56:568.
The Hofmann-Beckmann-Curtius-Lossen rearrangements. *Chem. Rev.* 14:219.

1935

The nitrogen system of compounds. American Chemical Society Monograph. New York: Reinhold Publishing Corp.

SELIG HECHT

February 8, 1892–September 18, 1947

BY GEORGE WALD[1]

O N SEPTEMBER 18, 1947, Selig Hecht, professor of bio-physics at Columbia University, died suddenly at the age of fifty-five. He was one of the most vivid scientific figures of his time, a pioneer in the development of general physiology in this country and, for more than two decades, the undisputed leader in his chosen field—the physiology of vision.

In Hecht, great scientific capacities combined with equally superb gifts as a teacher, writer, and lecturer. His interests ranged widely, and everywhere they touched, he made striking personal contributions. No less than his works, the world will miss his vigorous personality, his breadth of outlook, and his generosity of spirit.

Hecht instilled something of his own clarity, substance, and force into his special field. He drew together its scattered phenomena, ordered them, and gave them a secure foundation in physics and chemistry. In many areas of vision his laboratory contributed the most complete and accurate data we possess. He provided in addition a context of ideas and rigorous theory upon which workers in vision will rely for many years to come.

---

[1] An earlier version of this article first appeared in *The Journal of General Physiology* 32(1948):1–16, portions of which are reproduced here by copyright permission of the Rockefeller University Press.

Hecht cast his light widely and many found their way by it. In his death, his colleagues recognized the passing of a great scientist. They, and many others, feel as well the loss of a warm friend.

EDUCATION AND EARLY LIFE

Selig Hecht was brought to America as a young child from the village of Glogow, then Austrian Poland. The early part of the century was the period of the great migration to this country from Eastern Europe.[2] The family settled in New York's lower East Side, where young Selig went to public and Hebrew schools and was taught Hebrew at home by his father.

The early history of the Hecht family is filled with financial struggles. The eldest of five children, Selig ran errands after school to add to the family's small resources. During high school he found work as a bookkeeper in a woolen business, a position he kept all through college. The ideal of learning under difficulties was deeply embedded in the family's outlook, and Selig's father turned to serious study as soon as he could win some leisure. Over eighty and still vigorous, the elder Hecht read widely, warmly arguing problems in history and philosophy from Schopenhauer to Spinoza.

In 1909 Selig entered the College of the City of New York and began to concentrate in mathematics. He took his first course in zoology only late in his college career but then turned to it as his primary interest. A fellowship allowed him to spend the summer vacation before leaving college with his fellow student, William Crozier, at the Bureau of Fisheries Station in Beaufort, North Carolina. Out of that summer's work came two papers, one written jointly with Crozier on

---

[2] The pattern of life for these migrants can now be recaptured only in such accounts as Mary Antin's *Promised Land*.

the relation of weight to length in fishes, and one on the absorption of calcium during molting of the blue crab.

Graduating in February 1913, Selig went to work as a chemist in a fermentation research laboratory. Here he made his first contact with photochemistry, having been asked to study the effect of light on the deterioration of beer. On solving this problem, he was promptly discharged. He determined then and there to renounce industrial work forever.

Back at Beaufort for another summer, Hecht made plans to begin graduate study. To obtain funds for this he took a position as chemist in the Department of Agriculture in Washington. Within a year he had saved enough to enter Harvard for graduate training in zoology.

At Harvard he became one of a group of graduate students who were to play a major role in the development of general physiology in this country—Crozier, Fenn, Redfield, S. C. Brooks, Olmstead, and Minnick. He undertook research for the doctorate under G. H. Parker, studying also with Osterhout, Wheeler, Mark, and Rand. Summers were spent working at the Bermuda Biological Station on the physiology of *Ascidia atra*, the subject of his doctoral dissertation.

The Ph.D. was granted Hecht in June 1917, and on the following day he married Celia Huebschman, daughter of an immigrant Austrian family, whom he had met while at college in New York. It is difficult to think of either Hecht thereafter without the other. They shared an extraordinary community of interest and enjoyment and dealt with each other on an intellectual level few marriages attain. Wherever they were, Celia made a home warm with hospitality and grace to which Selig could bring his friends and his troubles, sure that both would be received with sympathy and understanding.

Their wedding was brightened by a characteristic incident. Selig had entered a portion of his doctoral thesis for the Bowdoin Prize "for essays of high literary merit," and was awarded two hundred dollars and a medal. With this puff to their fortunes, the young couple left for a honeymoon at the Oceanographic Institute at La Jolla. Ritter, then director of the Institute, gave Selig a fellowship for the summer, and under these circumstances he performed experiments on the sensitivity to light of the ascidian, *Ciona*, experiments that launched a lifetime of work on photoreception and vision.

The paper describing this investigation presented for the first time Hecht's view of the photoreceptor process. He sent it to Jacques Loeb for publication in the newly founded *Journal of General Physiology*, and it appeared in the first volume. From then on Hecht's entire scientific production, with only minor exceptions, was published in the pages of this journal. Though he never played a formal role in its direction, Hecht identified with its purposes and standards and never failed to send it the best of his achievements in their most definitive form.

PHOTORECEPTION STUDIES AND TRAVEL (1917–1926)

In the fall of 1917 Selig took the position of assistant professor of biochemistry in the Medical School of Creighton University, a Jesuit institution in Omaha, where he spent the next four years. But Hecht was made for the metropolis and it for him; he looked upon this as a period of exile made more onerous by lack of time and resources for research. He spent each summer at the Marine Biological Laboratory in Woods Hole, eagerly compensating for the year's frustrations and doing some of his most significant work.

He had by that time worked through the analysis of photoreception (introduced with the *Ciona* experiments) in detail using another relatively simple system, that of the clam *Mya*. As his theory became more firmly established, Hecht grew more confident of its generality and essential correctness and turned to the analysis of a human visual function—adaptation to darkness. Seeking direct information on the initial effects of light on the eye, he performed his classic studies of the bleaching of rhodopsin in solution.

Selig was now wholly caught up in what he believed to be a major scientific advance. He wanted to establish an adequate laboratory and to teach General Physiology—an area of science that inspired him with a mission[3]—and to develop about himself a group of research students. That no opportunity was made available to do these things was without question a source of deep disappointment.

With Jacques Loeb's sponsorship, Selig was awarded a National Research Council fellowship in biology, which he held for three years. After that, with no post in sight, he was a General Education Board fellow for another two years. Though rich in experience and fruitful in terms of his work, this was a trying period. For all his superb gifts and accomplishments, Hecht had to wait almost a decade after completing his formal training before he received an adequate academic appointment.

During this difficult period the warm friendship and confidence of Jacques Loeb, whom he had come to know at Woods Hole, was a continuing source of encouragement. In the fall of 1922 Loeb wrote to Hecht:

"I feel that in you the coming generation of scientists will have a leader and that I need not yield to my pessimistic mood in regard to the future of science in this country. You yourself may safely ignore the stupidity and even brutality of our times and keep that serenity which is required of a man who wishes to do his best work. The future needs you and belongs to you. . . ." [And, in a characteristically gracious postscript:] "Please remember me kindly to Mrs. Hecht—she may well be proud of you."

---

[3] The banner of General Physiology was raised in France by Claude Bernard (1813–1878) and, early in this century, came to inspire a whole generation of American biologists. It was a banner Hecht and all his students carried proudly and with great devotion. See Claude Bernard, *An introduction to the study of experimental medicine,* translated by H. C. Greene, with an introduction by L. J. Henderson (New York: Macmillan, 1927). See also J. M. D. Olmsted, *Claude Bernard, physiologist* (New York: Harper & Brothers, 1938).

Hecht spent his first year as a National Research Council fellow in Liverpool in the laboratory of the photochemist, E. C. C. Baly. There, with the help of R. E. Williams, he carried through a classic study of the spectral sensitivity of human rod vision.

The remaining two years of this fellowship were spent in the laboratory of L. J. Henderson, both at Harvard Medical School and at Woods Hole. During this period he extended his view of the photoreceptor process to a theoretical analysis of brightness discrimination—a characteristically global view that embraced the data for man and for the clam in one quantitative treatment. Here he pointed out for the first time that the data of human intensity discrimination are dual in origin, breaking on analysis into a low intensity portion (dependent on the rods), and a high intensity segment (governed by the cones).

In the spring of 1924 the Hechts' daughter, Maressa, was born. The family spent the following year in Naples, where Selig, then a General Education Board fellow at the Zoological Station, worked on *Ciona* and a new lamellibranch, *Pholas*.

The following year the Hechts lived in Cambridge, England, and Selig entered Barcroft's laboratory. One could hardly do this without being drawn into the lively controversy then raging over the question of whether the oxygen dissociation curve of hemoglobin is S-shaped or hyperbolic. For all his absorption in visual problems, Selig plunged into this work, devising a spectrographic procedure of which Barcroft wrote:

"This technique, so far as the making of all the estimations is concerned, is in many ways a decided advance on any of its predecessors. The improvement was aptly expressed by someone who, looking at one of Hecht['s] and Morgan's curves, said, 'This is the first dissociation curve I have seen where the points really lie on the curve.'"[4]

[4] J. Barcroft, *Respiratory Function of the Blood*, part 2, *Hemoglobin* (Cambridge: Cambridge University Press, 1928), p. 158.

In that same connection, Hecht told me the following story—
a nice example of Barcroft's exuberance. Just as Barcroft was
setting out for a meeting of the Physiological Society, Hecht
showed him one of his first oxygen dissociation curves of
hemoglobin, which looked to be a rectangular hyperbola.
Barcroft took it along with him to report on at the meeting.
But when he got back to Cambridge, Hecht, who had in the
interim done a more detailed job, told him that the curve was
S-shaped, after all. Nothing daunted, Barcroft—who had already written an abstract reporting that "the curve is clearly
a hyperbola"—crossed out "clearly" and over it wrote
"nearly."

The Cambridge interlude was the last of Hecht's *Wander-
jahre*. During these fellowship years, with their opportunities
for visiting and travel and at the Physiological Congress in
Stockholm in 1926, the Hechts formed many warm friendships abroad, which they maintained and cherished ever
afterward and renewed at every opportunity.

In this period Hecht also gained a wide international audience for his work. A general review he wrote for *Naturwis-
senschaften* in 1925 led to a published discussion with Lasareff.
In part because of associations formed in this earlier period,
Hecht continued to publish abroad: again in *Naturwissen-
schaften* in 1930, a comprehensive review in the Asher-Spiro
Ergebnisse der Physiologie (translated into German by Frau
Asher in 1931), a volume in the *Actualités Scientifiques* in 1938,
and invited papers in a number of British journals.

COLUMBIA YEARS (1926–1947)

In the spring of 1926, Selig was offered simultaneously a
post at Columbia and a projected chair at a major English
university. Much as he had valued his English associations,
he decided to return to this country. In September 1926, he
became associate professor and, in 1928, professor of bio-

physics at Columbia University—the post he held at the time of his death.

As the only physiologist in Columbia's Department of Zoology, Hecht had a large measure of autonomy within his special sphere to construct a situation after his own design. In the lofty isolation of the thirteenth floor of the new Physics Building, commanding a superb southern view of the city and the Hudson River, he fitted out a compact set of laboratories and workrooms with everything needed for physiological investigation and instruction.

There he began an advanced course in general physiology in which he imparted his highly original ordering of the subject before a small, well-prepared group of students. The students were given individual problems in the laboratory, and most of the initial group remained with him to complete their doctoral research.

Hecht took a quite extraordinary interest in his students, and the layout of the laboratory itself encouraged association. Tea was served every afternoon. There, and at weekly colloquia—indeed on any occasion in which Hecht or one of the students had something he wished to discuss—a group would gather. Under his influence conversation ranged over literature, politics, music, and art as well as science; and at one period students met at the Hechts' home one evening a week to read and discuss, as they appeared, L. J. Henderson's *Blood* and P. W. Bridgman's *Logic of Modern Physics*. Mrs. Hecht would join the group later in the evening over sandwiches and beer, and the conversation would broaden its scope.

This communal life of the laboratory articulated and clothed the bare bones of graduate instruction. It fostered in Hecht's students a strong and abiding attachment and sense of loyalty. Long after they left his laboratory, Hecht continued to hold a central place in their thoughts and affections.

Among Hecht's first students was Simon Shlaer, who became Hecht's assistant in his first year at Columbia and continued as his associate for twenty years thereafter. A man infinitely patient with things and impatient with people, Shlaer gave Hecht his entire devotion. He was a master of instrumentation, and though he also had a keen grasp of theory, he devoted himself by choice to the development of new technical devices.

Hecht and Shlaer built a succession of precise instruments for visual measurement, among them an adaptometer and an anomaloscope that have since gone into general use. The entire laboratory came to rely on Shlaer's ingenuity and skill. "I am like a man who has lost his right arm," remarked Hecht on leaving Columbia—and Shlaer—in 1947, "and his right leg."

In his Columbia laboratory, Hecht instituted investigations of human dark adaptation, brightness discrimination, visual acuity, the visual response to flickered light, the mechanism of the visual threshold, and normal and anomalous color vision. His lab also made important contributions regarding the biochemistry of visual pigments, the relation of night blindness to vitamin A deficiency in humans, the spectral sensitivities of man and other animals, and the light reactions of plants—phototropism, photosynthesis, and chlorophyll formation.

As Hecht's Columbia laboratory became one of the most productive centers of physiological investigation and training, he himself exercised an ever-widening influence and activity in contemporary science. Almost a score of his students went on to careers in physical and biological chemistry, physiology, chemical genetics, and ophthalmology.

In 1941, Hecht was awarded the Frederick Ives Medal of the Optical Society of America. He was elected to the National Academy of Sciences in 1944. A director-at-large of the Optical Society of America, he also served on the editorial boards of the *Journal of the Optical Society*, the *Biological Bulletin*, and *Documenta Ophthalmologica*.

War Work

Throughout the late years of World War II, Hecht devoted his energies and the resources of his laboratory to military problems. He and Shlaer developed a special adaptometer for night-vision testing that was adopted as standard equipment by several Allied military services. Hecht also directed a number of visual projects for the Army and Navy and was consultant and advisor on many others. He was a member of the National Research Council Committee on Visual Problems and of the executive board of the Army-Navy Office of Scientific Research and Development Vision Committee.

His influence, however, extended far beyond the scope of these formal commitments. He visited many military installations to acquaint himself with their problems at first hand, taking researches into the field whenever that seemed likely to bring quicker and more practical results. He had a strong sense of the urgency of the war and no civilian timidity whatever. His plain speech in high places won the esteem and affection of his military associates, who miss him now as deeply as do his academic colleagues.

Hecht had a high sense of the social obligations of science. He thought it imperative that science be explained to the layman in terms that he could understand and use in coming to his own decisions. For this task he himself had a special talent. When, for instance, he thought certain of his colleagues' statements regarding Heisenberg's "Uncertainty Principle" and the problem of human free will were misleading the lay public, he wrote an essay on the subject for *Harper's Magazine*. Early in the War he wrote another article for *Harper's* on night vision, which was later distributed in large numbers to the Air Force.

Educating the Public

Hecht greatly enjoyed teaching adults at the New School, where he gave courses in sensory physiology, physics, and atomic energy. His New School lectures on atomic energy grew into the book, *Explaining the Atom*, a lay approach to atomic theory and its recent developments that the *New York Times* (in a September 20, 1947, editorial) called "by far the best so far written for the multitude."

This popular book had one curious consequence: Hecht was asked to lecture on atomic energy before the War College. He accepted the invitation, characteristically changing the subject and lecturing instead on the relation of science to technology. In his speech Hecht pointed out the need, now that the war had ended, to foster basic scientific research. He was also deeply involved in the effort to abolish the military uses of atomic energy and to turn it toward constructive ends. An honorary vice-president of the Emergency Committee of Atomic Scientists, he was the only member of this small group who was not a nuclear physicist.

VISION RESEARCH

A man's work merits a biography of its own. It has its own ancestry, birth, and development; its own span of life. Selig Hecht's work was particularly vigorous, and it will long survive him.

All is grist to a mind as original as Hecht's, yet several early influences going back to his graduate years at Harvard made a particular impression on him. He often spoke of them, and they are apparent in his work over a long period. One was the nascent science of photochemistry, coming to fruition in the first decades of the century in the laboratories of Luther and his colleagues Weigert and Plotnikow. Another was Jacques Loeb's treatment of animal phototropism; his generalization of its fundamental mechanisms to include both animals and plants, and his insistence that phototropic excitation has its source in ordinary physicochemical processes. The third influence—Arrhenius's *Quantitative Laws in Biological Chemistry*, published in 1915—complemented the others. Hecht spoke of the excitement he and his fellow students at Harvard felt in the face of the promise that, by accurately measuring biological functions and fitting to them the simple equations of chemical kinetics, one could reveal their underlying physicochemical mechanisms.

Photoreception

Hecht launched his own investigations of photoreception with an intensive study of the relatively simple, unorganized systems associated with light reflexes in the ascidian *Ciona* and the clam *Mya*. These are highly manipulable organisms susceptible to wide temperature variation; their responses are definite and their reactions slow enough to be measured without elaborate apparatus. Hecht's experiments took full advantage of all these virtues.

His researches produced a picture of the photoreceptor process as a reversible (more properly, pseudo-reversible) system in which a photosensitive pigment is attacked by light and is simultaneously restored by ordinary thermal reactions. In light the concentration of photopigment declines to some constant, steady-state value; in darkness it is restored to a maximum level. Hecht recognized in these processes the chemical sources of light and dark adaptation.

The steady state achieved under constant illumination also has significant properties of its own. The simple animals with which Hecht began his work responded to *changes* in illumination; in the steady state they behaved as though light no longer stimulated them. Both the light-adapted and dark-adapted condition, therefore, provided a constant background upon which a stimulus could be superimposed—an absolute threshold upon the dark-adapted state, a differential threshold upon the light-adapted state.

Hecht had already worked out equations describing the steady state. By assuming that the visual threshold, whether absolute or differential, corresponds to a constant increment in the rate of breakdown of photosensitive material, he could also describe departures from the steady state—phenomena encountered in brightness discrimination, responses to flickering light, and the absolute threshold.

With no significant modification, Hecht turned the theoretical apparatus he had devised from studies of invertebrate systems to the examination of human vision. Never ceasing to test the validity of his ideas in the dialectic of organic evolution, he made the most comprehensive contribution to the field since Helmholtz. He explored adaptation to the dark in molluscs (*Mya* and *Pholas*), tunicates (*Ciona*), and primates (man); visual acuity in insects with compound eyes (the bee and fruitfly) and in man; intensity discrimination in *Mya*, *Pholas*, *Ciona*, the fruitfly, and man; and flicker in the clam and in man.

Color Vision

In 1929, at the Thomas Young Centenary celebration at Cornell University, Hecht presented a brilliantly original synthesis of the disorganized quantitative data on human color vision—the first attempt to provide a reasonably comprehensive theory in this field. Starting from the trichromatic theory propounded by Young, Helmholtz, and Maxwell, Hecht posited the existence of three types of cones. He then attempted to define their characteristics and physiological interrelations. The most distinctive outcome of this analysis was Hecht's ingenious conclusion that the sensitivities of all the cones must lie very close together in the spectrum—a theory that, though it differed sharply from all previous formulations, seemed highly persuasive until confuted later by direct measurements.

Assuming, more or less arbitrarily, that all three cone types make equal contributions to the brightness of white light, Hecht derived spectral sensitivity functions for each. The last investigation in which he took part, however—a comparison of the brightness function in normal and color-blind subjects—led him to conclude that each type of cone makes a different contribution to brightness, with the "red" group contributing the most and the "blue" the least. He had looked forward to exploring this possibility further.

Measuring Light Photons and Rod Stimulation

Hecht was also intensely interested in the relation of light quanta (photons) to vision. Reexamining earlier measurements of the minimum threshold for human rod vision, he and his colleagues confirmed that vision requires only fifty to 150 photons. When all allowances had been made for surface reflections, the absorption of light by ocular tissues, and the absorption by rhodopsin (which alone is an effective stimulant), it emerged that the minimum visual sensation corresponds to the absorption in the rods of, at most, five to fourteen photons. An entirely independent statistical analysis suggested that an absolute threshold involves about five to seven photons. Both procedures, then, confirmed the estimation of the minimum visual stimulus at five to fourteen photons. Since the test field in which these measurements were performed contained about 500 rods, it was difficult to escape the conclusion that one rod is stimulated by a single photon.

Hecht was in the process of determining the consequences of this fundamental discovery at the time of his death. Convinced that one has to deal with small numbers of elementary events at all levels of illumination, he was preparing to modify many of his earlier theories.

In the past, variations in the responses of organisms to physical stimuli were generally ascribed to variations in the reactivity of the organism. Yet in cases such as this, where the stimulus involved so few photons, statistical variations in the delivery of the stimulus became more significant than biological factors in varying the response. This new view also foreshadowed a fundamental revision in the idea of an absolute threshold of vision: the stimulation of a dark-adapted rod by a single photon set an absolute *physical* limit, for no smaller amount of light exists.

Hecht was deeply interested in the general implications this discovery held for biology. Some question still persists as to whether or not biological systems are subject to the ordinary restrictions of thermodynamics. Careful experiments have generally shown that they are. The process of vision, however, is initiated by so few photons and therefore involves so few photopigment molecules, it falls outside the province of thermodynamic treatment.

Indeed, the absolute threshold of human vision falls potentially *inside* Heisenberg's "Uncertainty Principle." There is no way to control the path of a single photon or the excitation of a single rod occasioned by a single molecule of rhodopsin. Were we able to see single events, our vision would be "noisy" even in complete darkness. Fortunately, to see even a minimal flash of light requires at least five such events happening simultaneously within a small patch of retina (1942). That "factor five" is what electronics engineers recognize as the proper signal-to-noise ratio needed to make sense out of what is otherwise meaningless chaos.

THEORIST, WRITER, TEACHER

Compared to earlier, more general statements regarding light reception in animals and plants, Hecht's contributions were particularly distinguished for their breadth, definition, and rigor. He expressed his theories in mathematical form at every turn and devised accurate measurements to test them. Believing it more important that a theory be definite and illuminating than that it attempt to cope with all complexities at once, he emphasized maximum simplicity and concreteness.

Hecht's contributions, furthermore, were presented strikingly and convincingly, and he often wrote several versions of a paper to expose its different facets. Carefully choosing each word, he spiced a vigorous prose style with graphic and telling phrases. He also drew and lettered all his own figures, devoting to them all the care he lavished on his paintings. Worked and reworked, his papers were models of design.

Hecht's scientific lectures were equally persuasive and well designed, and he had the gift of entering into close and earnest communion with large audiences. After he had, through persistent experimentation, testing, and examination, convinced himself of the fruitfulness of an idea, he was able to teach it unforgettably.

At Columbia Hecht set a rigorous standard for the work of his laboratory. He was imbued with the ideal of the "classic experiment," one done so thoroughly and well that it should never have to be repeated.

Hecht also had an unequalled grasp of the literature of his field. He worked constantly at drawing it together, rationalizing it, recalculating, cutting and fitting—attempting to achieve, through this process, an integrated view of the field that would guide him to fruitful experiment.

Before starting experiments in human dark adaptation, visual acuity, intensity discrimination, or color vision, he had already published theoretical approaches to these functions on the basis of existing data. Repeatedly frustrated by incomplete or inadequate information, he was determined that measurements from his own laboratory be precise and exhaustive.

THE PRIVATE MAN

Selig Hecht pursued his relaxations with all the wit and warmth with which he did science. He understood music as do few nonprofessional musicians. He was a painter talented in water colors. He read widely and critically. And to everything he did, he brought unfailing zest and taste.

Wherever he found the creative faculty at work, Hecht worked with it in spirit. He shared the problems of the composer at the symphony, the painter at the exhibition, the author of the book he read. Recognizing this for what it was, practitioners of all the arts dealt with him virtually as a colleague.

He took keen pleasure in all his activities and relationships, in science, painting, teaching, his family, friends, and colleagues. He was the most genial of companions—witty, stimulating, sympathetic. He loved good conversation and fruitful argument. He was a warm friend; in fair weather and foul one could rely upon his understanding and help.

In July, 1947, Hecht flew to England, coming together again with many old friends of earlier years at the Physiological Congress at Oxford. He went on to the Color Vision Conference in Cambridge and spent an absorbing week there in discussion and argument with most of Europe and America's workers in vision. During this period he reviewed the status of his own work, laying plans for the years ahead. One afternoon in Cambridge he walked across the river to the house in which his family had lived—and he had painted in the garden—twenty years before. He then returned to America for the wedding of his daughter. Two weeks later he died, without long illness or apparent suffering. It is good to think that such a life closed, like a sonata movement, recapitulating its main themes.

Selig Hecht conveyed a sense of wide spaces and clear light. The world is smaller and dimmer for his going.

SELECTED BIBLIOGRAPHY

1920

The photochemical nature of the photosensory process. *J. Gen. Physiol.* 2:229.
The dark adaptation of the human eye. *J. Gen. Physiol.* 2:499.

1921

The relation between the wave length of light and its effect on the photosensory process. *J. Gen. Physiol.* 3:375.
The nature of foveal dark adaptation. *J. Gen. Physiol.* 4:113.

1922

With Robert E. Williams. The visibility of monochromatic radiation and the absorption spectrum of visual purple. *J. Gen. Physiol.* 5:1.

1924

Photochemistry of visual purple. III. The relation between the intensity of light and the rate of bleaching of visual purple. *J. Gen. Physiol.* 6:731.
The visual discrimination of intensity and the Weber-Fechner law. *J. Gen. Physiol.* 7:235.

1927

The kinetics of dark adaptation. *J. Gen. Physiol.* 10:781.

1928

The relation between visual acuity and illumination. *J. Gen. Physiol.* 11:255.
On the binocular fusion of colors and its relation to theories of color vision. *Proc. Natl. Acad. Sci. USA* 14:237.

1929

With Ernst Wolf. The visual acuity of the honey bee. *J. Gen. Physiol.* 12:727.
The nature of the photoreceptor process. In: *The foundations of experimental psychology*, ed. C. Murchison, p. 216. Worcester, Mass.: Clark University Press.

1930

The development of Thomas Young's theory of color vision. *J. Opt. Soc. Am.* 20:231.

1931

Die physikalische Chemie und die Physiologie des Sehaktes. *Ergeb. Physiol.* 32:243.

1934

With George Wald. The visual acuity and intensity discrimination of *Drosophila. J. Gen. Physiol.* 17:517.

Vision: II. The nature of the photoreceptor process. In: *A handbook of general experimental psychology*, ed. C. Murchison, p. 704. Worcester, Mass.: Clark University Press.

1935

With Charles Haig and George Wald. The dark adaptation of retinal fields of different size and location. *J. Gen. Physiol.* 19:321.

1936

Intensity discrimination and its relation to the adaptation of the eye. *J. Physiol.* 86:15.

With Simon Shlaer. Intermittent stimulation by light. V. The relation between intensity and critical frequency for different parts of the spectrum. *J. Gen. Physiol.* 19:965.

With Emil L. Smith. Intermittent stimulation by light. VI. Area and the relation between critical frequency and intensity. *J. Gen. Physiol.* 19:979.

With Simon Shlaer. The color vision of dichromats. I. Wavelength discrimination, brightness distribution, and color mixture. II. Saturation as the basis for wavelength discrimination and color mixture. *J. Gen. Physiol.* 20:57.

1937

Rods, cones, and the chemical basis of vision. *Physiol. Rev.* 17:239.

1938

The nature of the visual process. *Bull. N.Y. Acad. Med.* 14:21; also in: *Harvey Lect.* 33:35.

1942

With Simon Shlaer and M. H. Pirenne. Energy, quanta, and vision. *J. Gen. Physiol.* 25:819.

1944

Energy and vision. *Am. Sci.* 32:159. (Sigma Xi National Lecture)

1947

Explaining the atom. New York: Viking Press.

1948

With Simon Shlaer, Emil L. Smith, Charles Haig, and James C. Peskin. The visual functions of the complete colorblind. *J. Gen. Physiol.* 31:459.

LIBBIE HENRIETTA HYMAN

December 6, 1888–August 3, 1969

BY LIBBIE H. HYMAN[1]
AND G. EVELYN HUTCHINSON[2]

"I was born in Des Moines, Iowa, December 6, 1888, of Jewish parents, both of whom were immigrants to the United States. My father, Joseph Hyman, came from a Polish village, name of Konin, located in a part of Poland that had been appropriated by Russia. It lay within the Russian Pale, where Jews were subject to brutal restrictions. At the age of fourteen he escaped across the border and made his way to London where he lived for some years, earning a living by plying the family trade of tailoring. Eventually he migrated to the United States, where he struck up a strong friendship with one David Goldman. The two men decided to migrate to what was then the far west (namely Iowa) and went to Des Moines, where they built a store, occupying the ground story with a clothing business.

"My mother, Sabina or Bena Neumann, was born in Stettin, Germany, one of eight children of a father who died young. She migrated to the United States and went directly to Des Moines, because she had a brother living there. He made a household slavey out of her and treated her roughly, after the best Prussian traditions. Finally she left him and went to work for a family named Posner. This Posner had married a sister of my father's, and my father—a bachelor in his late forties—was living with the Posners. He was twenty years older than my mother. The names Hyman and Posner are both invented names.

---

[1] Libbie Henrietta Hyman left with the Academy a brief autobiography of about 2,500 words, which I find so moving that I have quoted it here unedited. Since it is, however, overmodest, I have supplemented it with a more objective evaluation of her contributions to zoology.

[2] The Academy would also like to express its special thanks to Prof. James N. Cather of the University of Michigan for his editorial help in the preparation of this manuscript.

"My father and mother were married in 1884 and went to live in their own house in Des Moines where three children were born: my older brothers, Samuel and Arthur, then I. The family fortunes flourished as long as my father retained his partnership with Goldman. But my father had a scapegrace brother, name of Isaac, who persuaded him that big fortunes were to be made still farther west.

"My father therefore broke his partnership with Goldman and the family moved to Sioux Falls, South Dakota, where my last and youngest brother, David, was born. The Dakota venture failed and the family moved back to Iowa, settling into the town of Ft. Dodge, where I spent my childhood and youth. At first we lived in a rented house, then built our own house. My father opened a clothing store on the main street of the town but it was never successful and we lived mainly on the rentals from the Des Moines building.

"I was brought up in a home devoid of affection and consideration. My father, an aging man constantly worried about his declining fortunes, took practically no notice of his four children. My mother regarded children as property to be ordered about as she liked and to be used for her benefit. She seemed incapable of feelings of affection. She was also thoroughly infiltrated with the European worship of the male sex. My three brothers were brought up in idleness and irresponsibility, with the result that two of them never earned more than a bare living, whereas I, as a mere child, was required to participate in the endless work of the big ten-room house. For this reason I have violently hated housework all my life.

"My father was never cut out by nature to be a businessman. He was of a scholarly disposition and was particularly interested in travels and history, having a remarkable memory for historical dates. He had accumulated a small library of oddly assorted books, some of which could hardly be expected to interest anybody—as, for instance, a documentary history of New York state in several volumes. But there was also a complete Shakespeare, a Dante's *Inferno* with the Doré illustrations, and a complete set of the works of Dickens. I became acquainted with the novels of Dickens at an early age and have never ceased to admire and enjoy them.

"I was conscious from an early age of a strong interest in nature. This first took the form of a love of flowers. My earliest recollections concern flowers. As a child I roamed the woods that bordered the town, hunting the spring wild flowers. I learned their scientific names from a Gray botany book that my brothers had acquired in high school, but I puzzled over the classification until one memorable day when I suddenly realized that the flowers of a little weed known as cheeses had the same construction as hollyhock flowers. Thus I came to understand the families of flowering plants. Later in my teens I collected butterflies and moths and arranged them in a frame. I believe my interest in nature is primarily aesthetic.

"I received my elementary education in the public schools of Ft. Dodge. At the high school I failed to attract the attention of the science teachers, of which there were two, one teaching physics, the other biology and chemistry. I subsequently met the physics teacher on the campus of The University of Chicago, where he was studying for a Ph.D. in physics. It was the teacher of German and English, Mary Crawford, a graduate of Radcliffe, who took an interest in me.

"I graduated from the Ft. Dodge High School in 1905 but did not know what to do with myself. I took and passed the state examinations for teaching in the country schools but was informed that I was too young to be appointed. I have always considered this a great piece of luck, as even then I hated the idea of teaching. During 1906 I returned to the high school, taking advanced work in German, but when that came to an end I was again at loose ends. Finally I took a job in a factory, pasting labels on boxes.

"I was coming home from the factory one autumn afternoon when I met Mary Crawford. She asked me what I was doing and was shocked when I told her. She said the Ft. Dodge High School was one of a number of high schools that had been approved by The University of Chicago, which then offered a scholarship paying a year's tuition to top students. Hence, in the fall of 1906, I set off for The University of Chicago. To the best of my recollection it had never occurred to me to go to college. I scarcely understood the purpose of college.

"At The University of Chicago I planned to take a basic course in each of the physical and biological sciences and then decide which one suited me best. I began with botany, to which I was strongly inclined anyway. But I somehow made an enemy of the laboratory assistant, name of Burlingame, who tried to have me flunked. This Burlingame was responsible for the fact that I did not become a botanist. I then tried chemistry for a while but dropped it when I realized that chemical advance is based on quantitative procedures. I am not suited by temperament for quantitative work. In the zoology department I met with much encouragement and decided to make a career of zoology. I have never regretted that consideration.

"I received my B.S. in 1910 and again was at a loss what to do next. I made a feeble attempt to obtain a zoological job that did not involve teaching. Finally Professor C. M. Child suggested that I enter the graduate school and work for a Ph.D. degree. This I did, taking my doctor's degree under him in 1915. I had soon perceived that Child was the outstanding member of the Zoology Department, but his original ideas and thinking antagonized other zoologists and long prevented the recognition he deserved.

"After attaining my doctorate I again debated what to do other than teaching. Finally, Child got me appointed as his research assistant, and I occupied this position until his retirement. My work consisted of experiments on the physiology of planarians and other lower invertebrates. I do not regard any of this work as of outstanding importance. I am not a research type. I mainly accumulated data that bolstered Professor Child's ideas. My first publication was my doctor's thesis, entitled *An Analysis of the Process of Regeneration in Certain Microdrilous Olicochaetes*.

"In connection with my physiological work on hydras and planarians, it was necessary to have exact identifications of the species employed. I soon found that these common animals, used throughout the zoological world for a variety of purposes, were frequently misidentified, and in fact there had been no careful study of their taxonomy. In this way I became a taxonomic specialist on hydras and free-living flatworms. Such original work as I have published for the past thirty years or more consists mainly of such taxonomic studies.

"During my first year at the University I roomed with an uncle and aunt. In the winter of that year (1907) my father died. My return to attend his funeral was to be my last sight of Ft. Dodge, Iowa, until fifty years later.

"On my return to Chicago I took a room near the University. I had to work my way through college but was happy to escape from the unhappy atmosphere of my home. However, this escape was short-lived. My mother behaved after the manner of possessive mothers. She settled the family affairs in Ft. Dodge and moved the family to Chicago. Thus I was brought back into the same unhappy circumstances which lasted until the death of my mother in 1929.

"I never received any encouragement from my family to continue my academic career; in fact my determination to attend the University met with derision. At home, scolding and fault-finding were my daily portion. I have always considered it the great mistake of my life that I did not leave home after receiving my doctorate.

"I worked my way through graduate school by serving as laboratory assistant in various zoology courses. In the elementary course I felt that a better guide book was needed. Therefore I wrote *A Laboratory Manual for Elementary Zoology*, published in 1919 by The University of Chicago Press. It never occurred to me that it would find anything but local use; hence I was quite astonished when the Press informed me that the first printing had been rapidly exhausted. In 1929 I wrote a second expanded edition and this still has a considerable sale.

"Vertebrate anatomy was another subject in which I served as laboratory assistant and here, too, I felt that a better laboratory guide was badly needed. Therefore I wrote *A Laboratory Manual for Comparative Vertebrate Anatomy*, published in 1922 by The University of Chicago Press. Again I was surprised by the tremendous success of this book. I wrote the second edition in 1942 under the title, *Comparative Vertebrate Anatomy*, and this has continued to be highly successful. But I never liked vertebrate anatomy and since 1942 have abandoned all contact with the subject, refusing to consider making a third edition.

"Invertebrate zoology was always from the start my preferred subject. About 1925 I began thinking what I could do to further the teaching of this subject. I knew a good laboratory guide in this field was badly needed but was persuaded by colleagues to write an advanced text. I had no idea that this project would run to many volumes.

"By about 1930 I perceived that I could live on the royalties of my books. About this time, also, Professor Child came to the retiring age. Therefore I resigned my position as research assistant in the zoology department and have had no paid position since. I am amply supported by the royalties of my books, and so was left free to write a treatise on the invertebrates.

"The death of my mother left me with two bachelor brothers on my hands. Only my youngest brother ever married; he produced one daughter who has a son from the first of her two marriages. My bachelor brothers expected me to stay and keep house for them. To escape this situation I left Chicago in 1931, toured western Europe for fifteen months, and on return settled in New York to devote my entire time to the writing of a treatise on the invertebrates.

"I settled near the American Museum of Natural History in order to use the magnificent library of this institution. At first I worked at home but about 1937 was made research associate (honorary) of the Museum and assigned an office. Volume I of my treatise on invertebrates appeared in 1940, volumes II and III in 1951, volume IV in 1955, volume V in 1959. At present (1965) I am working on volume VI, which is near completion, but the rapid decline of my health and strength in the last few years makes it impossible for me to continue the project.

"I always wanted to live in the country and in 1941 bought a house in the village of Millwood in Westchester County, New York, about thirty-five miles north of Times Square. There I had full play for my passion for flowers and gardening. But it took me four hours daily to commute from my house to the Museum and back, and—added to this—the days I stayed home to work in the garden detracted seriously from work on my treatise.

If I had never bought that house I would undoubtedly be farther along with my treatise.

"Realizing that the house and garden were draining my time and strength, I sold the place in 1952 and returned to New York City, where I have lived ever since in a hotel apartment.[3]

"In 1961 my health was permanently impaired by surgery. I have never been really well since that time and have lived in a depressed state of mind. I never had much physical strength and was poor at sports, except swimming. In my youth I was a good swimmer and once saved a man's life. At the age of sixty I began losing strength and by now (seventy-six) have hardly any left. Lack of strength is the main reason that forces me to abandon my invertebrate project.

"The treatise on the invertebrates has brought me much fame and many honors but has given the zoological public an exaggerated idea of my scientific abilities. The treatise is essentially a compilation from the literature. My assets are some fluency in translating the main European languages and an ability to select and organize material in the literature.

"Member of Phi Beta Kappa, Sigma Xi, American Microscopical Society, Marine Biological Laboratory (Woods Hole), American Society of Zoologists (vice president, 1953), Society of Systematic Zoology (president, 1959), American Society of Limnology and Oceanography, Society of Protozoologists, American Academy of Arts and Sciences, National Academy of Sciences. Editor, *Systematic Zoology*, 1959–1963. Honorary degrees: Sc.D. The University of Chicago, 1941; Sc.D. Goucher College, 1958; Sc.D. Coe College, 1959; LL.D., Uppsala College, 1963. Daniel Giraud Elliot Medal, 1951; Gold Medal, Linnean Society of London, 1960." (L. H. Hyman's autobiography ends here.)

THE SCIENTIFIC WORK OF LIBBIE HENRIETTA HYMAN

In awarding the Linnean Society Gold Medal, Professor C. F. A. Pantin (by temperament perhaps the living person most qualified to judge and appreciate Hyman's work) said, after quoting Boswell, "What Boswell there says of Dr. Johnson's great *Dictionary* we can today say quite truly of Dr. Hyman's textbook of the invertebrate animal kingdom.

---

[3] I last saw her in a wheelchair, but most distinguished looking, being wheeled to the Museum Library.

Whole academies in more than one country have attempted to do what she has done. The debt of every zoologist to her is immense." Just before her death she received one final award, the Gold Medal of the American Museum of Natural History, presented to her at the centennial celebration of the Museum on April 9, 1969.

Hyman's earlier work, done under the direction of C. W. Child, primarily produced data, as she says, that bolstered Professor Child's ideas. His whole approach to the dynamics of form and development, usually subsumed under the title of the Axial Gradient theory, is now so neglected that it is doubtful if many of the current generation of postdoctoral fellows in developmental biology would have any idea what the expression means. But as the molecular processes under-lying differentiation are more fully elucidated, it is certain that the time will come when the biology of the whole embryo again becomes interesting. The various, perhaps seemingly contradictory, morphogenetic ideas of the first half of the century will then be disinterred and will be seen to be crude simulacra of the latest concepts. At that time, certain of Hyman's papers, which give some of the best evidence for the phenomena in which Child was interested, will perhaps come into their own.

Before she ceased to be Child's assistant, she had em-barked on the kind of research that made her the leading invertebrate zoologist of North America. Several papers on techniques for studying protozoans, flatworms, and coelen-terates appeared in the 1920s, and in 1926, a short but very interesting note on the chydorid, *Anchistropus minor*, as a predator of *Hydra*.

A little later, her long series of taxonomic contributions on both flatworms and the coelenterates of the genus *Hydra* began. These papers initiated the modern period in the study of the soft-bodied, freshwater invertebrates in America. In view of the great amount of experimental and ecological work that has been done during the last few decades, both on the planarian flatworms and the species of *Hydra*, the series on the taxonomy of North American species of these groups has had an importance rarely achieved by any systematizing work.

The discovery of a second species of the large brown hydra—then referred to a special genus, *Pelmato-hydra*, which has proved to be of some limnological importance—and of *Hydra littoralis*, now a well-known laboratory animal, may be mentioned. Her work on flatworms was very extensive, embracing all the major free-living groups, marine and terrestrial as well as freshwater. She was able to report the rediscovery of the peculiar large *Hydrolimax griseus* Haldeman, the sole member of a genus endemic to eastern Pennsylvania and New Jersey—a unique distribution that had not been found for nearly half a century and which, at the moment, may well be a somewhat forgotten endangered species.

She was greatly interested in the species that inhabit underground waters. Her work on flatworms was honored by a most important memorial symposium and volume, *Biology of the Turbellaria* (McGraw Hill, 1974), edited by N. W. Riser and M. P. Morse.

Significant as are these works to specialists, the great contribution of her life was the six volumes of *The invertebrates*. The only English precursor by a single author was Sedgewick's three-volume *Textbook of zoology* (1898–1909), which now—though sometimes useful—is quite naturally out of date. As Pantin pointed out, the only works that can be compared with Hyman's six volumes, containing over 4,000 pages, are of composite authorship.

In her autobiography she speaks of the work as "essentially a compilation from the literature," but it is a compilation by someone who had an extraordinary first-hand acquaintance with her materials. Fortunately the invertebrate phyla that she was able to cover included most of those of which she had greatest experience in her own researches. She worried that the scientific public regarded the book as based on her own work rather than on the researches of others. Actually, though she was technically correct, her enormous knowledge did indeed make it the result of the workings of her own mind.

In 1967, suffering from Parkinson's Disease and forced to discontinue work, she wrote at the end of the preface to Volume VI: "I now retire from the field, satisfied that I have accomplished my original purpose—to stimulate the study of invertebrates."

She had indeed.

SELECTED BIBLIOGRAPHY

1916

An analysis of the process of regeneration in certain microdrilous oligochaetes. *J. Exp. Zool.* 20:99–163.

1917

Metabolic gradients in amoeba and their relation to the mechanism of amoeboid motion. *J. Exp. Zool.* 24:55–99.

1919

A *laboratory manual for elementary zoology.* Chicago: University of Chicago Press.
Physiological studies on planaria. III. Oxygen consumption in relation to age (size) differences. *Biol. Bull.* 37:388–403.
With C. M. Child. The axial gradients in hydrozoa. I. Hydra. *Biol. Bull.* 36:183–223.

1920

The axial gradients in hydrozoa. III. Experiments on the gradient of tubularia. *Biol. Bull.* 38:353–403.

1922

A *laboratory manual for comparative vertebrate anatomy.* Chicago: University of Chicago Press.

1924

With B. H. Willier and S. A. Rifenburgh. Physiological studies on planaria. VI. A respiratory and histochemical study of the source of the increased metabolism after feeding. *J. Exp. Zool.* 40:473–94.

1925

Respiratory differences along the axis of the sponge grantia. *Biol. Bull.* 48:379–88.

1926

The metabolic gradients of vertebrate embryos. II. The brook lamprey. *J. Morphol.* 42:111–41.

1927

The metabolic gradients of vertebrate embryos. III. The chick. *Biol. Bull.* 52:1–38.

1929

A *laboratory manual for elementary zoology.* 2d ed. Chicago: University of Chicago Press.

1931

Studies on the morphology, taxonomy, and distribution of North American triclad turbellaria. IV. Recent European revisions of the triclads and their application to the American forms, with a key to the latter and new notes on distribution. *Trans. Am. Micros. Soc.* 50:316–35.

Taxonomic studies on the hydras of North America. IV. Description of three new species with a key to the known species. *Trans. Am. Micros. Soc.* 50:302–15.

1932

Relation of oxygen tension to oxygen consumption in Nereis virens. *J. Exp. Zool.* 61:209–21.

1940

The invertebrates. Vol. 1, Protozoa through ctenophora. New York: McGraw-Hill.

Observations and experiments on the physiology of medusae. *Biol. Bull.* 99:282-96.

1942

Comparative vertebrate anatomy. Chicago: University of Chicago Press.

1951

The invertebrates. Vol. 2, Platyhelminthes and rhynchocoela. New York: McGraw-Hill.

The invertebrates. Vol. 3, Acanthocephala, aschelminthes, and entoprocta. New York: McGraw-Hill.

1953

The polyclad flatworms of the Pacific coast of North America. *Bull. Am. Mus. Nat. Hist.* 100:265–392.
Posterior growth in annelids. *Am. Nat.* 87:395–96.

1955

The invertebrates. Vol. 4, Echinodermata. New York: McGraw-Hill.
How many species? *Syst. Zool.* 4:142–43.

1959

The invertebrates. Vol. 5, Smaller coelomate groups. New York: McGraw-Hill.

1967

The invertebrates. Vol. 6, Molusca I. New York: McGraw-Hill.

F. W. Loomis

FRANCIS WHEELER LOOMIS

August 4, 1889–February 9, 1976

BY FREDERICK SEITZ

FRANCIS WHEELER LOOMIS—or Wheeler Loomis as he preferred to be known—was a distinguished prototypical physicist of his generation who also possessed exceptional qualities of leadership.

He was born in Parkersburg, West Virginia, in 1889, just ten years before a small band of stalwarts created the American Physical Society in an attempt to foster physics on a national scale. For although physics in America had always been appreciated in a peripheral manner (one thinks of the remarkable work of Benjamin Franklin, Joseph Henry, Henry Rowland, Abraham Michelson and Willard Gibbs), it emerged relatively late here as a respected and respectable formal discipline. Striking exceptions to this rule were the Smithsonian Institution, the National Academy of Sciences, the Bureau of Standards, and a small number of universities (The Johns Hopkins University and, most notably, The University of Chicago, which established a research-oriented graduate Department of Physics in the last century). Nevertheless, the new Physical Society provided a forum throughout the country open to novice and skilled professional alike, and from its establishment onward, American physics was a cornerstone of science, a handmaiden to technology, and a key contributor to human enlightenment.

Loomis was destined not only to benefit from the new cohesive interest in physics in our country but also to be instrumental in raising the standards in his chosen profession to their present level of sophistication. Throughout his career he focused on two objectives: the pursuit of research of the highest quality and the building of research institutions upon a firm base. It was no accident that his student Polykarp Kusch won a Nobel Prize; it was no accident that the University of Illinois' Department of Physics that he headed for nearly thirty years was named after him and remains one of the most distinguished in the country.

EDUCATION AND EARLY YEARS

Loomis entered Harvard University as an undergraduate in 1906 and stayed on until he received his Ph.D. in 1917. He never spoke much about his Harvard years, though they were obviously highly formative ones. He was not much given to reminiscing, most of his conversation focusing rather on the present and future.

Loomis was presumably attracted to physics by a combination of his own natural talents and the stimulus provided by the revolutionary rise of quantum and relativity theories during his student days. He thoroughly enjoyed, moreover, the society of physicists, once commenting to the writer that he knew of no professional group with which he would rather be associated.

His thesis was carried out under the direction of Professor H. N. Davis and involved thermodynamic measurements on the element mercury—a field quite different from that in which he ultimately distinguished himself. In the early part of this century, Harvard doctoral candidates in physics were expected to do experimental theses and Loomis enjoyed experimental work. This fact did not, therefore, much affect his career, though it did reshape the careers of students like

David Locke Webster, who was of a more purely theoretical bent.

On completing graduate work Loomis accepted a position as a research physicist at the Westinghouse Lamp Company in Pittsburgh. When World War I intervened, he became a research investigator in the Army Ordnance Department with the rank of captain. He was put in charge of antiaircraft range-firing and the preparation of associated ballistic tables. Loomis served out the war at Aberdeen Proving Ground, which later became a major research center under the directorship of a former Harvard classmate, R. H. Kent.

NEW YORK UNIVERSITY: BAND SPECTRA OF DIATOMIC MOLECULES

Since he did not particularly enjoy the special challenges and pressures of industrial research, Loomis accepted, in 1920, a position in New York University's physics department. When Loomis joined the department, physics at New York University was as highly regarded as at Columbia University, and it appeared to some that NYU might become the leading department in the New York area.

Once there, Loomis decided to work on the analysis of band spectra of diatomic molecules. He rapidly gained a worldwide reputation as the discoverer of the influence of the isotopic composition of the constituent atoms upon the bands, the initial work being carried out with hydrogen chloride.

The 1920s proved to be very productive years for him, involving, among other things, close cooperation with Robert W. Wood in the analysis of a number of spectra. Loomis discovered new isotopes of carbon and oxygen and determined, with Wood, the nuclear spin of potassium. Work with band spectra remained his principal research interest, yet Loomis—ingenious and with wide-ranging interests—also experimented with the oil-drop technique for determining electric charge, using it to carry out (what for the times were) precision measurements of the ratio of the charge on the electron to that on the proton.

This was an enormously exciting period in the evolution of quantum theory. Quantum statistics and wave mechanics were finally achieving permanent form, at least in so far as they apply to atomic and molecular systems, and Loomis's research was central to the emerging structure.

UNIVERSITY OF ILLINOIS AT URBANA

In 1928 Loomis was awarded a Guggenheim Memorial Foundation Fellowship to study at Göttingen and Zürich. The association with European notables intrigued him, but his reflections on that period generally dealt with the European scientific environment of the day.

It was during that year, moreover, that he was invited to become head of the Department of Physics at the University of Illinois in Urbana, and he spent a significant fraction of his time dwelling on the offer. This involved a special trip back to the United States to look over the situation firsthand. By 1928 Loomis felt that the future of physics at NYU might prove to be limited, while Illinois, with a large and reasonably well-funded department, seemed very promising. Physics at Illinois had an interesting history, going back all the way to 1870, although a formal department was not established until 1889. The department's first head, Samuel W. Stratton, went on to become head of the Bureau of Standards and president of the Massachusetts Institute of Technology.

Loomis decided to accept the position at Illinois, and— aside from a four-year period as associate director of the Radiation Laboratory at MIT during World War II, and a two-year period as the organizer of the MIT Lincoln Laboratory—he remained in Urbana for the rest of the life. His wife, Edith, a native New Englander, learned to enjoy life as a faculty wife in a large midwestern university while still remaining true to her heritage. Throughout their long happy marriage, the Loomises spent long periods during the summer with her family on Martha's Vineyard.

During the next decade Loomis's outstanding qualities as an institution-builder came to the fore. Despite the rigors imposed by the Great Depression, and in part because of them, he had succeeded in gathering a distinguished faculty of young physicists at Urbana by 1939. These scientists contributed enormously—both at Illinois and in subsequent posts elsewhere—to the profession's evolution and standing in our country. Building an outstanding research institution, Loomis at the same time made certain teaching at all levels conformed to the highest standards.

In spite of the heavy administrative obligations associated with heading a large department that serves a number of university interests, Loomis continued doing excellent research. During this time, moreover, a number of outstanding graduate students carried out their Ph.D. research under his tutelage.

Since Urbana is what is sometimes called a centrally isolated community, Edith and Wheeler Loomis made certain that their home was a warm and happy mecca for a substantial fraction of the academic community, not least those in the physics department. They enjoyed, and indeed cultivated, people of all generations, a spirit that spilled over to the entire department. Many individuals who once spent time in the department later commented wistfully on the special atmosphere they had found there.

WORLD WAR II: THE RADIATION LABORATORY AT MIT

World War II intervened just at the time Loomis felt he had achieved his goal in developing a large, productive, modern Department of Physics. Inevitably, members of the staff were called away for various important aspects of military research. Early in 1941, Loomis received a plea from Dr. Lee A. DuBridge, director of the Radiation Laboratory at MIT, to join his administrative staff as associate director. One of their principal tasks was that of preserving the Laboratory's freedom of action in the face of meddling from Washington. They managed to do so with perfect tact. Both men earned the respect of the Laboratory staff for their dedication to all aspects of its functioning—not least for the attention given to both personal and professional needs of individuals in every rank.

Loomis's deep involvement with the Radiation Laboratory occupied his mind and physical energies completely and made a lasting imprint on him. The close personal associations he experienced there remained strong for the remainder of his life. Though not a man given to reminiscence, one of his fondest possessions was a framed panel of photographs of the twenty or so individuals who had led the Laboratory in its very successful wartime work.

RETURN TO ILLINOIS

In 1946 when Loomis and his family returned to Illinois they encountered a new world. Not only was the national physics community the object of considerable adulation, but an enormous flood of students, including returning veterans, decided to include physics in their curriculum. This required a rapid expansion of facilities and staff, and the opportunities for the employment of well-seasoned physicists was good everywhere. Some of the individuals who had been on the staff prior to the war, moreover, had left for special assignments elsewhere and decided for one reason or another not to return.

Many others in Loomis's position decided to fill their positions rapidly, but he wisely decided not to compromise on quality. He built Illinois' new, larger physics department gradually, as individuals who conformed to his standards became available.

In keeping with the interests of the time, he decided to focus first on developing a faculty of researchers in atomic, nuclear, and high energy particle physics. He noted, however, that solid state physics was beginning to emerge as a respectable field for study and in 1948 decided that some of the positions in his department should be devoted to it. One result of that decision was that he invited the author of this memoir to join the department and to help him expand that area of research. So began a long, close association and friendship that represents one of the most memorable facets of my own life.

Loomis was elected president of the American Physical Society in 1949. Addressing the Society on his retirement he spoke on the theme "Can Physics Serve Two Masters?" In this speech he expressed his deep conviction that, whatever else individual physicists became involved in, their principal obligation lay in the disclosure of the underlying properties of nature. This homely but profound advice was given at a time when it was easy for physicists to be diverted into applied work. Although he had great respect for applied research, Loomis made it clear that it was the profession's duty to give precedence to basic work.

During the Korean War in 1951, Loomis was asked to organize a new laboratory that would be attached to MIT. He spent the next two years at that task. Today the Lincoln Laboratory, one of the many products of his splendid organizational ability, occupies a leading position among defense laboratories everywhere.

Upon returning to Illinois after this second, relatively brief, sojourn in the Boston area, he took up campus life again and remained active as department head until his retirement in 1957. By this time he was much revered on campus. His advice was sought and respected, but—unlike many other campus leaders—he was not one to dominate discussions at the University Senate meetings. When he did offer advice, his recommendations were generally taken.

Of everything that occurred at Illinois during the years following World War II, that of which he was perhaps most proud was the evolution within the department of the term "Loomis tenure." This expression was applied to the ironclad promise Loomis occasionally made to nontenured staff who had been offered attractive positions elsewhere. Once he had promised to give individuals tenure at a certain rank as the positions became available, it was done. (This would, of course, be somewhat more difficult today given the dubiously useful proliferation of committees in the decision-making chain.)

As was the practice in the University Senate at that time, Loomis sometimes delivered an obituary statement for a deceased member of the faculty, many of whom were old friends. He once confided to me that he labored hard in the preparation of such obituaries because he hated to think that, in paying the last tribute to an old associate, he would bore his colleagues to death. I trust that I have not done so in this account of his own richly productive life.

SELECTED BIBLIOGRAPHY

1917

The heat of vaporization of mercury. (Ph.D. diss., Harvard University)

With L. S. Marks. The physical properties of anhydrous ammonia.

1920

Absorption spectrum of hydrogen chloride. *Nature* 106:179.

Infra-red spectra of isotopes. *Astrophys. J.* 52:248; also in *Phys. Rev.* 17(1921):436-A.

1922

The ratio of the two elementary charges. *Phys. Rev.* 20:15; 19: 535-A.

Oil-drop experiments as proof of the invariance of electric charge. *Phys. Rev.* 10:111-A.

1926

Chapters on fluorescence and on isotope effect. In: *Nat. Res. Counc. Bull.* 2, pt. 3, No. 57.

Correlation of the fluorescent and absorption spectra of iodine. *Phys. Rev.* 27:802-A; 29:112.

1927

New series in the spectrum of fluorescent iodine. *Phys. Rev.* 29: 355-A.

1928

Vibration levels and heat of dissociation of Na_2. *Phys. Rev.* 29:607-A; 31:323, 705-A.

With R. W. Wood. Rotational structure of the blue-green bands of Na_2. *Phys. Rev.* 31:1126-A; 32:223.

With R. W. Wood. Optically excited iodine bands with alternate missing lines. *Philos. Mag.* 6:231; also in *Phys. Rev.* 31:705.

With S. W. Nile, Jr. New features of the red band system of sodium. *Phys. Rev.* 31:1135-A; 32:873.

1929

With A. J. Allen. Ultraviolet fluorescence of IBr and I_2. *Phys. Rev.* 33:639-A.

1930

Iodine fluorescence in the infra-red. *Phys. Rev.* 35:662-A.

1931

With R. W. Wood. Nuclear spin of potassium. *Phys. Rev.* 38:854.

With R. E. Nusbaum. The magnetic rotation spectrum and heat of dissociation of the lithium molecule. *Phys. Rev.* 37:1712-A; 38:1447.

Rotational structure of the red bands of potassium. *Phys. Rev.* 38:2153; 39:189-A.

1932

With R. E. Nusbaum. Heats of dissociation of Na_2 and K_2. *Phys. Rev.* 39:179-A.

With H. Q. Fuller. The enhancement of iodine absorption by the admixture of oxygen. *Phys. Rev.* 39:180-A.

With R. E. Nusbaum. Magnetic rotation spectrum and heat dissociation of the potassium molecule. *Phys. Rev.* 39:89.

With R. E. Nusbaum. Magnetic rotation spectrum and heat dissociation of the sodium molecule. *Phys. Rev.* 40:380−86.

With J. G. Winans. Über einen Versuch zur Auffindung des Ramaneffekts en Metallelektronen. *Z. Phys.* 73:658−61.

1934

With T. F. Watson. New band system of tin oxide. *Phys. Rev.* 45:805−6.

With M. J. Arvin. Band spectrum of NaK. *Phys. Rev.* 46:286−91.

With P. Kusch. Band spectrum of caesium. *Phys. Rev.* 46:292−301.

1936

With W. H. Brandt. Band spectrum of OH^-. *Phys. Rev.* 49:55−66.

With P. Kusch. Band spectrum of caesium. *Phys. Rev.* 49:217−18.

1939

With P. Kusch. The magnetic rotation spectra of SO_2 and CS_2 in the ultraviolet. *Phys. Rev.* 55:850−57.

1950

Can physics serve two masters? *Bull. At. Sci.* 6:115.

Jacob Marschak

JACOB MARSCHAK

July 23, 1898–July 27, 1977

BY KENNETH J. ARROW

ORN IN 1898 IN KIEV, capital of the Ukraine, Jacob
Marschak died seventy-nine years later in Los Angeles,
California, still in active service as professor of economics and
business administration at the University of California at Los
Angeles and president-elect of the American Economic Association. These facts only barely suggest the long and varied
odyssey of his career and his high—though slowly developed—position in American economics.

Marschak's scholarly career spanned fifty-five years and
three very different environments: Germany of the Weimar
period, the United Kingdom of the Great Depression, and
the United States from World War II on. The world economy
and economists' perceptions and theories were altering rapidly, and Marschak experienced, in addition, international
variances in academic environment—especially in traditions
and modes of economic thought. To all these influences must
be added the fact that he was a Russian and a Jew, whose
educational and political formation derived from a particular
period of Russian history that had little in common with the
life of his host countries.

It is not surprising, therefore, that Marschak's focus as an
economist showed considerable changes of direction over his
long and productive lifetime. His early empirical and prac-

tical interests later yielded to theoretical and methodological themes; his youthful political enthusiasms subsided, and he became increasingly aloof from political affairs and even from specific proposals of economic policy.

For all the changes marking Marschak's thought and work, his extraordinary ability to synthesize enabled him to maintain in his work an underlying continuity of purpose and approach. He looked at the problem in hand from every useful angle, drawing on every good idea and theoretical presupposition, then subjected it to severe criticism regarding utility, clarity of expression, and contribution to the understanding of economic issues. This process allowed him to be remarkably open to new ideas and methods, which he would then transform with his own improvements and clarifications.

Marschak became a leader of research organizations at a relatively young age in Germany, and later—with his increasing recognition—was director of the Oxford Institute of Statistics (1935–1939) and of the Cowles Commission for Research in Economics at The University of Chicago (1943–1948)—a fertile period that greatly influenced the course of economic analysis in several diverse fields. Only after 1948 did he begin to make the contributions to economic analysis that are most distinctively his own. Yet in curious ways, the subject matter of his later studies was consonant with his earlier career. An organizer of economic research, he became a theorist of organization. A student and critic of new developments in economic analysis, he developed the economics of information. A skeptic distrustful of received dogma, he studied the economics of uncertainty.

Another characteristic of Marschak's work was his consistently interdisciplinary approach. Some of his early papers dealt with class structure and the emerging phenomenon of Italian fascism. From 1928 to about 1953, though his titles stayed more narrowly within the field of economics as it was then understood, the papers themselves not infrequently contained broader notions derived from politics, sociology, and—later—individual psychology. His work on information and organization, for example, led to a series of experimental and theoretical studies on the psychology of decision making, while during his last fifteen years he organized an interdisciplinary behavioral sciences seminar that proved a main source of contact among mathematical modelers with widely divergent interests.

EDUCATION AND EARLY LIFE

Marschak's parents were well-to-do Russian Jews assimilated to the local culture. Their son received some formal Jewish education but was never religious. His family sympathized with the revolution of 1905, but Marschak later remembered the pogrom that followed. He learned German and French from governesses but at age nine was refused admittance to gymnasium because of the very small Jewish quota. He went instead to the First Kiev School of Commerce.

In 1915, after engaging in the very common group discussions about which revolutionary group to join, he became a Marxist and, in the same year, entered the Kiev School of Technology. He joined the Menshevik Internationalist (antiwar) faction, was arrested with others in December 1916, and was released with the fall of the Czar in February 1917. He then joined the Kiev municipal government, but in October that coalition broke into a three-cornered struggle: Bolsheviks, supporters of the Kerensky government, and Ukrainians wanting a separate state. The last group won.

Marschak and his entire family left Kiev to settle in a resort in the Terek region of the northern Caucasus, where political activity was also intense. Bolsheviks there were organizing all Russian political parties against the Moslem mountaineers—a coalition also intended as a counterweight to the Cossacks, with whom there was an uneasy alliance. In this government Marschak became Secretary of Labor, leading the Menshevik and Socialist Revolutionary movement to withhold recognition of the Bolshevik government in Petrograd until the elected constituent assembly was allowed to meet.

But by June 1918 another three-sided conflict had arisen—this time among Mensheviks, Cossacks, and Bolsheviks (who were by then allied with the mountaineers). Marschak composed manifestos explaining the Menshevik government's aims, acting essentially as a press relations officer. But when the government eventually came under the control of a local dictator, he and his family returned to Ukrainian-run Kiev.

By this time Marschak, like many of his friends and political colleagues, had decided there was no longer a viable political cause in Russia to support. In 1919, after studying statistics briefly at the Kiev Institute of Economics, he decided to study economics at the University of Berlin for six months. This brief period was, according to his later accounts, extremely important in his life, for it was in the lectures of Berlin economist and statistician Ladislaus von Bortkiewicz that he first learned the importance of mathematical and statistical methods in economic analysis. He then moved to the University of Heidelberg, where he received his Ph.D. in 1922.

Economics in Germany at that time was a broad subject. Not only did Marschak study with economist Emil Lederer— a strong advocate of quantitative analysis—but also with philosopher Karl Jaspers and sociologist Alfred Weber.

Because of the good relations between Mensheviks and German Social Democrats, the latter helped Marschak get started in his career. From 1924 to 1926 he was an economics reporter for the famous newspaper, the *Frankfurter Allgemeiner Zeitung*, after which he joined the staff of the *Forschungsstelle für Wirtschaftspolitik* (Research Center for Economic Policy) in Berlin, sponsored by the labor unions and the Social Democratic Party.

His interests and aspirations shifted increasingly toward the academic, and he spent some months in England in 1927 on a Rockefeller Foundation travelling fellowship—the first of several support grants from that source. Back in Germany he joined the staff of the University of Kiel's *Institut für Seeverkehr und Weltwirtschaft* (Institute for Maritime Shipping and World Economics), headed by Bernhard Harms, an academic entrepreneur with a good eye for quality in those who had had difficulty finding academic posts. In 1930, overcoming the liability of his Russian accent and Jewish origin, he was appointed *Privatdozent* at the University of Heidelberg.

THE 1920S: THE ECONOMICS OF INDUSTRY

Outside journalism, Marschak's work during the 1920s was largely devoted to studies of industry. At Kiel he directed a large study on export industries for the Reichstag (1929,1). Among the papers with the greatest permanent interest were his first, about the raging debate (started by Ludwig von Mises) on the possibility of a rationally planned socialist society (1923,1). The market system, argued Marschak, could not only be used under socialism, it was likely to work better under socialism than under the monopolistic distortions of capitalism. It is interesting to see here the earliest manifestation of his later interests in organization theory.

Marschak's other major pioneering paper of this period was his detailed, empirical study of the "new middle class"—white-collar workers who, he argued, though economically workers, were sociologically middle class. (1926,3).

Marschak's empirical work led him into studies of demand. He began to participate in the growing econometric movement (not yet so-named) in which formal statistical methods and economic theory were used jointly to interpret empirical economic data. His careful work on the elasticity of demand (1931,1) was—with the contemporary works of Wassily Leontief and Ragnar Frisch—a major contribution to the development of the field.

With financing from the Rockefeller Foundation, he and Walther Lederer also conducted a major empirical study of capital formation. Because of the political upheavals in Germany at that time, however, it was not published until 1936, when it came out in England in the original German (1936,1). He was also one of the young German economists who advocated compensatory public works policy as a response to the Depression (1931,3), years before the publication of Keynes's *The General Theory of Employment, Interest, and Money* (1936).

Marschak immediately perceived the consequences of the Nazi accession to power in 1933. He had by this time achieved sufficient international reputation to have been invited to write two articles in the *Encyclopaedia of the Social Sciences* (1933,1,2). Through the good offices of Redvers Opie, he was appointed Chichele Lecturer at All Souls College, Oxford— a position designed for refugees.

English economics was in general far in advance of German at that time, but Marschak brought with him quantitative skills that Oxford lacked. Two years after his arrival, the Oxford Institute of Statistics was created (again with Rockefeller Foundation support) for systematic empirical work, and through Opie and Roy F. Harrod, Marschak was made director. Though treated with great reserve by most of the Oxford economics faculty, the Institute became a world-recognized center for empirical analysis in economics. In 1938, Marschak, Helen Makower, and H. W. Robinson carried out a study of the geographical mobility of labor that was probably the first true fusion of theoretical reasoning with formal statistical analysis in this area (1938,3). As befits the period, differentials in unemployment rates among cities were found to be a chief determinant of mobility.

THE 1930S: DEMAND AND CAPITAL FORMATION

Marschak's work on demand and on capital formation deepened and developed into more theoretical and methodological studies. The earliest of his papers that are still influential today were two on money and the theory of assets—in the one written with Makower he introduced the portfolio approach to the demand for money as one among a set of assets (1938,1,2). Choosing a new tack from the Cambridge and Fisher approaches, he stressed the relationship of money holdings to wealth rather than income and, above all, derived the demand for different kinds of assets from the uncertainties connected with their holding. Although ideas of this kind had long been informally expressed, this was their first true modeling. Since the expected-utility theory of behavior under uncertainty was then in limbo because it appeared to conflict with the ordinal concept of utility, Marschak had an alternative criterion function—an indifference map in the space of the first two or three moments of the probability distribution of returns.

In 1939 Marschak published a number of methodologically and practically important papers on demand analysis (1939,1,2,6). They studied, in particular, the usefulness of budget studies in developing the consumption function. They also showed how to combine budget and time series studies and aggregate individual demand functions into a national total.

New York (1938–1943)

Marschak spent December 1938 to August 1939 in the United States as a Rockefeller Foundation travelling fellow.

Anticipating the outbreak of World War II, he arranged for his family to be brought over. In 1940 he was appointed professor of economics in the graduate faculty of the New School for Social Research—a faculty created largely to accommodate the flood of German refugee scholars and to make use of their talents. At the same time, through the National Bureau of Economic Research, he organized a seminar in mathematical economics and econometrics that served as a clearinghouse for a flood of new ideas—primarily, though not exclusively, for the growing group of European scholars. After the outbreak of the war, they came not only from Germany, but also from such occupied countries as Norway and the Netherlands.

One of the great motivating forces in quantitative research in this period was Jan Tinbergen's massive 1939 study of business cycles conducted for the League of Nations.[1] Like many large-scale studies, its most important scientific effect occurred after it was completed: reflections by participants and critics on ways it could be done better. Ragnar Frisch had perceived while the investigation was under way that statistical inference in the case of simultaneous relations posed new problems not dreamed of in the philosophy of regression analysis. His student, Trygve Haavelmo, who was in the United States during the war, developed the principles of maximum likelihood estimation of simultaneous equations (1943), one of the papers presented at Marschak's seminar.

A small circle of economists in New York immediately recognized the importance of Haavelmo's work. As early as 1942 Marschak wrote a paper on its general philosophy (1942,1). The theoretical statisticians Henry B. Mann and Abraham Wald proved a fundamental consistency property of the es-

[1] J. Tinbergen, *Statistical Testing of Business Cycle Theories*, 2 vols. (Geneva: Economic Intelligence Service of the League of Nations, 1939; reprint ed., New York: Agatha Press, 1956).

timates.[2] Tjalling Koopmans, who had earlier worked on Tinbergen's study and found the distribution of the serial correlation coefficient (a closely related statistical problem), was drawn into the field of simultaneous-equations estimation.

THE UNIVERSITY OF CHICAGO AND THE COWLES COMMISSION FOR RESEARCH IN ECONOMICS (1943–1955)

At this moment there occurred an unusual conjunction of opportunities. In 1943 Marschak was appointed director of the Cowles Commission for Research in Economics and professor of economics at The University of Chicago. The Commission, founded and supported by Alfred R. Cowles III, an investment manager who had also been treasurer of the Econometric Society in its early days, had pioneered the use of econometric methods. In particular, its prewar summer conferences at Colorado Springs had attracted the leaders of the leading econometricians. Marschak had attended the 1937 summer conference and in 1943 was offered the directorship.

During Marschak's directorship from 1943 to 1948, the central focus of the Commission's work was to develop economy-wide models for predictive and structural analysis. Two elements were needed: appropriate statistical methods and an economic theory with which to derive equations that fit the data.

The theoretical impetus came from John Maynard Keynes and his American followers. Marschak's receptivity to arguments about purchasing power enabled him to accept Keynesian theory with little of the difficulty experienced by others. By the same token he lacked the dogmatism of many

[2] H. B. Mann and Abraham Wald, "On the Statistical Treatment of Linear Stochastic Difference Equations," *Econometrica* 11 (1943):173–220.

of the newly converted English and American economists. Several of his 1941 papers (1,2,3), expounded Keynesian policies and theories and related them to earlier European thought—especially that of Knut Wicksell. In an important paper (1942,2), Marschak cleared up many of the confusions regarding identities, equilibrium, and stability—essentials of Keynesian methodology—then current in the literature. At the New School he supervised Franco Modigliani's dissertation, for a long time the most influential exposition of Keynes. But the highly specific discipline of fitting a complete model meant that the Keynesian apparatus had to be defined in far more detail than had been needed for more general expositions and policy statements.

A small, but increasing, band of young economists was finding mathematics and formal thinking useful. Statistical theory, moreover, was just beginning to attract significant numbers of students. Still, neither of these groups was in great demand. The academic market during the war and the immediate postwar period was not strong; mathematical economics was little regarded; and theoretical statistics had yet to find a suitable academic home.

Marschak seized the opportunity to secure a remarkable staff at bargain prices. Though he managed a tenure faculty appointment for Koopmans, he was forced to appoint the rest purely on a research basis. Lawrence Klein developed the model and the data. Haavelmo was there for a few years working on both model development and statistical methodology. The main developments in theoretical statistics were carried out by Koopmans and the theoretical statisticians, Theodore W. Anderson and Herman Rubin. Though sometimes going far afield, Kenneth J. Arrow and Leonid Hurwicz worked on problems in economic theory and statistical inference suggested by the basic modeling effort. Among The University of Chicago graduate students drawn into the work, mention must be made of Don Patinkin, whose thesis under Marschak's supervision was a milestone in the integration of Keynesian and monetary theory with neoclassical general equilibrium analysis. His subsequent appointment at the Hebrew University of Jerusalem, where he refashioned the Economics Department, stemmed from a recommendation by Marschak to Fritz Naphtali, who had headed the Forschungsstelle für Wirtschaftspolitik during Marschak's stay. Indeed, the Commission in this period was producing scholars as well as scholarship, and it is a close question which was the more valuable.

Marschak did not impose direction; he provided vision and drive. Recognizing the creative energies of his research associates, he saw to it that they flowed in their own most productive channels. He insisted on understanding the essence of the most technical developments and, by requiring explanations, forced the staff to reevaluate repeatedly the content and significance of their work. His clear, terse introductions to the statistical methodology publications penetrated remarkably deeply into the essentials of the issues (1950,1, 1953,1; see also 1947,2).

With William H. Andrews he carried out one major study of his own: the first application of the simultaneous equations technique to the estimation of production functions (1944,2). Using new statistical approaches, this study resolved the difficulties of interpretation that had been found in the pioneering work of Paul Douglas.

During the same period Marschak reverted once to his old field of industry studies, though in a new context. Through his personal relations with Leo Szilard and the other European scientists at Chicago who had participated in the Manhattan Project, he came to feel that the economist's perspective was important in assessing the future of atomic energy. At the Cowles Commission he initiated a study on the problem. The bulk of this study was done by others, particularly Sam Schurr and Herbert Simon, but Marschak's judgment, expressed in a summary introduction to the publication of the project (1950,4), was amply confirmed. Straightforward economic analysis showed that the impact of atomic energy could be nothing like the total technological transformation envisaged by many scientists and intellectuals.

The Economics of Information and Team Theory

Turning the directorship of the Cowles Commission over to Koopmans in 1948, Marschak moved very rapidly into pure scholarship and into more abstract and theoretical work than ever before. He was greatly excited by John von Neumann and Oskar Morgenstern's revival of the expected utility theory in its axiomatic form, by Abraham Wald's exploration of the foundations of statistical decision theory, and (at his own Cowles Commission) by Leonard J. Savage and Rubin and Herman Chernoff's axiomatic development of subjective probability theory. To apply these theories he turned most immediately to his old subject, the demand for money and other assets (1949,1).

Then his interests found new focus. Attempts by Marschak, Albert G. Hart, and others to clarify the concept of liquidity had shown how important anticipating new information was to economic behavior and launched Marschak on a series of studies regarding the economics of information. The value, or demand price, of information in any context was governed by the additional benefit that could be obtained by its optimal use, an approach he initiated in 1954 (1954,2) and summarized in 1971 (1971,2). This subject, originally broached by Marschak, has since become a major research area. His most noteworthy immediate influence in this field was on his student, Roy Radner, and on a colleague at the University of California, Jack Hirshleifer.

Investigating the importance of communication and its limits in the transmission of information led Marschak to a new approach to the study of organization—a simplification of the theory of games he called "the theory of teams."[3] A team is an organization in which the members have the same preferences and prior beliefs but have different information and choose different actions. The problem is how to devise optimal decision rules prescribing each member's action as a function of his information. Characteristically for Marschak, his analysis does not so much solve this problem as put it in an entirely different—and much more varied—setting. His work with Radner on this subject was embodied in the book *The Economic Theory of Teams* (1972,1).[4]

Stochastic Decision

The third major area of Marschak's research after 1948 was stochastic decision, which, while recognizing that individuals are not thoroughly consistent, also recognizes that the theory of rational behavior has some foundation. Individuals are assumed to make choices randomly about a rational (transitive and connected) pattern, a thesis that was developed both theoretically and experimentally (see 1960,1; and, with G. Becker and M. DeGroot, 1963, 3,4,5). Stochastic decision work so far has had greater impact on psychologists than on economists, though it was recently used as the basis for

[3] Marschak first introduced the notion of team theory, in French, at an extraordinarily interesting conference on the theory of risk-bearing (1953,2). Its first English publication took place in the same paper in which he discussed the evaluation of information (1954,2).

[4] Marschak's team theory makes precise the meaning of "informational decentralization," of central importance to the controversy on socialist planning that was the subject of his first published paper.

Daniel McFadden's work on choice among alternative modes of transportation.[5]

HONORS AND LATER LIFE

In 1955 Marschak and the Cowles Commission, now renamed the Cowles Foundation for Research in Economics, left Chicago for Yale University. He did not stay long; in 1960 he accepted the post of professor of economics and business administration at the University of California at Los Angeles. Official retirement did not change his activities at all; he remained as active in teaching and research when emeritus as he had been before.

Throughout most of his career in America, Marschak had a reputation as being rather esoteric, and his later broad interests did not change that view. But widespread recognition of his work grew—especially as his former students and junior colleagues became information disseminators. He was elected a fellow of the American Academy of Arts and Sciences in 1962, a distinguished fellow of the American Economic Association in 1967, and a member of the National Academy of Sciences in 1972. He received honorary degrees from the University of Bonn in 1968, from his old University of Heidelberg in 1972, and from Northwestern University in 1977.

In 1976 he was nominated and elected president-elect of the American Economic Association for the year 1977. According to the custom of the association, the president-elect prepares the annual meeting and becomes president the following year. Marschak had completed all arrangements for the December 1977 meeting but died in the summer of that year.

[5] D. McFadden, "Quantal Choice Analysis: A Survey," *Ann. Econ. Soc. Meas.* 5 (1976):363–90.

THIS ARTICLE WAS BASED largely on personal communications and reminiscences of Lawrence Klein, Tjalling Koopmans, Karl Lachman, Carl Landauer, Walther Lederer, Adolph Lowe, Helen Makower, Redvers Opie, Don Patinkin, Roy Radner, Hans Speier, and the author. Important material on Marschak's early life is found in an interview with him conducted by Richard A. Pierce, "Notes on Recollections of Kiev and the Northern Caucasus, 1917–1918," on file at the Regional Oral History Office, Bancroft Library, University of California, Berkeley.

SELECTED BIBLIOGRAPHY

1923

Wirtschaftsrechnung und Gemeinwirtschaft. *Arch. Sozialwiss.* 51: 501-20.

1926

Der neue Mittelstand. *Grundriss der Sozialökonomik* 9(1):120–41.

1931

Elastizität der Nachfrage. Tübingen: J. C. B. Mohr.

1933

Consumption (Measurement). *Encyclopedia of the social sciences.*
Wages (Theory). *Encyclopedia of the social sciences.*

1938

Money and the theory of assets. *Econometrica* 6:311-25.*
With H. Makower. Assets, prices and monetary theory. *Economica* N. S. 5:261–88.*
With H. Makower and H. W. Robinson. Studies in the mobility of labour. *Oxford Econ. Pap.* 1:83–123; 2:70–97; 4:39–62.

1939

Family budgets and the so-called multiplier. *Can. J. Econ.* 5: 358–62.
On combining market and budget data in demand studies. *Econometrica* 7:332–35.
Personal and collective budget functions. *Rev. Econ. Stat.* 21: 161–70.*

1941

Lack of confidence. *Soc. Res.* 8:41–62.*
The task of economic stabilization. *Soc. Res.* 8:361–72.
Wicksell's two interest rates. *Soc. Res.* 8:469–78.*

* Reprinted in 1974,1.

1942

Economic interdependence and statistical analysis. In: *Studies in mathematical economics and econometrics in memory of Henry Schultz*, eds. O. Lange et al., pp. 135–50. Chicago: University of Chicago Press.*

Identity and stability in economics. *Econometrica* 10:61–74.*

1944

With W. H. Andrews. Random simultaneous equations and the theory of production. *Econometrica* 12:143–205.*

1947

Economic structure, path, policy, and prediction. *Am. Econ. Pap. Proc.* 37:81–84.

1949

Role of liquidity under complete and incomplete information. *Am. Econ. Rev.* 39:182–95.*

1950

Statistical inference in economics: an introduction. In: *Statistical inference in dynamic economic models*, ed. T. C. Koopmans, pp. 1–50. New York: Wiley.

Economic aspects of atomic power, eds. Sam Schurr and Jacob Marschak. Princeton: Princeton University Press.

1953

Economic measurements for policy and prediction. In: *Studies in econometric method*, eds. W. C. Hood and T. C. Koopmans, pp. 1–26. New York: Wiley.*

Équipes et organisations en régime d'incertitude. *Économetrie: colloques internationaux du Centre National de la Recherche Scientifique*, 40:201–11. (From a CNRS colloquium held May 12–17, 1952, in Paris)

1954

Towards an economic theory of organization and information. In: *Decision processes*, eds. R. M. Thrall, R. L. Davis, and C. H. Coombs, pp. 187–220. New York: Wiley.*

1960

Remarks on the economics of information. In: *Contributions to scientific research in management*, Western Data Processing Center, pp. 79–100. Los Angeles: University of California at Los Angeles.*

1963

With J. G. Becker and M. DeGroot. Stochastic models of choice behavior. *Behav. Sci.* 8:41–55.*

With J. G. Becker and M. DeGroot. An experimental study of some stochastic models for wagers. *Behav. Sci.* 8:199–202.*

With J. G. Becker and M. DeGroot. Probabilities of choices among very similar objects: An experiment to decide between two models. *Behav. Sci.* 8:306–11.*

1971

Economics of information systems. In: *Frontiers of quantitative economics*, ed. M. Intriligator, pp. 32–107. Amsterdam: North-Holland.*

1972

With R. Radner. *Economic theory of teams.* New Haven: Yale University Press.

1974

Economic information, decision and prediction, 3 vols. Dordrecht and Boston: Reidel.

DONALD HOWARD MENZEL

April 11, 1901–December 14, 1976

BY LEO GOLDBERG AND LAWRENCE H. ALLER

D ONALD H. MENZEL, one of the first practitioners of theoretical astrophysics in the United States, pioneered the
application of quantum mechanics to astronomical spectroscopy. He was the first to establish the physical characteristics
of the solar chromospheres and he initiated the modern era
of investigations of physical processes in gaseous nebulae.
Although primarily a theorist, he organized and conducted
more than a dozen solar-eclipse expeditions and established
two major solar observatories in the western United States.
As a naval officer in World War II, he showed how solar
observations could be used to anticipate large changes in conditions of long-distance radio wave propagation. He later
played a leading role in establishing the Central Radio Propagation Laboratory of the National Bureau of Standards. As
director of the Harvard College Observatory from 1952 to
1966, he established one of the first university programs for
research and instruction in radioastronomy and space astronomy. He was elected to the National Academy of Sciences
in 1948.

EARLY LIFE

The Menzel family was of German origin, his great grandfather, Johann Theodor Menzel, being a member of the

mounted police in Magdeburg. His grandparents emigrated from Germany to America as children, and his father, Charles Theodor, Jr., was born in Brooklyn, New York. When Charles was six, the Menzel family moved to Denver, Colorado. But when Charles was twelve years old his father died, leaving the family in difficult circumstances. Forced to leave school to support the family, the boy found a job with the Denver & Rio Grande Railroad, first as a telegraph operator, then as clerk to a ticket salesman, and finally as the Railroad's passenger agent in Florence, Colorado. In 1900 he married Ina Zint, and Donald was born in Florence a year later, on April 11, 1901.

Four years later Donald's father was transferred to Leadville, Colorado, a famous pioneer mining camp that—at 10,200 feet—was the highest community in the United States. There Donald grew up and received most of his primary and secondary education. In 1910 Donald's father invested his mining savings and proceeds in a partnership in Leadville's largest general store, and the family's financial condition improved markedly.

Young Donald displayed a remarkable ability as a "quick study." By age five he was reading *Gulliver's Travels*, and even before that his father had taught him to send and receive simple messages in Morse code. Fortunately for the precocious young Menzel, the school superintendent had initiated a program of progressive education that allowed exceptional students to advance at an accelerated pace, and Donald was able to graduate from high school at age sixteen.

As a schoolboy Donald pursued hobbies that helped satisfy his scientific curiosity and provided outlets for the almost limitless energy that was to characterize his entire life. Only five when attracted by the sight of brightly colored ores that had spilled from railway cars near Leadville, he soon owned a rapidly growing collection. He actively traded specimens and peddled ore samples to tourists on the trains, once giving a choice sample to President William Howard Taft. In ten years his collection grew to at least two tons; it was eventually donated to the University of Denver.

As a teenager, Menzel built a radio transmitter and receiver with a crystal detector, fabricating all the components himself except the earphone. Years later, in the 1930s, he acquired a "ham" (short for Hammerlund) radio transmitter and receiver with the call letters W1JEX.

Menzel's most absorbing hobby was laboratory chemistry, to which a young friend initiated him at age eleven. A great leap forward in his experiments was made possible by the failure of a leading drugstore in town, for it was purchased by Menzel's father and Donald was able to acquire a huge stock of chemicals and other interesting substances. He and his pals performed many experiments with this expanded laboratory, some prompted by ideas gained from the library chemistry books he read so voraciously, others inspired simply by the urge to mix chemicals and see what happened. Although some of this involved the development and manufacture of explosives, good fortune prevailed, and there were no disasters.

COLLEGE DAYS AND A CHANGE OF PLAN

In 1916 Donald's family moved to Denver, where he graduated from high school in 1917 and enrolled in the University. He earned an A.B. in three years at the University of Denver in his beloved chemistry, but a boyhood friend, Edgar Kettering, had aroused his interest in another subject: astronomy. In later years, Donald always credited Kettering, the total solar eclipse of June 8, 1918, and the outburst of Nova Aquilae almost immediately thereafter with awakening his interest in the field.

Further encouragement came from James Whaler, an inspiring English professor from whom Donald acquired much of his skill in writing. A Princeton alumnus, Dr. Whaler suggested Donald contact Professor R. S. Dugan, a variable star expert, who sent him instructions for making observations and put him in touch with the American Association of Variable Star Observers. Eagerly taking up a program of observing, young Donald was able to use the 20-inch telescope by the start of his senior year. Classes by day and observation by night did not exhaust his energy; he taught a course of college algebra to forty students, took a surveying course, and in his spare time surveyed fields for farmers and laid out the boundaries of the football field!

After graduating with an A.B. degree, young Menzel decided to continue for an additional year to obtain an M.A. He secured the degree under the guidance of Professor Dugan of Princeton, fulfilling the requirements with astronomy courses and a thesis based on observations of eclipsing stars. Now he was ready to study for the Ph.D., for which he already had several offers of fellowships in chemistry.

It was James Whaler who urged him to apply for an astronomy scholarship at Princeton, though Donald's father—worried, like many fathers of future astronomers, that his son would not make a living in astronomy—urged him to stay in chemistry. Yet the head of the Denver University chemistry department pointed out that, while astronomy jobs were few, astronomers were fewer, and urged Donald to do what he really wanted to do. Fortunately for astronomy, he decided to go to Princeton.

WIDE NEW HORIZONS AT PRINCETON

Menzel continued to observe variable stars for Professor Dugan as a means of support, but he was most enthusiastic about the lectures of Professor Henry Norris Russell. Theoretical astrophysics was new; it had been spawned around

1920 by Saha's derivation of the ionization equation and Eddington's stellar interior modeling that led to his famous relation between mass and luminosity. Russell was the first practitioner of theoretical astrophysics in the United States. Inspired by his example, Donald set out to master as many courses in mathematics and physics as possible. Among his teachers were Oswald Veblen, Luther Eisenhart, Augustus Trowbridge, and K. T. Compton, whom he especially admired.

As his thesis for his Ph.D., Menzel sought to establish a stellar temperature scale by applying the Fowler-Milne theory based on application of the Saha equation to stellar spectra. Harlow Shapley employed him at Harvard as a research assistant during the summers of 1922, 1923, and 1924, but when Menzel arrived at Harvard, he found that a young British lady, Cecilia Payne, had been assigned the same topic. Shapley resolved the conflict in Solomon-like fashion, assigning the hot stars to Miss Payne and the cooler ones to Menzel.

While working as Harlow Shapley's assistant, Donald discovered star clusters on the periphery of the Large Magellanic Cloud. Using their apparent diameters, he and Shapley determined that the Large Cloud was some 100,000 light years distant from us.

At the same time, he analyzed Coblentz and Lampland's published observations and measurements of so-called "water-cell transmissions" of radiation from planets. Menzel found that, contrary to popular belief, at least the upper atmospheres of the planets Jupiter, Saturn, and Uranus were extremely cold. His interest in planets later led to an important deduction concerning the atmosphere of Mars. A planet with a dense atmosphere—such as the Earth—would look blue from a great distance because of the strong color-dependence of light-scattering by gas molecules. Conversely,

Mars's red color indicated that the overlying atmosphere was too thin to modify the reflected light by color-dependent molecular scattering. Menzel deduced that the pressure at the surface of the planet was hardly more than one-tenth that of the surface of the Earth.

Upon receipt of his Ph.D. from Princeton in 1924, Donald found that opportunities for an astronomer were few, especially for a new theoretical astrophysicist. He spent the next two years chiefly teaching courses in elementary astronomy, first at the University of Iowa and then at Ohio State University.

In mid-1926 he married Florence Kreager, who had been a student at Ohio State. The pair made an excellent team for the life that lay ahead, and Florence was the ideal hostess. They had two daughters, Suzanne and Elizabeth, and six grandchildren.

AN OPPORTUNITY AT LICK OBSERVATORY

Meanwhile, Henry Norris Russell had convinced authorities at Lick Observatory that they should acquire a staff member conversant with the newer developments in astrophysics. He suggested Menzel, who was offered an appointment. Despite its meaning a cut in salary, Donald accepted the post as a real opportunity to establish himself in research.

He was eager to apply the new developments in atomic physics to the interpretation of astronomical spectra but soon found that the promise of theoretical astrophysics was not at all appreciated by Lick's conservative astronomers. His principal task was to take spectrograms for radial velocity measurements. Fortunately, the director also assigned him the task of analyzing the magnificent collection of solar chromosphere spectra that had been obtained by W. W. Campbell during four different total solar eclipses. This effort was hampered a bit by the fact that Campbell had not calibrated the photographic plates to establish the relationship between blackness of the image and intensity, a limitation Donald ingeniously managed to overcome.

He soon discovered that what was expected of him was to catalogue wavelengths, identify lines with chemical elements, and give crude intensities; whereas his own aim was to apply the newest atomic theory to the study of atomic processes in the solar chromosphere. Despite periodic scoldings by Director Aitken, who admonished him to leave theory to the "poor, underprivileged British astronomers like Milne and Eddington, who have no decent telescopes," Menzel persevered.

After several years of hard labor, he published his results in a large volume that has become a classic in theoretical astrophysics as one of the earliest examples of quantitative astronomical spectroscopy. He found the temperature of the solar chromosphere to be about 4700°K, but the emission lines of H, He I, and He II revealed large deviations from thermodynamic equilibrium. He also derived the fundamental equations of the curve of growth for emission lines. From observed chromospheric density gradients, he found evidence for a mean molecular weight of about 2 in the lower chromosphere, a result that finally persuaded Russell and others that hydrogen and helium are overwhelmingly the most abundant elements in the sun.

While at Lick, Menzel developed an interest in the physics of gaseous nebulae and directed a thesis by Louis Berman, who made a pioneering spectrophotometric study of planetary nebulae. Donald and J. H. Moore made the first spectroscopic determination of the rate and direction of the rotation of the planet Neptune. He wrote a paper with R. T. Birge in which they pointed out that a discrepancy in the molecular weight of hydrogen could be removed if there existed an isotope of mass 2, a suggestion that led Harold Urey to seek and find the predicted isotopes. Finally, Donald made many lasting friendships with physicists and chemists at Berkeley.

PREWAR DAYS AT HARVARD OBSERVATORY

In 1932, to the dismay of friends and students in California, Menzel accepted an offer from Harvard University. Harvard was seeking a replacement for H. H. Plaskett, who had gone to Oxford. Lick Observatory, whose director was quite oblivious to the value of Menzel's work, made no effort to retain him. At Harvard, where theoretical activity was encouraged, the next nine years were to be scientifically the most productive of Menzel's career.

He promptly became acquainted with Harvard and Massachusetts Institute of Technology physicists and persuaded them to work with him on problems of astrophysical interest. He and his students studied quantum mechanics intensively and applied it to radiation and atomic structure calculations pertinent to interpretations of spectroscopic data. Menzel and Leo Goldberg, for example, made use of the concept of fractional parentage to invent a new method for calculating the strengths of multiplets. This early program helped to inspire modern laboratory astrophysics, which is being pursued today at the Joint Institute for Laboratory Astrophysics in Boulder, Colorado, and at the Division of Atomic and Molecular Physics at the Harvard-Smithsonian Center for Astrophysics.

Menzel maintained his interest in the solar chromosphere and used spectra from the 1932 Lick Observatory expedition to Fryeburg, Maine, for pioneering investigations of departures in the solar atmosphere from local thermodynamic equilibrium. In the Soviet Union he and MIT's J. C. Boyce carried out a well-planned program of spectroscopic observations of the 1936 solar eclipse—some 800 spectra were obtained during two minutes of totality.

During this epoch Menzel also developed an improved theory of the curve of growth that related the measured-equivalent widths, or "total intensities," of absorption lines to the corresponding numbers of absorbing atoms. This also laid the groundwork for determining the chemical compositions of solar and stellar atmospheres.

Seeing the dominance of hydrogen in astronomical spectra, Menzel collaborated with C. L. Pekeris in 1935 to improve and extend quantum mechanical calculations of line and continua intensities in the spectrum of hydrogen. In 1937 this study inspired him to initiate, in collaboration with a number of other physicists and astrophysicists, a series of eighteen papers on physical processes in the highly ionized plasmas of gaseous nebulae. Their work on the solar chromosphere and gaseous nebulae was the first realistic investigation of nonequilibrium conditions in celestial plasmas and represented a major advance in the level of sophistication in the analysis of astronomical spectra.

The impact of the nebular series on astronomy has been far-reaching. In the words of D. E. Osterbrock:

"The investigation of the physical processes in gaseous nebulae by Menzel, Goldberg, Aller, Baker, and others before World War II led naturally to the theory of H II regions developed by Strömgren, which in its turn stimulated the observational work on the spiral arms of M31 and other galaxies by Baade, and on the spiral arms of our own galaxy by Morgan. Much of what we know of the galactic structure and dynamics of Population I objects, about abundances of light elements, and of the ultraviolet radiation emitted by hot stars, has been learned from the study of H II regions. Observations of planetary nebulae have led to considerable knowledge of the elemental abundances in highly evolved old objects, the galactic structure and dynamics of Population II objects, and the final stages of evolution of stars with masses of the same order as the Sun's mass."

Although, at that time, high-quality spectrographic equipment had been developed for eclipse work, nothing more advanced than the objective cameras used in the late nineteenth century by Pickering et al. was available at Harvard for work on stellar and nebular spectra. To complement the theoretical work on gaseous nebulae and stellar atmospheres with suitable observational data, it was necessary to secure high-quality spectra from other observatories, among them Lick.

After the Siberian eclipse expedition, Menzel investigated the possibility of observing the solar corona outside of eclipse in broad daylight. After an unsuccessful effort with a device called the coronavisor, he turned to the coronagraph which had been perfected recently by B. Lyot in France.

The first model with a 10-cm objective lens was built and tested in Cambridge with the collaboration of a graduate student, Walter Orr Roberts. They put the equipment into operation on a high mountain at Climax, Colorado, in 1940. By the time Roberts gave up the leadership of the High Altitude Observatory to become the first director of the National Center for Atmospheric Research in Boulder, HAO had become one of the world's leading centers for solar coronal research.

Within the space of eight years, while the country was in deep financial depression and the government provided no financial support, astronomers under Menzel's guidance did ground-breaking theoretical research in atomic and solar physics and on gaseous nebulae, conducted an ambitious eclipse expedition, founded the first coronagraphic observatory in the western hemisphere, and established a school of theoretical astrophysics.

TEACHER, DIPLOMAT, FRIEND

Those of us who were fortunate enough to study with Don in the 1930s—J. G. Baker, J. W. Evans, W. O. Roberts, and the authors, to mention only a few—remember him with affection and awe. His imagination, powers of concentration, and productivity were outstanding. In addition to his heavy research program, he taught courses ranging from elementary astronomy to advanced theoretical astrophysics.

His graduate courses, of necessity, contained liberal doses of atomic physics and quantum mechanics, subjects in which graduate students of that era were often ill-prepared. It also must be remembered that in 1934, though theoretical astrophysics—thanks to such luminaries as Eddington, Jeans, Milne, McCrea, Strömgren, Pannekoek, Minnaert, Unsöld, and Rosseland—was well established as a subdiscipline in Europe, in the United States it was still a novelty. Until the late 1930s, Menzel and his former teacher, H. N. Russell, were the only active theoretical astrophysicists in the land. Much of what Menzel taught, consequently, was the product of his own research.

He was relentless in demanding that his students acquire literacy in written English. He detested excessive use of the passive voice and abominated dangling participles. One of his favorite examples was: "Sitting on a park bench and eating bananas, the sun sank slowly in the west."

His influence was also strongly felt in the summer schools of astronomy organized by Harlow Shapley, in which lectures relevant to theoretical astrophysics were offered by such experts as H. N. Russell, A. Pannekoek, B. Edlén, J. C. Slater, O. Struve, P. Merrill, I. S. Bowen, G. H. Shortley, and S. Rosseland.

Menzel was diplomatic and persuasive in his dealings with bureaucrats and administrators, as the following anecdote will show.

In a chimerical hunt for gold, a cruel and irresponsible father dragged his son out of high school after only two years. Yet despite the discouraging environment of a primitive mining camp and the objections of his family, the teenager continued to pursue his studies in astronomy and related sciences.

On reading an article in *Publications of the Astronomical So-*

ciety of the Pacific by Menzel, the boy wrote him and, by an incredible stroke of luck, managed to meet him at Berkeley, where Menzel was teaching one semester. Menzel gave the would-be astronomer the final examination in Astronomy 1, and he did better than any of the regular students. Menzel promptly recommended that Merton Hill, then director of admissions at UC-Berkeley, admit the young man as a special student. But according to the rules, special students could not be admitted under the age of twenty-one.

Undaunted, Menzel kept hammering on the way the young chap had persevered under miserable conditions and the fact of his having already passed a university course. Why not admit him? Hill relented; the young man was admitted and continued on to have a career in astronomy.

Although he demanded high standards of performance from his students, Don welcomed them as personal friends, and the doors of his home and his office were always open to them without an appointment. In those days he often worked at home until very late, and it was not unusual for students to drop in on him at 10:00 or 11:00 P.M. for a chat on some vexing problems. He was always helpful. This pattern of accessibility greatly enhanced his popularity with students and accelerated the pace of research.

WORLD WAR II AND ITS IMPACT

Pearl Harbor terminated the most scientifically active and rewarding period of Don Menzel's career. After a year of organizational duties and teaching courses in cryptanalysis, Don was offered and accepted a commission as lieutenant commander in the U. S. Navy. He was assigned to the Office of the Chief of Naval Communications as an expert on wave propagation, for which his previous training in solar physics, mathematics, cryptanalysis, and shortwave radio made him uniquely qualified. He soon became an expert on matching radio frequencies to radio communication conditions, making, for example, significant contributions to the success of the Navy's program for the detection of enemy submarines by radio-direction finding.

In particular Menzel showed how solar observations could be used to anticipate profound changes in radio communication conditions and to dictate appropriate changes in radio frequencies. Foreseeing the need for an agency that could provide similar services after the war, he played a leading part in establishing the Central Radio Propagation Laboratory of the National Bureau of Standards, now located in Boulder, Colorado.

AFTER THE WAR

After the war ended, Don returned to his professorship at Harvard, but his agenda had undergone major revision. He resumed teaching and research, but there was no longer the single-minded devotion to pure scholarship that had distinguished his pre-war career. The availability of federal funds in significant amounts, furthermore, offered unparalleled opportunities for the creation of new astronomical facilities, and Don was uniquely situated to seize the moment.

No branch of astronomy at that time offered better prospects for major support than solar physics, where Don had helped demonstrate to the military the importance of monitoring solar phenomena in order to improve the forecasting of radio propagation conditions. His efforts at the Pentagon resulted not only in a major expansion by the Navy of facilities at Climax but also in the establishment by the Air Force of a new solar observatory at Sacramento Peak, New Mexico. Under the directorship of J. W. Evans, a former student of Menzel's, the Sacramento Peak Observatory became a leading research institution. Later the Air Force supplied funds to build a solar radio-wave observatory at Fort Davis, Texas. For many years this observatory supplemented the Sacramento Peak Observatory by providing sweep frequency measurements of solar radio bursts.

DIRECTOR OF THE HARVARD COLLEGE OBSERVATORY, LATER YEARS

In 1952, upon the retirement of Harlow Shapley, Don was appointed acting director of Harvard College Observatory and was chosen to be its permanent director two years later.

This was a critical time in the Observatory's history. After more than twenty years of depression and war, it was severely understaffed and underfunded; buildings and equipment were in a state of disrepair and obsolescence. Ancient buildings were torn down and replaced, sometimes in the face of opposition from the old-timers, new faculty positions were created, and new sources of funding sought.

The most far-reaching step was a cooperative arrangement with the Smithsonian Institution, agreed upon in 1955, to transfer the Smithsonian's Astrophysical Observatory to the grounds of Harvard Observatory. Designed to provide Harvard's astronomy effort with a permanent source of financial support, the arrangement evolved into what is now the Center for Astrophysics, whose success stands as a monument to Menzel's wisdom.

He also assisted Bart J. Bok in the acquisition of a sixty-foot radio telescope and participated in efforts that eventually led to the establishment of the National Radio Astronomical Observatory.

During the 1960s Menzel's activity was slowed by a serious circulatory problem, but he continued to work as his strength permitted. In his later years he developed interests in and wrote papers on a wide range of physical and astronomical topics, including radiative transfer, magnetohydrodynamics, and lunar research.

DONALD H. MENZEL—THE MAN

Menzel's versatility and successful pursuit of a vast range of interests were possible only to a person of enormous energy and ability. Among his diversions while he was a student at Princeton was writing contributions for the magazine, *Science and Invention*, and science fiction articles under a variety of pseudonyms. In addition, he found time to win the chess championship of Princeton and to participate in several Ivy League matches.

He had many hobbies throughout his life, including playing the zither, the piano, the guitar, bridge, and chess; ballroom dancing; necktie collecting; and operating a ham radio. He loved to travel and had a vacation home in Costa Rica. But his best known hobby was doodling sketches of Martians and flying-saucer creatures, the originals of which are now highly prized.

Don's writing skills made him a popular author and editor. He wrote many books on popular science and served as a newspaper correspondent. Among his technical writings was a text on theoretical physics, a book written with Bruce Shore on atomic spectra, and a useful collection of physical formulae.

Astronomers have always had to contend with astrologers and other charlatans, but after World War II the problem became more severe. Menzel's devastating criticism of Velikovsky's *Worlds in Collision* in *Physics Today* provided one of the earliest exposés of this pseudoscientific rubbish. His careful analysis of the UFO phenomenon did much to debunk the claims of visitations by extraterrestrial vehicles.

Don Menzel's great personal charm was nowhere better illustrated than in his love of children. He gave talks on astronomy to children from four to eleven years of age at the Harvard Observatory but was at his best in less formal settings. He was Donald Duck to all of them: Donald le Canard in France, Pasto Donald in Latin America, and Donald Utka in the Soviet Union.

Outstanding as were Menzel's research, writing, and administrative accomplishments, they are equalled by his contributions as a teacher. He was an inspiration to his students, who enjoyed all the benefit of his sound physical insights and technical expertise. Many astrophysicists practicing in the United States today do not realize how much of what they learn originated with Menzel, whose tradition carries on through his many and devoted disciples.

SELECTED BIBLIOGRAPHY

1924

A study of line intensities in stellar spectra. *Harv. Circular*, 258.

1926

The atmosphere of Mars. *Astrophys. J.* 63:48–59.

1927

With W. W. Coblentz and C. C. Lampland. Temperatures on Mars, 1926, as derived from the water-cell transmissions. *Publ. Astron. Soc. Pac.* 39:97–100.

1931

A study of the solar chromosphere. *Publ. Lick Obs.* 17:1–302.[1]

1932

With R. T. Birge. The relative abundance of the oxygen isotopes, and the basis of the atomic weight system. *Phys. Rev.* 53:950(A).

1935

With C. L. Pekeris. Absorption coefficients and hydrogen line intensities. *Mon. Not. Roy. Astron. Soc.* 96:77–111.

1936

With L. Goldberg. Multiplet strengths for transitions involving equivalent electrons. *Astrophys. J.* 84:1–10.
The theoretical interpretation of equivalent breadths of absorption lines. *Astrophys. J.* 84: 462–73.

1937

Physical processes in gaseous nebulae. I. Absorption and emission of radiation. *Astrophys. J.* 85:330–39.
With J. G. Baker. Physical processes in gaseous nebulae. II. Theory of the Balmer decrement. *Astrophys. J.* 86:70–77.

---

[1] *Authors' note*: This was probably Menzel's single most important publication.

1938

With J. G. Baker and L. Goldberg. Equivalent widths and the temperature of the solar reversing layer. *Astrophys. J.* 87:81–101.

With J. G. Baker. Physical processes in gaseous nebulae. III. The Balmer decrement. *Astrophys. J.* 88:52–64.

With J. G. Baker and L. H. Aller. Physical processes in gaseous nebulae. IV. The mechanistic and equilibrium treatment of nebular statistics. *Astrophys. J.* 88:313–18.

With J. G. Baker and L. H. Aller. Physical processes in gaseous nebulae. V. Electron temperatures. *Astrophys. J.* 88:422–28.

1939

With L. H. Aller and J. G. Baker. Physical processes in gaseous nebulae. VII. The transfer of radiation in the Lyman continuum. *Astrophys. J.* 90:271–80.

With J. G. Baker and L. H. Aller. Physical processes in gaseous nebulae. VIII. The ultraviolet radiation field and electron temperature of an optically thick nebula. *Astrophys. J.* 90:601–10.

1940

With M. H. Hebb. Physical processes in gaseous nebulae. X. Collisional excitation of Nebulium. *Astrophys. J.* 92:408–23.

1941

With G. H. Shortley, L. H. Aller, and J. G. Baker. Physical processes in gaseous nebulae. XI. Strengths of forbidden lines in p^2, p^3, and p^4 as a function of coupling. *Astrophys. J.* 93:178–93.

With L. H. Aller and M. H. Hebb. Physical processes in gaseous nebulae. XIII. The electron temperatures of some typical planetary nebulae. *Astrophys. J.* 93:230–35.

With L. H. Aller. Physical processes in gaseous nebulae. XVI. The abundance of O III. *Astrophys. J.* 94:30–36.

With L. H. Aller. Physical processes in gaseous nebulae. XVII. Fluorescence in high-excitation planetaries. *Astrophys. J.* 94:436–48.

1945

With L. H. Aller. Physical processes in gaseous nebulae. XVIII. The chemical composition of the planetary nebulae. *Astrophys. J.* 102:239–63.

1955

With G. Athay, C. Pecker, and R. Thomas. The thermodynamic state of the outer solar atmosphere. V. A model of the chromosphere from the continuum emission. *Astrophys. J.* (Supp.) 1:505–19, no. 12.

1963

With L. Doherty. The evolution of solar prominences, pp. 159–61; Magnetohydrostatic models of the solar corona, pp. 307–15. In *The Solar Corona: I.A.U. Symposium XVI in Cloudcroft, New Mexico, August 28–30, 1961*, ed. J. W. Evans. New York: Academic Press.

With G. E. Moreton. The sun's magnetic field and the stability of solar markings, pp. 315–31. In *The Solar Corona: I.A.U. Symposium XVI in Cloudcroft, New Mexico, August 28–30, 1961*, ed. J. W. Evans. New York: Academic Press.

1968

With B. Shore. *Principles of atomic structure*. New York: J. Wiley & Sons.

N. M. Newmark

NATHAN M. NEWMARK

September 22, 1910–January 25, 1981

BY WILLIAM J. HALL

NATHAN MORTIMORE NEWMARK, internationally known educator and engineer, died January 25, 1981, in Urbana, Illinois. Dr. Newmark was widely known for his research in structural engineering and structural dynamics at the University of Illinois at Urbana-Champaign, for his contributions to the design of earthquake-resistant structures—including the Latino Americana Tower in Mexico City—and, most recently, for his work on the design of the trans-Alaska pipeline.

EDUCATION AND EARLY CAREER

Nathan M. Newmark was born in Plainfield, New Jersey, on September 22, 1910, to Abraham S. and Mollie Nathanson Newmark. He married Anne May Cohen on August 6, 1931, and is survived by his wife and three children, Richard, Linda (Mrs. James Bylander), and Susan (Mrs. Paul Mayfield).

After receiving his early education in North Carolina and New Jersey he attended Rutgers University. There he accumulated a number of prizes and graduated in 1930 with high honors—including special honors in civil engineering—giving evidence of his unusual skills and talents at a young age. He then enrolled as a graduate student at the University of Illinois in Urbana where he worked under the late professors

Hardy Cross, Harold M. Westergaard, and Frank E. Richart, receiving his M.S. and Ph.D. degrees in 1932 and 1934, respectively.

UNIVERSITY OF ILLINOIS AT URBANA-CHAMPAIGN

Beginning in 1930 as a graduate research assistant, Nate Newmark held a succession of positions for over half a century at the University of Illinois. He was appointed research professor of civil engineering in 1943, skipping the intermediate rank of associate professor. Early in his career he contributed significantly to the fields of structural analysis and structural materials and received national and international recognition for his work pertaining to highway bridges. His contributions in the area of structural dynamics, including consideration of impact, wave action, wind, blast, and earthquakes, greatly influenced structural and mechanical design throughout the world.

In 1956 he was appointed head of the Department of Civil Engineering of the University of Illinois at Urbana-Champaign, a position he held until 1973. He retired from his university position in 1976. Although the reputation of the department had been great almost since its founding, under Professor Newmark's leadership its stature rose to new heights.

From 1947 to 1957 he was chairman of the Digital Computer Laboratory at the university. During this period he had a major hand in developing one of the first modern, large-scale, digital computers (ILLIAC-II)—work that eventually led to the university's eminent position as a developer of computer science for engineering.

Newmark served in many important leadership capacities in the university and had the distinction of the longest tenure to date on the University Research Board. This board was in large part responsible for making the university one of the world's great research institutions, and Nate's vision and foresight played no small role in the success of this effort.

THE WORLD'S EARTHQUAKE ENGINEER

During World War II Dr. Newmark was a consultant to both the National Defense Research Committee and the Office of Scientific Research and Development. Part of his national service time was spent in the Pacific War Zone. In 1948, he was awarded the President's Certificate of Merit. In addition to serving on numerous Department of Defense boards and panels, he made major contributions to the development of the Minute Man and MX missile systems.

As a practicing engineer he was instrumental in developing the design criteria for many of the largest and most complex projects of the world.

In the late 1940s and early 1950s, Newmark served as the earthquake consultant on the forty-three story Latino Americana Tower in Mexico City. A plaque is mounted on that building, which withstood a strong earthquake in 1957 without damage, attesting to his design accomplishment.

Newmark was also responsible for developing the seismic design criteria for many other large projects, including the Bay Area Rapid Transit System and the trans-Alaska Oil Pipeline System, now the largest privately financed project in the history of the world. During the seventeen years before his death he carried the major responsibility for developing earthquake design and review criteria for about seventy nuclear power plants and for proposed liquid natural gas facilities on the West coast; at the time of his death, he was the consultant on seismic design for the Alaska-Canada Gas Pipeline.

Professor Newmark's publications include over 200 papers, books, and chapters in books. He is the coauthor of the following books on earthquake engineering: *Design of Multi-*

Story Reinforced Concrete Buildings for Earthquake Motion, with John A. Blume and Leo Corning (Chicago: Portland Cement Association, 1961) and *Fundamentals of Earthquake Engineering,* with Emilio Rosenbluth (Englewood Cliffs, New Jersey: Prentice-Hall, Inc., 1971).

HONORS AND AWARDS

Nate played a major role in many of the most important technical activities of the American Society of Civil Engineers. He was one of the founding members of the Engineering Mechanics Division and a prime mover in furthering the Society's computer application activities. Having received virtually every major award given out by the American Society of Civil Engineers and the Engineering Foundation Founders Society, he was an honored member of the many learned societies to which he belonged.

He was elected a fellow of the American Academy of Arts and Sciences in 1962, a founding member of the National Academy of Engineering in 1964, and a member of the National Academy of Sciences in 1966. Among his many NAE/NAS/NRC activities were the following: NAE Council, 1964–1968; NAE/NAS Joint Board, 1966–1968; NAE Committee on Earthquake Engineering Research, 1965–1970; NAS/NAE Committee on Scientific and Technical Communication, 1966–1969; and NAE/NRC Committee on Natural Disasters, 1971–1977 (member and chairman).

In 1968, Nathan Newmark received the National Medal of Science from President Lyndon B. Johnson. A year later he received the Washington Award—a joint award given annually by the major engineering societies of the United States. In 1979, Dr. Newmark was presented the John Fritz Medal, an all-engineering society award. In 1980 he received the sixteenth Gold Medal in the fifty-seven-year history of the Institution of Structural Engineers of Great Britain—the second American engineer to be so honored. He also received honorary degrees from several universities: Rutgers University (his *alma mater*) in 1955, the University of Liège in Belgium in 1967, the University of Notre Dame in 1969, and the University of Illinois in 1978.

On February 19, 1981, three weeks after his death, the Board of Trustees of the University of Illinois renamed the Civil Engineering Building the Nathan M. Newmark Civil Engineering Laboratory, in commemoration of his contributions to the university.

IN CONCLUSION

Nate Newmark was a university unto himself. Whether in academia or professional practice, engineers young and old sensed the challenge of this man's education and intellect. His penetrating insight, his keen engineering judgment, and his genuine interest in people were a constant source of inspiration to all who had the privilege of working with him.

Professor Newmark possessed an unusual ability to attract young people to the field of civil engineering, to inspire them with the confidence for undertaking new and varied tasks, and to guide but not direct their thinking. He insisted they receive appropriate recognition as individuals for their accomplishments. His unceasing devotion to research, his noteworthy and continuing contributions to the betterment of structural design practice, and his leadership in engineering education, teaching, and professional activities had a profound influence on civil engineering. It is no accident that there grew up around him one of the most active research centers in civil engineering in this country, or that the alumni of this group have assumed broad leadership in education, industry, and government throughout the world.

SELECTED BIBLIOGRAPHY

1933

With W. M. Wilson. The strength of thin cylindrical shells as columns. *Ill. Eng. Exp. Sta. Bull.* 255. 45 pp.

1935

Simplified computation of vertical pressures in elastic foundations. *Ill. Eng. Exp. Sta. Cir.* 24. 19 pp.

1936

Interaction between rib and superstructure in concrete arch bridges. *Proc. ASCE* 62:1043–61, based on Newmark's doctoral dissertation. See also author's closure to discussion, *Proc. ASCE* 64(1938):341–43 and *Trans. ASCE* 103(1938):62–88, with discussions.

1938

A distribution procedure for the analysis of slabs continuous over flexible beams. *Ill. Eng. Exp. Sta. Bull.* 304. 118 pp.

1941

Note on calculation of influence surfaces in plates by use of difference equations. *J. Appl. Mech.* 8:A-92.

1942

Influence charts for computation of stresses in elastic foundations. *Ill. Eng. Exp. Sta. Bull.* 338. 28 pp.

1943

Numerical procedures for computing deflections, moments, and buckling loads. *Trans. ASCE* 108:1161–1234.

1947

Influence charts for computation of vertical displacements in elastic foundations. *Univ. Ill. Eng. Exp. Sta. Bull.* 367. 11pp.
With E. C. Colin, Jr. A numerical solution for the torsion of hollow sections. *J. Appl. Mech.* 14:A313–15.

1948

Design of I-beam bridges and highway bridge floors—a symposium. *Proc. ASCE* 74:305–30.

With F. E. Richart, Jr. An hypothesis for the determination of cumulative damage in fatigue. *Proc. Am. Soc. Test. Mat.* 48:767–98.

1949

Numerical methods of analysis of bars, plates, and elastic bodies. In: *Numerical methods of analysis in engineering,* ed. L. E. Grinter, pp. 138–68. New York: Macmillan.

A simple approximate formula for effective end-fixity of columns. *J. Aeronaut. Sci.* 16:116.

1950

With W. H. Bruckner. Axial tension impact tests of structural steels. *Weld. J.* 29:212–16.

With C. P. Seiss. Moments in two-way concrete floor slabs. *Univ. Ill. Eng. Exp. Sta. Bull.* 385. 124pp.

1952

With A. S. Veletsos. A simple approximation for the natural frequencies of partly restrained bars. *J. Appl. Mech.* 19:563.

Bounds and convergence of relaxation and iteration procedures. *Proc. 1st Nat. Congr. Appl. Mech.,* pp. 9–14.

A review of cumulative damage in fatigue. In: *Fatigue and fracture of metals,* pp. 197–228. New York: John Wiley and Cambridge: MIT Press.

1954

With C. P. Siess. Research on highway bridge floors at the University of Illinois, 1936–1954. *Proc. Highway Res. Board* 33:30–53. (Also issued as *Univ. Ill. Eng. Exp. Sta.,* reprint no. 52)

1955

With L. E. Goodman and E. Rosenblueth. Aseismic design of firmly founded elastic structures. *Trans. ASCE* 120:782–802.

1956

An engineering approach to blast-resistant design. *Trans. ASCE* 121:45–64.

With Leonardo Zeevaert. Aseismic design of Latino Americana Tower in Mexico City. *Proc. World Conf. Earthquake Eng.*, pp. 35(1)–35(11). Berkeley: Earthquake Engineering Research Institute.

1957

With A. S. Veletsos. Natural frequencies of continuous flexural members. *Trans. ASCE* 122:249–85.

1958

With L. A. Harris. Effect of fabricated edge conditions on brittle fracture of structural steels. *Welding Res. Suppl., Welding J.* 37:137.

1959

With S. T. Rolfe and W. J. Hall. Brittle-fracture tests of steel plates containing residual compressive strain. *Welding Res. Suppl., Welding J.* 38:169(S)–175(S).

The place of the university in the education of civil engineers. I. Undergraduate study and the curriculum, pp. N10–11. II. Postgraduate education, pp. N18–19. III. The place of engineering research in universities, pp. N24–25. IV. Concluding remarks, p. N24. *Proc. Inst. Civil Eng., Great Britain*, vol. 12.

1961

With A. S. Veletsos. Effects of inelastic behavior on the response of simple systems to earthquake motions. *Proc. 2nd World Conf. Earthquake Eng.*, Tokyo, vol. 2, pp. 895–912.

Failure hypotheses for soils. Opening address, *Res. Conf. Shear Strength Cohesive Soils*, American Society of Civil Engineers, pp. 17–32.

With J. A. Blume and Leo Corning. *Design of multi-story reinforced concrete buildings for earthquake motions.* Chicago: Portland Cement Association. 350 pp.

1962

Educación en ingenieria. *Ingenieria (Mexico City)* 32:73–78.

A method of computation for structural dynamics. *Trans. ASCE* 127:1406–35, with discussion. Paper No. 3384.

1963

Design of structures for dynamic loads including the effects of vibration and ground shock. *Symposium on Scientific Problems of Protective Construction,* Swiss Federal Institute of Technology, Zürich, pp. 148–248.

1965

Structural engineering. In: *Listen to leaders in engineering,* eds. Albert Love and James Saxon Childers, pp. 73–84. Atlanta: Tupper and Love.

Effects of earthquakes on dams and embankments. Fifth Rankine Lecture, Institute of Civil Engineers, London. *Geotechnique* 15:139–59.

With A. S. Veletsos and C. V. Chelapati. Deformation spectra for elastic and elasto-plastic systems subjected to ground shock and earthquake motions. *Proc. 3rd World Congr. Earthquake Eng., New Zealand,* vol. 2:(II)663–(II)682.

1968

With W. J. Hall. Dynamic behavior of reinforced and prestressed concrete buildings under horizontal forces and the design of joints (including wind, earthquake, blast effects). *8th Congr., Intl. Assoc. Bridge Struct. Eng., September 1968, New York.* Preliminary publication, pp. 585–613 (with French and German translations).

With M. A. Sozen, P. C. Jennings, R. B. Matthiesen, and G. W. Housner. *Engineering report on the Caracas earthquake of 29 July, 1967.* Committee on Earthquake Engineering Research, Division of Engineering, NRC-NAE. Washington, D.C.: National Academy of Sciences. 217 pp.

1969

Relation between wind and earthquake response of tall buildings. *Proc. 1966 Ill. Struct. Eng. Conf., February 1969*, pp. 137–56.

Design criteria for nuclear reactors subjected to earthquake hazards. *Proc. IAEA Panel on Aseismic Design and Testing of Nuclear Facilities*, pp. 90–113. Tokyo: Japan Earthquake Promotion Society. (Supplement by N. M. Newmark and W. J. Hall, pp. 114–19)

Torsion in symmetrical buildings. *Proc. 4th World Conf. Earthquake Eng., 1969, Santiago, Chile*, vol. 2, pp. (A3)19–(A3)32.

With W. J. Hall. Seismic design criteria for nuclear reactor facilities. *Proc. 4th World Conf. Earthquake Eng., 1969*, Santiago, Chile, vol. 2, pp. (B4)37–(B4)50.

With S. J. Fenves. Seismic forces and overturning moments in buildings, towers, and chimneys. *Proc. 4th World Conf. Earthquake Eng.*, Santiago, Chile, vol. 2, pp. (B5)1–(B5)12.

1970

Current trends in the seismic analysis and design of high rise structures. In *Earthquake Engineering*, ed. Robert L. Weigel, pp. 403–24. Englewood Cliffs, N.J.: Prentice-Hall.

1971

With E. Rosenblueth. *Fundamentals of earthquake engineering.* Englewood Cliffs, N.J.: Prentice-Hall.

1972

Earthquake response analysis of reactor structures. *Nuclear Eng. Des.* 20:303–22.

1973

With W. J. Hall. Procedures and criteria for earthquake resistant design. *Building practices for disaster mitigation*, National Bureau of Standards Building Science Series 46, vol. 1:209–36.

With J. A. Blume and K. K. Kapur. Seismic design spectra for nuclear power plants. *Proc. ASCE* 99:287–303.

With W. J. Hall and B. Mohraz. *A study of vertical and horizontal earthquake spectra.* Directorate of Licensing, U.S.A.E.C. Report WASH-1255, April 1973.

1974

With W. J. Hall. Seismic design spectra for trans-Alaska pipeline. *Proc. 5th World Conf. Earthquake Eng., Intl. Assoc. Earthquake Eng., Rome 1974*, vol. 1, pp. 554–57.

Interpretation of apparent upthrow of objects in earthquakes. *Proc. 5th World Conf. Earthquake Eng., Intl. Assoc. Earthquake Eng., Rome 1974*, vol. 2, pp. 2338–343.

1975

Seismic design criteria for structures and facilities, trans-Alaska pipeline system. *Proc. U.S. Natl. Conf. Earthquake Eng., June 1975, Ann Arbor, Michigan.* Earthquake Eng. Res. Inst., pp. 94–103.

With W. J. Hall. Pipeline design to resist large fault displacement. *Proc. U.S. Natl. Conf. Earthquake Eng., June 1975, Ann Arbor, Michigan.* Earthquake Eng. Res. Inst., pp. 416–25.

1976

With W. J. Hall and B. Mohraz. *Statistical studies of vertical and horizontal earthquake spectra.* Division of Systems Safety, U.S. Nuclear Regulatory Comm. Report NUREG-0003.

With W. J. Hall. Vibration of structures induced by ground motion. In *Shock and vibration handbook*, 2nd ed., eds. Cyril M. Harris and Charles E. Crede, pp. 1–19. New York: McGraw-Hill.

1978

With W. J. Hall. *Development of criteria for seismic review of selected nuclear power plants.* U.S. Nuc. Reg. Comm. Report NUREG/CR-0098.

N. M. Newmark et al. *Tentative provisions for the development of seismic regulations for buildings.* Appl. Tech. Council Report ATC 3-06, NBS Special Publ. 510; NSF Publ. 78-8, June 1978. 506 pp.

With W. J. Hall. Seismic design criteria for pipelines and facilities. *Proc. ASCE* 104:91–107.

1980

With Anil K. Chopra. Analysis. In: *Design of earthquake resistant structures*, ed. E. Rosenblueth. London: Pentech Press.

With R. Riddell. Inelastic spectra for seismic design. *Proc. 7th World*

Conf. Earthquake Eng., September 8–13, 1980, Istanbul, vol. 4, pp. 129–36.

1982

With R. Villaverde. Computation of seismic response of light attachments to buildings. *Proc. 7th World Conf. Earthquake Eng., September 8–13, 1980, Istanbul*, vol. 5, pp. 343–50.

With W. J. Hall. *Earthquake spectra and design.* Berkeley, Calif.: Earthquake Eng. Res. Inst. Monogr. Ser.

Lars Onsager

LARS ONSAGER

November 27, 1903–October 5, 1976

BY H. CHRISTOPHER LONGUET-HIGGINS
AND MICHAEL E. FISHER[1]

ONE DAY IN 1925 Pieter Debye was sitting in his office at the Eidgenössische Technische Hochschule in Zürich when a visitor from Norway was announced. In came a tall young man, who walked silently across the room, bent over the desk, and said solemnly: "Professor Debye, your theory of electrolytes is incorrect." Whereupon Debye, after begging the stranger to sit down and inviting him to discuss his objections, offered him an assistantship for the following year. The young man's name was Lars Onsager.[2]

Forty-three years later Onsager was awarded the Nobel Prize in Chemistry for the "discovery of the reciprocal relations bearing his name, which are fundamental for the thermodynamics of irreversible processes." A group of physicists and chemists at Cornell had written of him: "We believe that his work is unique for its penetration, breadth, and influence in the development of theoretical and experimental studies of condensed matter. He is surely one of the outstanding physicists of this century."

---

[1] This essay originally appeared in the *Biographical Memoirs of Fellows of the Royal Society*, London, vol. 24 (London: Royal Society, November 1978):443–71. The text presented here corrects the original in various places, contains a few new references, and includes a completed bibliography of Onsager's published work.

[2] T. J. Murphy and E. G. D. Cohen, "The Motion of Ions in Solution," *BioSystems* 8(1977):255–60.

NORWAY (1903–1925)

Lars was born in Oslo on 27 November, 1903, to Erling and Ingrid Kirkeby Onsager. Erling was a barrister, and it is said that the family had interests in the steel industry, though Lars was later at pains to deny that his father was "a steel tycoon." His early education was liberal; his friends found him, in later life, extraordinarily well read in classical literature and philosophy and admired his taste in music and the fine arts. He attended high school in Oslo and at an early age familiarized himself with Norwegian literature, including the verse epics he loved to recite to his family and friends in later life, both in the original and in his own English translations.

In 1920 Lars was admitted to the Norges Tekniske Hogskole in Trondheim to study chemical engineering in preparation for a technical career. But his inclinations were mainly intellectual; he had already bought a copy of Whittaker and Watson's classic monograph, *Modern Analysis*,[3] and he worked through most of the (notoriously difficult) examples in his spare time. This early discipline equipped him for some of his most spectacular later achievements, notably his famous solution of the Ising problem in two dimensions.

In other ways as well, Onsager's time as a student at the Norwegian Institute of Technology was prophetic of his later scientific work. As a freshman chemist he was introduced to the current theory of electrolyte solutions, according to which the properties of an electrolyte should be additive, not just over molecules, but even over the constituent ions.

"In spite of some idealization," he declared later, "it sufficed for a great many purposes; it eased many tasks no end, and we were eternally grateful for that. However, very soon the journals rather than the textbooks taught

---

[3] E. T. Whittaker and G. N. Watson, *A course of modern analysis* (Cambridge: Cambridge University Press, 1902), 4th ed., 1927.

me about numerous observations which did not quite fit into the picture, and of tentative explanations for the discrepancies. . . . Suspicion centered on the long-range forces between the ions." (1969,1)

This passing reference to "the journals" shows that Onsager was already exercising an independence of mind that later blossomed into a deep scientific originality. When, in 1923, Debye and Hückel published their new theory of electrolyte solutions,[4] Onsager was quick to master their ideas and to detect a flaw in their account of electrolytic conduction and diffusion. It was his own ideas about these processes that ultimately led him to the reciprocal relations that now bear his name; but a parallel influence on his thinking was the experimental work of C. N. Riiber[5] on the kinetics of tauto-merism, which he had already begun to consider in 1924 in the light of the principle of microscopic reversibility. Onsager saw that this principle would supply a sufficient condition for detailed balancing to prevail—for there to be no chemical "circulation" when three or more tautomers were present under equilibrium conditions. The same principle might, he suspected, be brought to bear on the relative rates of other naturally occurring processes.

In his five years at Trondheim, Onsager not only acquired the mathematical skill that he later put to such impressive use and an interest in electrolytes to which his attention was to return continually throughout his life, he also developed a deep appreciation of the relation of theory to experiment and of the duty of a theorist to propose experimental tests of his ideas. It is at least likely that his later interests in ther-

[4] P. W. Debye and E. Hückel, "Zur Theorie der Elektrolyte. I. Gefrierpunktser-niedrigung und verwandte Erscheinungen," *Phys. Z.* 24(1923):185–206; "Zur Theorie der Elektrolyte. II. Das Grenzgesetz für die elektrische Leitfähigkeit," pp. 305–25.

[5] C. N. Riiber, "Über Mutarotation I. Mitteilung," *Chem. Ber.* 55B(1922):3132–43; and "Über Mutarotation II. Metteilung," *Chem. Ber.* 56B(1923):2185–94.

mal diffusion (1939,2,3,4; 1940,1), in colloidal solutions (1942,1; 1949,1), and in turbulence (1945,2; 1949,3) were also engendered by his training as a chemical engineer. At any rate, when he finally graduated with a Ch.E. in 1925, a most formidable intellect stepped onto the scientific scene.

ZÜRICH (1926–1928)

It was Onsager's interest in electrolytes that first took him to Zürich in 1925. Debye and his assistant Erich Hückel had put forward a new theory of electrolyte solutions founded on the idea that the electrostatic field of a dissolved ion is screened by an "atmosphere" of opposite net charge, the effective screening distance being inversely proportional to the square root of the ionic strength c, defined as

$$c = \sum_i c_i z_i^2, \tag{1}$$

where c_i is the concentration of ion i, and z_i is its electric charge in elementary units. The activity coefficient f_i of any ion—its thermodynamic activity divided by c_i—could then be calculated, for small c, from the equation

$$\ln f_i = A_i \sqrt{c}, \tag{2}$$

in which A_i was a function of the charge z_i, the temperature T, and the dielectric constant D of the solvent. The theory was quantitatively successful in accounting for the thermodynamic properties of dilute salt solutions, but Debye and Hückel's extension of their theory to deal with the conductivities of electrolytes ran into difficulties. Their equation

$$\Lambda = \Lambda_0 + \Lambda_1 \sqrt{c} \tag{3}$$

for the molar conductivity Λ appeared to be correct in form, but the calculated value of Λ_1, also dependent on T and D, differed considerably from the experimental value.

This was puzzling because the most important physical effects had, it seemed, been allowed for: an "electrophoretic effect" in which the counter-ions in the atmosphere pull the solvent in the wrong direction, making it necessary for the central ion to "swim upstream"; and a "relaxation effect" in which the ion is held back by the net attraction of the atmosphere itself.

Accepting the general correctness of the physical picture, Onsager himself had explored its implications and in 1923 produced, as he himself put it, 'a modest but firm result':

"The relaxation effect ought to reduce the mobilities of anion and cation in equal proportion. Much to my surprise, the results of Debye and Hückel did not satisfy that relation, nor the requirement that wherever an ion of type A is 10 Å west of a B, there is a B 10 Å east of that A. Clearly something essential had been left out in the derivation of such unsymmetrical results." (1969,1)

By the time he visited Debye in his office in 1925, Onsager had pinpointed the origin of the discrepancy. Debye and Hückel had evaluated Λ_1 by assuming one particular ion to move uniformly in a straight line but allowing the other ions to undergo Brownian motion subject to the fields of their distorted atmospheres. All that was required was to relax the constraint that the central ion move uniformly, and to allow it to move as freely as its neighbors—subject, of course, to their influence and that of the external field. In this way the desired symmetry could be restored, and the calculated value of Λ_1 brought into good agreement with experiment.

Debye must have been deeply impressed by this astonishing insight. It is no wonder that he proclaimed his young critic a genius. In April 1926 he demonstrated his sincerity by taking Onsager on as a research assistant and in 1927 by promoting his ideas at a discussion meeting of the Faraday Society in Oxford. (1927,2)

The Onsager Limiting Law, as it came to be called, was first put forward in the second of a pair of papers in the *Physikalische Zeitschrift* (1926,1; 1927,1). The evident thoroughness and maturity of these papers doubtless owed much to the influence of Debye himself. Onsager would have been the first to admit that he stood on Debye's shoulders both in his work on electrolytes and in his later investigations of the dielectric constants of polar liquids and solutions of polar molecules. During the next few years the meticulous experimental work of Shedlovsky[6] confirmed the Limiting Law to a high degree of accuracy, and Onsager was to continue to develop his theory of electrolytic transport—especially in collaboration with Raymond M. Fuoss—for many years after that. But in the meantime his thoughts were beginning to turn to problems of greater generality and to horizons of wider scope.

JOHNS HOPKINS UNIVERSITY (1928)

In 1928 Onsager emigrated to the United States and was appointed an associate in chemistry at The Johns Hopkins University. The appointment was brief. In the words of Robert H. Cole, who was one of Onsager's associates for more than forty years: "They made the mistake there of assigning Onsager to the basic Chemistry I, II course. He just couldn't think at the level of a freshman. Frankly, he was fired."[7]

Onsager's difficulties in communicating with weaker intellects were acute and remained so throughout his life. It

[6] T. Shedlovsky, "The electrolytic conductivity of some uni-univalent electrolytes in water at 25°," *J. Am. Chem. Soc.* 54(1932):1411–28.

[7] J. F. Barry, Jr., "Lars Onsager: The greatest theoretical chemist," *Brown Univ. Alum. Mo.* (November 1976):2.

may seem strange that a man who could see so deeply into physical reality should have been so conspicuously lacking in imagination when it came to reading other minds, but almost everyone who met him became immediately aware of this disability.

"I won't say he was the world's worst lecturer," Professor Cole continues, "but he was certainly in contention. He was difficult to understand anyway, but he also had the habit of lecturing when his back was to the students and he was writing on the blackboard. To compound matters, he was a big man, and students had to peer round him just to try and see what was being written."

Onsager's problems in communicating with lesser mortals were certainly not due to impatience or arrogance. The theoretical chemist Julian Gibbs, of Brown University, who got to know him some years later describes Onsager as a "very, very friendly man" who would always assume that his listeners were as advanced in their thinking as he was. "He assumed that if he knew it, others in the field automatically knew it," whatever the subject under discussion.

Yet it was not only students who found Onsager difficult to understand; his colleagues had the same difficulty. Oliver Penrose, who worked with him as a postdoctoral associate, recalls a lecture to the Kapitza Club in Cambridge, many years later, at which Onsager was explaining his joint work with Bruria Kaufman on the Ising lattice. He had been warned that non-theoreticians would be present and that he should phrase his talk in not too technical language. He plunged, nevertheless, into the mathematics of spinor algebras. After about twenty minutes, one of the many experimentalists in the audience had the courage to ask him what a spinor was. Onsager replied, thoughtfully: "A spinor—no, a set of spinors—is a set of matrices isomorphic to the orthogonal group." With that he gave the famous Onsager grin, twinkled his Nordic blue eyes at the bewildered faces around him, and continued the lecture as if nothing had happened.

"In private discussion," wrote Cyril Domb, "it was much easier to communicate with Onsager provided you were courageous enough to persist in questioning when you did not understand. He would drop the level one stage at a time until the gap could be bridged."[8]

In their introduction to the proceedings of a conference held in his honour in 1962, Shedlovsky and Montroll said in his defense:

"Whether deserved or not, Onsager has the reputation of being verbally obscure, or at least enigmatic. However, those who know him well will testify that he is clarity itself and often responds at great length, if the question presented to him refers to Norse mythology, gardening, the more subtle aspects of *Kriegspiel* (a form of blindfold chess involving two opponents and a referee) and even encyclopedic facts about organic chemistry."[9]

And everyone who actually worked with him testified to his unfailing generosity with his time and ideas.

Onsager's interest in *Kriegspiel*, incidentally, is confirmed by Penrose: "I never played this with him although I did play a game of chess with him once. He was a good player at chess, but very slow. At *Kriegspiel* he had worked out how to force the win with a king and two bishops—it may even have been king, bishop, and knight—against king alone; something which I had not believed could be done until he showed me." Onsager regarded chess, so he said, as too much like real problem-solving to spend much time on it. When he wanted to unwind from his work he would play solitaire, and bridge was a good relaxation in company.

---

[8] C. Domb, C., Obituary, *Nature, Lond.* 264(1976):819.

[9] T. Shedlovsky and E. Montroll, Introduction, Proc. Conf. Irreversible Thermodynamics and the Statistical Mechanics of Phase Transitions (Onsager Symposium), *J. Math. Phys.* 4,2(1963).

BROWN UNIVERSITY (1928–1933)

So Onsager had to move. Fortunately, an opening appeared at Brown, where Charles A. Kraus was chairman of the Chemistry Department. The two men were very different—Onsager the young high-powered theorist and Kraus the hard-headed experimentalist. "But Kraus," reports Cole, "knew that Onsager would be good for Brown, and he signed him up as a research instructor. . . . A look at the University catalogues for the Onsager years at Brown reveals that he was listed at the bottom of the page simply as 'Mr. Onsager.' The fact was that he had no Ph.D. He did all his work at Brown that led to his Nobel Prize without the 'advantage' of a Ph.D."

A lesser scientist might have been discouraged by the intellectual isolation in which Onsager must have found himself during those five years. The problems on which he was working and the ideas he was developing can hardly have appealed to his departmental colleagues. Speaking in 1973 of his now classic work on irreversible processes, which appeared in 1931, he said: "It wasn't doubted, but completely ignored." "It was not until after the Second World War," confirms Stig Claesson, commenting on the length of time before the full import of Onsager's ideas was recognized, "that it attracted great attention. The man was really ahead of his time."[10]

As chairman of the department Kraus was always after Onsager to do an experiment of some sort rather than spending all his time on theoretical work. One day Onsager told him he had decided to try an experiment on the separation of isotopes by thermal diffusion. "Fine," said Kraus, and was

[10] S. Claesson, "The Nobel Prize for Chemistry" (presentation speech), *Les Prix Nobel en 1968*, p. 42 (Stockholm: Imprimerie Royale P. A. Norstedt & Söner, 1972). Also in: *Nobel Lectures—Chemistry 1963–1970*, p. 269 (Amsterdam: Elsevier).

doubly pleased when Lars told him that the only equipment he would need was a long tube. But his encouragement was quickly withdrawn when Onsager explained that the tube must be made of platinum and would have to stretch from the basement to the third floor of the chemistry building. Kraus never pestered him again about doing an experiment, which "was too bad," writes Julian Gibbs, "because no one succeeded in conducting this experiment until more than a decade later, when it was needed as part of the Manhattan Project for the atomic bomb."[11]

Onsager's pedagogic endeavours at Brown were hardly more effective than at Johns Hopkins, but they resulted in one major conversion. John F. Ryan, a Brown alumnus, re-calling Onsager's "Sadistical Mechanics" course, as it was known, says that in the year he took the course a New Boy was attending it. Early in the second lecture Lars wrote a typically complicated equation on the blackboard, and turned to his audience with a hopeful "You see?" The gloomy silence that followed was broken by the New Boy: "But shouldn't it be 'times unit vector?'" Lars wheeled round to the board, shouted "Yah! Yah!" scribbled in the unit vector symbol and beamed at the class and the world in general. He had found a disciple who understood him, and the rest of the course was a duet between the two, witnessed with irri-tated incomprehension by the rest of the students. The New Boy was Ray Fuoss, who took his Ph.D. with Onsager and became his first co-author (1932,1). Together again at Yale, he and Onsager collaborated on many joint papers during the next thirty-five years (1932,1; 1957,3; 1958,1; 1961,2; 1962,1; 1963,1,2; 1964,2; 1965,2).

While he was at Brown struggling to meet the demands of the educational system, Onsager's mind was preoccupied

---

[11] Barry, *Brown Univ. Alum. Mo.* (1976):2.

with the rates of irreversible processes. He had already given much thought to the motion of dissolved ions in electric fields and felt that he could gain a better perspective by generalizing the problem to the case of combined diffusion and electrical conduction. The force on an ion could be represented by the equation

$$k_i = -\nabla\mu_i - e_i \nabla\phi, \qquad (4)$$

where $\nabla\mu_i$ and $\nabla\phi$ were the gradients of chemical and electrical potential, and e_i was the ionic charge. His own theory of transport in electrolytes gave the ionic fluxes J_i as linear combinations of the forces acting on the ions:

$$J_i = \sum_j L_{ij}k_j \qquad (5)$$

and the coefficients L_{ij} invariably formed a symmetric matrix.

It was soon evident, he reports in his Nobel Lecture (1969,1), that this symmetry did not depend on any mathematical approximations in the theory.

"For the relaxation effect I could depend on Newton's principle of action and reaction; for all the complications of hydrodynamics a 'principle of least dissipation' derived by Helmholtz assured the symmetry. Admittedly, I did assume some consistent scheme of Brownian motion kinetics; but even that seemed non-essential."

At this point his thoughts returned to the precise experimental work of Riiber on the mutarotation of sugars.[12] Riiber had discovered that galactose existed in at least three tautomeric forms, the interconversion of which

". . . gave rise to a little problem in mathematics. In analysing it I assumed, as any sensible chemist would, that in the state of equilibrium the reaction $1 \rightarrow 2$ would occur just as often as $2 \rightarrow 1$, and so forth, even though this is

[12] Riiber, *Chem. Ber.* 55B(1922):3132–43; and *Chem. Ber.* 56B(1923):2185–94.

not a necessary condition for equilibrium, which might be maintained by a cyclic reaction—as far as the mathematics goes."

In other words, Onsager felt sure on physical grounds that such equilibrium states must conform to the principle of detailed balancing, and he was able to show that this principle was thermodynamically equivalent to the principle of least dissipation.

"I developed a strong faith in the principle of least dissipation and recognized that it had been used somehow by Helmholtz in his theory of galvanic diffusion cells and by Kelvin in his theory of thermoelectric phenomena."

Kelvin had put forward a quasithermodynamic theory of thermoelectricity that linked the Seebeck effect—the generation of an electric current in a thermocouple—with the Peltier effect, in which a temperature gradient is established in a bimetallic circuit by passing a current through it. Kelvin's theory could not, however, be derived from thermodynamic first principles—nor could Helmholtz's theory of diffusion potentials.

"Some years later in Zürich, in a conversation with P. Scherrer, I found that he had been strongly impressed by the ideas of G. N. Lewis about detailed balancing. This made me put the cart behind the horse. Now I looked for a way to apply the condition of microscopic reversibility to transport processes, and after a while I found a handle on the problem: the natural fluctuations in the distribution of molecules and energy due to the random thermal motion. According to a principle formulated by Boltzmann, the nature of thermal (and chemical) equilibrium is statistical, and the statistics of spontaneous deviation is determined by the associated changes of the thermodynamic master function—that is, the entropy. Here was a firm connection with the thermodynamics, and we connect with the laws of transport as soon as we may assume that a spontaneous deviation from the equilibrium decays according to the same laws as one that has been produced artificially."

In order to exploit this line of thought Onsager had to find some measure (analogous to the excess concentration of a reacting substance) with which to describe the small fluctuations of spatially inhomogeneous systems away from equilibrium and the associated entropy deficiency. With characteristic simplicity and depth of physical insight he chose for his non-equilibrium parameters the displacements α_i of certain centres of mass and energy from their equilibrium positions. Thus a small temperature gradient in a solid body could be represented by assigning a small finite value to the vector displacement of the center of energy from its equilibrium position, and the consequent flow of heat would appear as a regression of this displacement towards the value zero. The non-equilibrium state itself would be represented by an ensemble that maximized the entropy S subject to the α_i having specified values; the "forces" conjugate to the α_i would be the partial derivatives of S with respect to the displacements:

$$X_i = (\partial S/\partial \alpha_i). \tag{6}$$

As soon as a specified fluctuation has begun to regress, one can proceed to define the corresponding set of fluxes by the equation:

$$J_i = \langle \alpha_i(t + \tau) - \alpha_i(t) \rangle/\tau, \tag{7}$$

where the angle brackets indicate an average over the ensemble representing a fluctuation occurring at time t; τ is a time interval, short compared to the regression time, but long compared to the molecular collision time.

Now the statistical weight of the fluctuation $(\alpha_1, \alpha_2, \ldots)$ in the equilibrium ensemble is, by Boltzmann's theory, equal to

$$\exp(\delta S/k) = \exp(\sum_j \alpha_j X_j/k) \approx [1 + \sum_j \alpha_j X_j/k]. \tag{8}$$

To this approximation, then,

$$J_i = (kT)^{-1}\langle[\alpha_i(t + \tau) - \alpha_i(t)]\sum_j \alpha_j(t)X_j\rangle, \qquad (9)$$

where now the average is over the equilibrium ensemble and use has been made of the fact that the mean values of the α_i are zero in equilibrium. Regarding J_i as a function of the X_j, one may write:

$$J_i = \sum_j L_{ij}X_j \qquad (10)$$

with

$$L_{ij} = (kT)^{-1}\langle\alpha_i(t + \tau)\alpha_j(t) - \alpha_i(t)\alpha_j(t)\rangle. \qquad (11)$$

It is at this point that the principle of microscopic reversibility becomes relevant. If the dynamical equations of motion of the system are reversible in the time—as they will be if no magnetic field or Coriolis forces are present—then the cross-correlation function $\langle\alpha_i(t + \tau)\alpha_j(t)\rangle$ between the displacements α_i and α_j must be symmetrical in τ. It follows directly that $L_{ij} = L_{ji}$, or, more generally, that in a magnetic field H:

$$L_{ij}(H) = L_{ji}(-H). \qquad (12)$$

This set of equations is Onsager's famous Reciprocal Relations.

Onsager first announced this result in 1929 (1929,1), but "in view of the very general claims I felt that concepts and conditions ought to be defined with great care, and a complete exposition did not appear until 1931." The claims were general indeed, and the Reciprocal Relations are now often referred to as the Fourth Law of Thermodynamics.

Like the other equations of thermodynamics, they are at the same time mathematically simple and physically deep.

Though they arose in Onsager's mind from his studies of electrolytic conduction, he soon recognized their application to the cross-coefficients for the diffusion of pairs of solutes in the same solution (1932,1) and the varied interactions that can occur between thermal conduction, diffusion, and electrical conduction.

Thermal diffusion was an important special case: the temperature gradients set up by the interdiffusion of two gases have their counterpart in the partial separation that occurs when a temperature gradient is applied to a mixture of gases. At the beginning of World War II Onsager published two important papers on this subject (1939,2 and 1940,1). In a comprehensive review of the experimental evidence several years later, D. G. Miller[13] concluded that the reciprocal relations were obeyed, within experimental error, in all the varied physical situations in which they had yet been checked. Eight years later still, they earned their discoverer the Nobel Prize.

Onsager himself set much store by the Principle of Least Dissipation, which—for systems very close to equilibrium—he showed to be mathematically equivalent to the reciprocal relations. The passage of time has perhaps modified this judgment; though the Principle was later generalized by Onsager and Machlup (1953,1,2) and supplied with new theoretical foundations, it does not in fact hold for substantial departures from equilibrium and, in any case, it is the reciprocal relations that are directly accessible to experimental test.

Onsager remained at Brown until 1933, when the economic depression made it necessary for his appointment to be discontinued. It would have been impossible for the Chemistry Department to convince the University that his services as a teacher were indispensable.

[13] D. G. Miller, "Thermodynamics of irreversible processes: the experimental verification of the Onsager reciprocal relations," *Chem. Revs.* 60(1960):15–37.

In the summer of that year Lars was in Europe and went to visit H. Falkenhagen, the Austrian electrochemist. Falkenhagen was unwell at the time and asked his sister, Gretl (Margarethe Arledter), to entertain Lars. Gretl saw him coming up the stairs—a very handsome young man who, her brother had told her, was "well ahead of his times." They went out to dinner, but Lars was his usual reticent self. After dinner he fell asleep on the patio, then woke up and said: "Are you romantically attached?" They became engaged eight days later—Margarethe at twenty-one and Lars at twenty-nine—and got married on September 7, 1933.

YALE—THE PREWAR YEARS (1933–1939)

In 1933 Onsager was appointed Sterling and Gibbs Fellow at Yale University, where he was to remain for the greater part of his life. Having awarded him a postdoctoral fellowship, the Chemistry Department was embarrassed to discover that he had no Ph.D.

The Reciprocal Relations had been published two years before, but an outline of his results, submitted to his *alma mater* in Trondheim, had been judged unacceptable for a doctorate as it stood. This setback naturally upset him, and he felt uncomfortable at being addressed as "Dr. Onsager" when he had no such entitlement. His colleagues suggested he try for a Yale Ph.D. Lars had already taken the relevant course work and orals, and as for the thesis, any of his published work would do.

Lars felt, however, that he should write something new. It was soon ready—a thesis entitled *Solutions of the Mathieu Equation of Period 4π and Certain Related Functions* (1935,1). The chemists were quite out of their depth, and the physicists, too. Eventually the thesis was sent over to the Mathematics Department, where Professor Einar Hille, himself an expert in the subject matter of Whittaker and Watson's

Modern Analysis[14] (Lars's favorite text), read it with enjoyment. He suggested to Professor Hill, chairman of chemistry, that if the Chemistry Department felt uneasy at doing so, the Mathematics Department would be happy to recommend the award of the degree. Not wishing to be upstaged, the chemists sponsored the thesis.[15]

One can see this incident as an illustration of Onsager's pride in his mathematical skill—a skill that, throughout his life, was more evident to his colleagues in theoretical physics than to the vast majority of his fellow chemists. Before publishing new results he always insisted on making sure that there were no mathematical loopholes in any of his arguments, but he never lost his sense of proportion to the extent of cultivating mathematical rigor for its own sake. On a new derivation of Birkhoff's strong ergodic hypothesis he once remarked in exasperation: "To be any more immaculate they will have to begin sterilizing the paper as well as the theorem!"

In 1934 Onsager was appointed an assistant professor in the Chemistry Department at Yale and, in 1935, was awarded his Ph.D. He settled down to family life on Whitney Avenue in New Haven, and in the course of the next few years Gretl bore him four children, Erling Frederick (named after his grandfather), Inger Marie (now Mrs. Kenneth R. Oldham), Hans Tanberg, and Christian Carl. The eldest son and the youngest later graduated from Yale, but none of the children went into science.

At about this time the Onsagers bought a farm in Tilton, New Hampshire, with a farmhouse and about a hundred acres of land. Lars used to grow vegetables with enthusiasm and engaged in carpentry and other practical pursuits. A

[14] See n. 3 above.
[15] B. Hille, "Ionic channels of nerve: questions for theoretical chemists," *BioSystems* 8(1977):195–99.

scholar to the core, he would regale his guests with the complete life cycles of all the parasites that might attack his delicious lettuces and could name the chemical compound that would deal most effectively with each one of them. He always seemed surprised if anyone else did not know anything that he had found interesting—about horticulture or any other subject: "Why, it's in all the standard textbooks of paleontology." (He had a theory, based on his reading, that the dinosaurs were warm-blooded; so they probably were.)

The family made the most of their country life. Lars was a keen walker and enjoyed swimming and cross-country skiing up to the end of his life. Even when he was an old man, he would not allow people to carry heavy suitcases for him; he could not bear to think that his physical strength might be declining.

His scientific output might have been judged relatively slender, especially during the early years at Yale, but its quality was beyond reproach. He preferred to work alone rather than with graduate students or colleagues, though later he liked to collaborate with postdoctoral fellows. He earned himself the reputation of being something of an individualist. He displayed no ambition to build up a research group of his own and may have disappointed some of his colleagues by making little attempt to bring other theoretical chemists into the department. His lecturing showed no visible signs of improvement—his courses on statistical mechanics (1952,3; 1961,3) were popularly known as "Advanced Norwegian I" and "Advanced Norwegian II." But he made firm friendships both in and outside Yale, and his natural warmth, kindness, and integrity—coupled with a complete absence of malice—won the affection of virtually everyone who got to know him.

His best-known papers of that period were a paper on the Wien effect and one on the dipole moments of molecules in solution. Wien had discovered that weak electrolytes such as acetic acid, which are only partly dissociated in solution, display at high electric fields a conductivity in excess of the low-field value.

Onsager (1934,2) saw that this effect must be due to a disturbance by the field of the rate at which associated pairs of ions dissociate into effectively free ions, the rate of reassociation being virtually unaffected by the field. On this bold, simplifying assumption he derived a remarkable formula that implied—correctly—that the effective dissociation constant ought to be shifted by a factor proportional to the absolute value of the field (at high fields), but independent of the concentration. In a much later paper with C. T. Liu (1965,1), he revised the details but not the central message of this work. In the intervening years Onsager's theory of the Wien effect was exploited by Eigen and DeMaeyer in their experimental studies of very fast reactions, particularly in biological systems.[16]

The paper on dipole moments (1936,1) disturbed a number of chemists because it called into question the Debye formula relating the dielectric constant of a polar substance to the molecular dipole moment. The formula had been widely used for determining dipole moments from the temperature variation of gaseous dielectric constants but was known to fail for polar liquids, presumably because of molecular association or hindered rotation. Onsager suspected that there was a flaw in the underlying theory, since it predicted a ferroelectric Curie point for all polar solutions, whereas no such transition had ever been observed.

Onsager's first account of his own theory took the form of a paper he sent to Debye for publication in the *Physikalische Zeitschrift*, but Debye found the paper "unreadable" and

[16] M. Eigen, "Die 'unmessbar' schnellen Reaktionen," Nobel Prize lecture, 11 December, 1967, in *Les Prix Nobel 1967* (Stockholm: P. A. Norstedt & Söner, Imprimerie Royale, 1969), 151–80.

turned it down. This rebuff from his old teacher hurt Onsager deeply, and it was not until some years later that he was prevailed upon by J. G. Kirkwood to submit an English version to the *Journal of the American Chemical Society* (1936,1). In his anonymous, third-person, scientific autobiography,[17] Onsager concealed his feelings about the incident behind the lighthearted remark that he would not have had "the heart to throw cold water on the rising tide of enthusiasm for the study of dipole moments" if Kirkwood had not pointed out to him that Jeffries Wyman's recent measurements on polypeptide solutions[18] fitted well with his new ideas. It was, however, many years before Onsager's theory of dielectrics received the attention it deserved. Debye eventually accepted Onsager's amendment to his theory; but it must, to say the least, have been unendurably galling to the great physicist to have yet another of his famous theories taken apart by the extraordinary young man whose scientific career he himself had launched.

The last four papers of the prewar period were all, in their way, indicative of what was to come. A paper on the electrostatic interactions of molecules in crystals (1939,1) pointed the way to his later work on the statistical mechanics of phase transitions in more than one dimension. Two papers on the separation of isotopes by thermal diffusion (1939,2,3) foreshadowed the use of this technique in the Manhattan Project for extracting the fissile isotope ^{235}U from natural uranium, which is mostly ^{238}U. A paper on turbulence in thermal diffusion columns (1939,4) hinted at an interest that was later to lead Onsager to rediscover Kolmogoroff's theory of

---

[17] Lars Onsager (autobiography), in *Modern men of science* (New York: McGraw-Hill, 1966), 1:357–59.

[18] J. Wyman, Jr., and T. L. McMeekin, "The dielectric constant of amino acids and peptides," *J. Am. Chem. Soc.* 55(1933):908–14; "The dipole moments of esters of amino acids and peptides," 915–22.

isotropic turbulence, put forward in 1941 but unknown in the West until after the War.

The fact that Gretl was an Austrian and Lars not yet an American citizen spared the Onsagers the dislocation of active war service. Perhaps, indeed, the lowered tempo of academic life at Yale made it easier for Lars to concentrate on his own research. Whatever the reason, he was able to find the time to think as hard, or harder, than ever before and to solve a key problem in physics others might well have believed to lie beyond the reach of human intelligence.

The problem was this: Can the fundamental postulates of statistical mechanics account for the distinct phases of matter, and more specifically, do they imply the occurrence of a sharp phase transition in a regular array of particles that interact only with their nearest neighbors in the array?

It was known that, for a one-dimensional crystal, the answer was in the negative: Whatever the (finite) range of interactions, no sharp phase transition was possible. There was, however, a simple model system in which a phase transition was suspected to occur, namely the two-dimensional Ising lattice. (The prospect of deriving from statistical mechanics the thermodynamic properties of any higher-dimensional cooperative assembly was, at that time, too remote to be worth considering.)

The Ising model, which can serve as a model of ferromagnetism, of antiferromagnetism, of gaseous condensation, or of phase separation in fluid mixtures and metallic alloys, looks innocuous enough to the nonspecialist—like the four-color problem in topology (to which, in fact, it is not entirely unrelated). An Ising model is an assembly of particles or "spins" located at the vertices of an infinite space lattice—in the simplest nontrivial case, a two-dimensional planar square lattice. Each particle or spin can exist in either of two states, and the total energy of the lattice is additive over neighboring pairs of particles. The energy of any such pair is either $+J$ or $-J$ according as the particles are in the same state or in different states, or as the spins are parallel or antiparallel. (Onsager actually considered the significantly more general problem in which the interaction energy has different magnitudes, J and J', for the two directions—horizontal and vertical—of a square lattice. An essentially one-dimensional system is obtained when $J'/J \to 0$.)

Earlier treatments of the "Ising problem"—namely the task of evaluating the partition function and hence the free energy—had been improved by H. A. Bethe and R. E. Peierls, and later by H. A. Kramers and G. H. Wannier, but all of these authors had been forced to employ methods of approximation that could be extended only by the greatest labor and were of an accuracy most difficult to assess, and which—in the final outcome—proved quite inadequate. Kramers and Wannier had, however, discovered one important clue, essentially by symmetry arguments: that if there indeed existed a unique point of phase transition, i.e. a critical point, then the value of the critical temperature must be a rather simple function of J and J'.

"With fascination, Onsager examined their methods and saw that he could add a trick or two, then followed up one encouraging lead after another until he had computed the partition function, which determines the thermodynamic properties. The result was obtained in 1942; he took time to tidy up various details and published it in 1944."[19]

Onsager, in fact, utilized the transfer matrix method introduced by Kramers and Wannier in which the partition function of a square lattice of m rows, each containing n particles or spins, is expressed as a trace; explicitly one has

[19] L. Onsager (autobiography), *Modern men of science.*

$$Z_{mn}(T) = \text{Tr}\{[\mathbf{K}_m(T)]^n\}, \tag{13}$$

where the matrix $\mathbf{K}_m(T)$ serves to build up the lattice column by column. The matrix elements are the Boltzmann factors for the pair interactions and hence depend simply on the temperature, T, and the interaction energies, J and J'. To obtain the free energy, $F(T)$, per particle of a long lattice, one must take the so-called thermodynamic limit, $n \to \infty$, which yields

$$-F(T)/k_B T = m^{-1}\ln[\lambda_{0,m}(T)], \tag{14}$$

where $\lambda_{0,m}(T)$ is the largest eigenvalue of $\mathbf{K}_m(T)$ (and is necessarily unique and positive). In the one-dimensional case ($m = 1$) the transfer matrix is of size only 2×2 and Ising's original exact solution is trivially recaptured. In general, however, $\mathbf{K}_m$ is a $2^m \times 2^m$ matrix and, furthermore—to obtain a truly two-dimensional result—one must calculate for $m \to \infty$. Indeed, Onsager's work proved that a sharp phase transition occurs *only* when the lattice becomes infinite in both dimensions.

Onsager has related how he first attacked the problem by solving the two-row case ($m = 2$) where $\mathbf{K}_m$ is a 4×4 matrix. Then he calculated in detail for $m = 3$ and $m = 4$—not a very easy exercise! At that point he felt he had some ideas on how the general result might go. He checked these out on the $m = 5$ case and they worked. From there he saw how to reduce the eigenvalue problem from that for a $2^m \times 2^m$ to that for a $(2m) \times (2m)$ matrix and he thence found the eigenvalues for general m.

Among the "trick or two" Onsager added were results taken from branches of mathematics almost unheard of in the theoretical physics of his day—generalized quaternion algebra and the theory of elliptic functions, as expounded by his unknowing mentors, Whittaker and Watson. Joseph B.

Hubbard, Onsager's postdoctoral associate thirty years later, tells how, on suspecting an error in the treatment of analytic continuation in *Modern Analysis*, he went to consult Onsager, who dug out his own copy. The book was a wreck, with notes, corrections, and extensions jotted all over it. It had disintegrated into several parts but had never been replaced.

Onsager's solution of the Ising problem was first revealed as a discussion remark following a paper by Gregory Wannier at a meeting of the New York Academy of Sciences on February 18, 1942. It took the world of theoretical physics by storm:

"The partition function for the Ising model of a two-dimensional 'ferromagnetic' has been evaluated in closed form. The results of Kramers and Wannier concerning the 'Curie point' T_c have been confirmed, including their conjecture that the maximum of the specific heat varies linearly with the logarithm of the size of the crystal. For an infinite crystal, the specific heat near $T = T_c$ is proportional to $-\ln|(T - T_c)|$." (1942,2)

As Pippard wrote, in 1961:

"Onsager's exact treatment, which created a sensation when it appeared, showed that the specific heat in fact rose to infinity at the transition point, a phenomenon which profoundly disturbed those who were sure that fluctuations always smoothed over the asperities which were created by approximations in the analysis. This work gave a new impetus to the study of cooperative phenomena, . . . and it is certainly the most important single achievement in this important field."[20]

The instant recognition of its importance is reflected in a letter Wolfgang Pauli wrote to H. B. G. Casimir immediately after the War. Casimir was concerned at having been cut off for so long from the theoretical physics of the Allied countries, but Pauli reassured him by saying that nothing much of interest had happened anyway, apart from Onsager's so-

[20] A. B. Pippard, private communication to the Royal Society, 1961.

lution of the Ising problem.[21] And in later years, Lev D. Landau, whose own general phenomenological theory of phase transitions was fatally undermined by Onsager's results, told V. L. Pokrovskii that while the work of other theorists of his generation presented no real challenges to him, he could not envisage himself accomplishing Onsager's solution of the Ising model.

The full paper was published in 1944 (1944,1), and two years later at a conference in Cambridge, Onsager reported a slightly less exacting route to the summit using spinor algebras, which he had discovered in collaboration with Bruria Kaufman (1946,1).

But as he once remarked to Joseph Hubbard, "Obsession with partition functions maketh a dull man," and he was soon on the track of the other properties of the two-dimensional Ising ferromagnet. In August 1948 he silenced a conference at Cornell by writing on the blackboard an exact formula for the spontaneous magnetization. During the discussion following a paper by G. S. Rushbrooke at the first postwar I.U.P.A.P. statistical mechanics meeting in Florence, he exhibited the formula again. This intervention is worth quoting in full:

"Mathematically, the composition-temperature curve [coexistence curve] in a solid solution presents the same problem as the degree of order in a ferromagnetic with scalar spin. B. Kaufman and I have recently solved the latter problem (unpublished) for a two-dimensional rectangular net with interaction energies J, J'. If we write $\sinh (2J/kT) \sinh (2J'/kT) = 1/k$, then the degree of order for $k < 1$ is simply $(1 - k^2)^{\frac{1}{8}}$." (1949,3, p. 261)

In modern terminology one would say that the spontaneous magnetization, or coexistence curve, varies as

[21] Cited in E. W. Montroll's "Obituary, Lars Onsager," *Physics Today* 30,2(February 1977):77.

$$M_0(T) \approx B(T_c - T)^\beta \tag{15}$$

with critical exponent $\beta = \frac{1}{8}$. This contrasts with all previous approximate theories such as those of van der Waals, Curie and Weiss, Bragg and Williams, etc., which inevitably lead to the parabolic law $\beta = \frac{1}{2}$. In reality, three-dimensional magnetic and fluid systems have since been found to be characterized accurately by $\beta \approx 0.31$ to 0.36; but for effectively two-dimensional and layered magnetic materials, experiments yield $\beta \approx 0.11$ to 0.14—in striking accord with Onsager's formula.[22]

Onsager never published his derivation of this result, though in 1949 he and Kaufman produced a paper on the short-range order or, more correctly, on the set of pair-correlation functions of the square lattice Ising model (1949,2). It was left to C. N. Yang[23] to rederive the result independently. Only twenty years later, at the Battelle Symposium in Gstaad, did Onsager reveal fully that in computing the long-range order he had been led to a general consideration of Töplitz matrices and determinants but did not know how "to fill out the holes in the mathematics—the epsilons and the deltas" (1971,1). By the time he had done this, he found that "the mathematicians" had got there first—although, in fact, the generality and depth of Onsager's results were not matched for many years.

Although Onsager's 1944 result for the critical singularity in the specific heat was rapidly and widely acclaimed, other

[22] See, for example, R. J. Birgeneau, H. J. Guggenheim, and G. Shirane, "Neutron scattering from K_2NiF_4: a two-dimensional Heisenberg antiferromagnet," *Phys. Rev. Lett.* 22(1969):720–22; "Neutron scattering investigation of phase transitions and magnetic correlations in the two-dimensional antiferromagnets K_2NiF_4, Rb_2MnF_4, Rb_2FeF_4," *Phys. Rev. B.* 1(1970):2211–30. See also H. K. Kim and M. H. W. Chan, "Experimental determination of a two-dimensional liquid-vapor critical-point exponent," *Phys. Rev. Lett.* 53(1984):170–73.

[23] C. N. Yang, "The spontaneous magnetization of a two-dimensional Ising model," *Phys. Rev.* 85(1952):808–15.

aspects of the original paper—in many ways of deeper significance—took longer to be appreciated. Onsager showed that the general ideas of Ornstein and Zernike concerning the propagation of order *away* from the critical point were quite correct for the square lattice Ising model. Explicitly, he found that the correlation function, $G(R,T)$, for a pair of particles or spins at separation R must decay as $e^{-R/\xi(T)}$ where the correlation length or range of correlation obeys

$$\xi(T) \approx D^+/(T - T_c)^\nu \quad \text{as} \quad T \to T_c+ , \qquad (16)$$
$$\approx D^-/(T_c - T)^{\nu'} \quad \text{as} \quad T \to T_c- ,$$

with critical exponents $\nu = \nu' = 1$ and amplitude ratio $D^+/D^- = 2$. From the work of Kaufman and Onsager (1949,2) it further followed that at the critical point itself the correlations decay as:

$$G(R,T_c) \approx D_c/R^{d-2+\eta}, \qquad (17)$$

where, for $d = 2$ dimensions, one has $\eta = \frac{1}{4}$.[24] It is now realized that these exact results have most profound consequences for the theory of critical fluctuations and, furthermore, lead directly to the concept of the "anomalous dimensions" of operators in quantum field theory.

Again, in the 1944 paper, Onsager obtained (by an ingenious device) an explicit result for the surface tension between two coexisting phases below the transition; this may be written:

$$\Sigma(T) \approx E(T_c - T)^\mu \quad \text{with} \quad \mu = 1, \qquad (18)$$

a conclusion that also led to extensive reevaluation of theory and experiment.

[24] M. E. Fisher, "The susceptibility of the plane Ising model," *Physica* 25 (1959):521–24.

"In the days of Kepler and Galileo," wrote Montroll, "it was fashionable to announce a new scientific result through the circulation of a cryptogram which gave its author priority and his colleagues headaches. Onsager is one of the few moderns who operates in this tradition."[25]

The I.U.P.A.P. meeting in Florence provided him with the opportunity of letting off two more fireworks—one on the theory of turbulence and the other on the motion of superfluid helium.[26]

"To read this nowadays," wrote Pippard in 1961, "in the light of Feynman's later theory of helium, is to see that several of the essential ideas were well known to Onsager, particularly the view that the critical velocity for superfluid flow is conditioned by the quantization of circulation—a view which has received strong support from the experiments of Hall and Vinen. This is perhaps the first important example of what has become a marked characteristic of Onsager in the last ten years—a reluctance to publish anything except fully-polished work, combined with the habit of dropping valuable hints couched in gnomic terms. The obscurity of his utterances is not due to a desire to mislead; rather it is a result of an inability to appreciate the limitations of his hearers. To those who have been able to appreciate what he tries to say, he has been a source of deep stimulation."[27]

A lesser man than Onsager might have been embittered at the reappearance of his ideas, without acknowledgment, in the published work of other scientists, but he invariably gave his competitors the benefit of the doubt:

"Onsager suggested the existence of such vortices in 1949, R. P. Feynman independently a few years later," he wrote in his anonymous autobiography.

---

[25] E. W. Montroll, R. B. Potts, and J. C. Ward, "Correlations and spontaneous magnetization of the two-dimensional Ising model," *J. Math. Physics* 4(1963):308–22.

[26] L. Onsager, "Statistical hydrodynamics," *Nuovo Cim. Suppl. 9* 6(1949):249 on the theory of turbulence; see also pp. 279–87 on the motion of superfluid helium.

[27] Private communication to the Royal Society of London.

And again, in referring to his theory of the de Haas-van Alphen effect:

"In 1952 Onsager showed, this time followed independently by E. Lifschitz, how highly significant information about the distribution of electrons . . . in a metal could be extracted from studies of the de Haas-van Alphen effect. . . . "[28]

Joseph Hubbard reports that Onsager could not be persuaded to give his opinion of Feynman's theory of liquid helium, but Richard Feynman has given us a vivid account of some personal encounters with Onsager. They met in 1953 at a conference in Japan:

"I had worked out a theory of liquid helium, which was a new field for me so at that meeting I met many of the people in that field for the first time. At a dinner the day before I was to speak, I was seated next to Onsager. He said 'So you think you have a theory of liquid He II?' I said, 'Yes, I do,' to which he simply answered 'hmpf' and said nothing more. I took it to mean he didn't believe my theory could be anything but nonsense.

"The next day at the meeting I presented my paper, in which I claimed to explain everything except, I made clear apologetically, there was the serious flaw that I did not understand adequately the detailed nature of behavior of the thermodynamic functions right at the transition. In the period for questions, Onsager spoke first.

'Mr. Feynman is new in our field, and there is evidently something he doesn't know about it, and we ought to educate him.' I was petrified; this was even worse than the grunt last night—what had I left out—what stupid mistake had he found? He continued, 'So I think we should tell him that the exact behavior of the thermodynamic functions near a transition is not yet adequately understood for any real transition in any substance whatever. Therefore, the fact that he cannot do it for He II is no reflection at all on the value of his contribution to understand the rest of the phenomena.'"

[28] L. Onsager (autobiography), *Modern men of science* 1(1966):357–59.

This sketch of Lars Onsager, made by the late Otto R. Frisch, F.R.S., is reproduced by permission of the *Biographical Memoirs of Fellows of the Royal Society,* London.

Feynman was quick to recognize, behind Onsager's habit of talking in riddles, a kindly and generous man. Later they met on several occasions at scientific gatherings.

> "On one occasion when we were standing together, a young man came up to explain his ideas on superconductivity to us both. I didn't understand what the fellow was saying—so I thought it must be nonsense (a bad habit I have). I was surprised to hear Onsager say: 'Yes, that seems to be the solution to the problem.' Did he mean the puzzle of superconductivity was solved—and I didn't even know what the young man said? I guess so."

Feynman thinks the young man may well have been Leon Cooper, but Cooper is unable to recall the incident.

YALE—THE LATER YEARS (1949–1972)

To outward appearances, the year 1949 was Onsager's *annus mirabilis.* It saw the publication, not only of his third paper on the Ising lattice (1949,2) and his remarks on spontaneous magnetization and quantized vorticity (1949,3, p. 261), but also a fundamental paper on anisotropic solutions of rod-shaped molecules (1949,1). This paper set the theory of liquid crystals on a firm statistical basis (he used elliptic functions again for determining one of the cluster integrals) and made it unnecessary to postulate the existence of mysterious "biological" forces between the particles in a solution of, say, tobacco mosaic virus.

But he had by no means shot his bolt. In 1951–52 he went to Cambridge as a Fulbright Scholar to work at the Cavendish Laboratory and there produced his beautiful theory of diamagnetism in metals. The de Haas-van Alphen effect—the periodic variation, with magnetic field, of the magnetic moment of a metallic crystal—had already attracted the attention of theorists, but the current theories gave little insight into its origin.

With customary penetration Onsager went straight to the root of the matter—the geometry of the Fermi surface—and explained the periodicity in terms of quantized electron orbits circumscribing the surface at right angles to the applied field. He gracefully acknowledged the contribution of his experimental colleagues at the Mond:

"Within a few years, D. Shoenberg rose to the challenge and applied intense magnetic fields by a pulse technique, then picked up the fine ripples of the magnetic response as the field changed."

During the same year he gave a seminar in Oxford about his ideas on liquid helium, but on this occasion even the theorists were baffled. Onsager's final comment in reply to a question was: "The results are not bad when you consider the enormity [sic!] of the swindle which I have perpetrated!"[29]

His interest in superfluids continued, and in 1956 he and Oliver Penrose published an important paper on Bose-

---

[29] C. Domb (obituary), *Nature, Lond.* 264(1976):819.

Einstein condensation (1956,1). In it they eschewed the description of a Bose-Einstein liquid as a highly perturbed Bose-Einstein gas and defined the condensed (or superfluid) state as one in which the leading term in the one-particle density matrix is an extensive rather than an intensive property of the system. The concept of long-range order in such a system could be associated with the behavior of the off-diagonal elements of the density matrix; this idea was later taken up and carried still further by C. N. Yang.[30] It is a crucial component of the modern understanding of phase transitions, ordering phenomena, and broken symmetries.

By this time the scientific world had at last awoken to the fact that a rare genius was in their midst. Onsager had become an American citizen in 1945 and was elected to the National Academy of Sciences in 1947. In 1953 he was awarded the Rumford Gold Medal of the American Academy of Arts and Sciences, and in the following year Harvard conferred on him his first honorary doctorate of science. (It was just twenty-one years since Gretl had been told by their friends not to mind his eccentricities, he was twenty years ahead of his time.)

Honors and invitations came thick and fast: the Lorentz Medal of the Royal Netherlands Academy of Sciences in 1958; an honorary *Dr. Technicae* in 1960 from the Norwegian Institute of Technology, his penitent *alma mater*; and in 1962 no fewer than three more honorary doctorates (one of them from Brown University) and three medals of the American Chemical Society: the Lewis Medal, the Gibbs Medal (Yale had appointed him J. Willard Gibbs Professor of Theoretical Chemistry in 1945), and the Kirkwood Medal, which had been endowed in memory of his old friend and Yale col-

---

[30] C. N. Yang, "Concept of off-diagonal long-range order and the quantum phases of liquid helium and of superconductors," *Rev. Mod. Phys.* 34(1962):694–704.

league Jack Kirkwood, who died prematurely. The Debye Medal of the American Chemical Society, which followed in 1965, was no less fitting a tribute to his old teacher, Pieter Debye, than to Onsager himself.

Kirkwood and Onsager had been at Yale together for some years, and though both men added lustre to the Sterling Chemical Laboratory, they were a study in contrasts. Kirkwood had a passion for formal rigor but less of a taste for bold simplifying physical assumptions. He was a conscientious teacher and supervisor of research students, a diligent correspondent, and a pillar of the department. Onsager was a hopeless teacher and an appalling correspondent; it is said that he used to take his letters out of the mailbox one by one, glance at them, and tear them up.

When Kirkwood died, Onsager was pressed to write a short note of appreciation for *Molecular Physics*, but he failed to reply, even when the invitation was renewed a month later. Perhaps, though, he had other reasons for ignoring the request.

Shedlovsky and Montroll[31] relate that, at a conference in 1942, there was a sharp exchange between Kirkwood and Onsager just before the break. Kirkwood had lit his pipe, and Onsager took the last cigarette from a pack and straightened out the tinfoil. Suddenly he laid it on Kirkwood's bald head, and Kirkwood was just about to explode with fury when Onsager grinned and said: "Jack, you forgot the screening effect!" Tempers relaxed in a burst of laughter.

Onsager himself never strayed far from physical reality. On another occasion, when asked by Longsworth how he would explain the electrophoretic effect in "physical terms," he picked up Longsworth, chair and all, and carried him across the room.

[31] Shedlovsky and Montroll, Introduction, Onsager Symposium, *J. Math. Phys.* 4,2(1963).

Onsager's sense of humor occasionally verged on the mischievous, especially when he felt the urge to deflate a pompous colleague. At the 1948 I.U.P.A.P. meeting in Florence a lecture was delivered by an eminent British physical chemist who had a reputation for making cutting remarks in public, especially about the work of younger scientists. The blackboard was rapidly covered with symbols; Onsager reposed in the front row, apparently asleep. At the end of the talk, the chairman of the session asked for questions or comments. Onsager awoke and raised his hand. The chairman eagerly gave him the floor. Onsager walked to the blackboard and picked up the eraser; silently, with back to the audience and starting at the top left-hand corner, he erased every formula, figure, and comment recorded during the lecture. Having completed his handiwork, he turned to the audience, grinned, and sat down. The chairmen sensed that justice had been done and hastily terminated the discussion.

Another story, which we owe to Sir Denys Wilkinson, concerns a paper that Onsager was asked to referee at the beginning of his year in Cambridge. Months passed, but no report was forthcoming. Eventually, just before he left, Onsager was prevailed upon to return the paper. His report consisted of the single word "Somehow."

It is hardly surprising that the journals eventually stopped asking him to act as a referee. But a personal approach might yield dividends; on rare occasions (we know of at least two), an aspiring young scientist would receive a terse but encouraging letter of reply to a suggestion or idea that caught Onsager's fancy.

Between 1955 and 1965 Onsager's thoughts turned repeatedly to his first scientific problem—the properties of electrolytes. Raymond Fuoss, the New Boy at Brown, had joined the department at Yale in 1945, and the two of them continued to develop the ideas they had first expounded in 1932

(1932,1). The theory became more sophisticated but not obviously better; the real trouble was that the new and important problems were now largely structural rather than merely kinetic.

Onsager realized this and turned his attention to the electrical properties of ice, where the structure and its various defects are of paramount importance. He felt that a full understanding of this fascinating solid might throw light on the structures and properties of biological membranes. His interest in these matters may have been fired by conversations with Max Perutz when he was in Cambridge. At that time, says Perutz,[32] "we had several discussions about the possible location and manner of binding of this water [to hemoglobin], but it was only recently that my colleagues and I found where some of it is actually bound." In spite of much theoretical dexterity in collaboration with Dupuis (1962,3) and others (1974,2), he never really hit the biological jackpot. It would have been a miracle if he had.

In the early 1960s two conferences were inspired by Onsager's work: an International Conference, held in his honor, on "Irreversible Thermodynamics and the Statistical Mechanics of Phase Transitions" at Brown University in June 1962 (reported in *J. Math. Phys.*, Feb. 1963) and an International Conference on "Phenomena in the Neighborhood of Critical Points," held at the National Bureau of Standards in Washington in the spring of 1965.

In 1966 he received the Belfer Award at Yeshiva University, and in 1968 he was nominated—not for the first time—for the Nobel Prize. The faculty at Cornell nominated him both for the Physics and the Chemistry prize, mentioning especially his fundamental work on phase transitions; in the

---

[32] M. F. Perutz, "The role of bound water in hemoglobin and myoglobin," *BioSystems* 8(1977):261–63.

event he was awarded the 1968 Nobel Prize in Chemistry for his discovery of the reciprocal relations—which had failed to secure him a Norwegian Ph.D. Other academies soon followed suit, including the University of Cambridge. In 1970 the Battelle Symposium at Gstaad commemorated the 25th anniversary of his first paper on the two-dimensional Ising lattice (1944,1); and in 1972, on his retirement from Yale, his colleagues presented him with a dedicatory volume to remind him of his achievements and of the esteem in which they held him.

CORAL GABLES (1972–1976)

On his retirement in 1972, Yale offered Onsager an office as emeritus professor but denied him facilities for continuing collaborative research with postdoctoral associates. Specifically, the Provost's office cited a rule that prohibited an emeritus professor from being a "principal investigator" on a research proposal to a granting agency. Onsager resented the blind application of the rule and appealed against the decision but without success. By the time others in the University discovered the situation and protested to President Kingman Brewster, Jr., it was too late. Onsager had, in the meanwhile, accepted an appointment as Distinguished University Professor at the University of Miami, Coral Gables, and joined the University's Center for Theoretical Studies directed by Behram Kursunoglu, where his research was generously funded by national agencies. The Onsagers kept their house in New Haven for some time, however, with the hope of returning.

On his seventieth birthday, the Center for Theoretical Studies arranged in his honor a conference in Miami entitled "Quantum Statistical Mechanics in the Life Sciences." Lars presented a paper on "Life in the Early Days," outlining some of his ideas about the origin of life on earth, a subject which he had discussed from time to time over the years, with Manfred Eigen.

During the last few years of his life, Onsager took much interest in biophysics and regularly attended the meetings of the Neurosciences Research Program, of which he was an Associate. (He was a regular attender at conferences of all sorts, but his interventions were few and far between; he preferred listening, usually with his eyes closed, to holding forth.) But he never underestimated the task of understanding the brain; of the electroencephalogram he once remarked: "It is like trying to discover how the telephone system works by measuring the fluctuations in the electric power used by the telephone company."

Joseph Hubbard, who first met Onsager at Yale as a postdoctoral fellow in 1971 and accompanied him to Coral Gables, has given us a number of personal glimpses of the last few years. On first setting eyes on his new postdoc, Lars embraced him in Russian style and took him to his office to show him a reprint. There was chaos on every surface, including the floor. Suddenly Lars disappeared, and Hubbard found him underneath the desk, where he had located the reprint (which turned out to be a 400-page thesis) and a two-month-old paycheck. Observing Onsager's contortions, Hubbard thought to himself: "Here's a fellow who scratches his left ear by reaching round the back of his head with his right hand. I wonder how he ties his shoes!"

Lars had a number of strong opinions on the way to do research. "There's a time to soar like an eagle and a time to burrow like a worm. It takes a pretty sharp cookie to know when to shed the feathers and" (long pause) "to begin munching the humus!" (characteristic Onsager giggle).

About a certain Belgian theoretical chemist: "He's a bright fellow. But there are a lot of folks, some quite talented, who arm themselves with methods and then go hunting for vulnerable problems; but to accept a problem on its own terms and then forge your own weapon—now that's real class!" (Experts, beware!)

In defense of Hubbard, under cross-examination as to why it took so long to get a self-consistent kinetic theory of ion-solvent interactions: "The theory of dielectrics has more booby traps than a gamma function has poles!"

In an argument with Hubbard about crystal acoustics: "If I said what you just said, I wouldn't have any idea what I was talking about!"

To John F. Nagle, while he was a graduate student at Yale, about the three-dimensional Ising problem: "I'm afraid it's one dimension too many." (But Michael J. Stephen, who knew Onsager as a faculty colleague at Yale, says that on being questioned about the problem Onsager once remarked that in his more optimistic moments he thought analytic progress could be made, though he did not expect to see the solution in his lifetime.)

About someone's new, generalized, unified field theory: "I might give it more credence if only he weren't so sure he was right!"

The Royal Society elected Onsager a Foreign Member in 1975.

In the autumn of 1976, Lars went to a conference in Canada on radiation chemistry—a relatively new interest, but touching on some of his early ideas (1974,3). He had not been feeling too well of late; he was having some pain in his breathing (he was a confirmed smoker) and had contracted phlebitis in his legs, but was too embarrassed to complain of these ailments to his friends. His wife was staying at their farm in Tilton, and Lars returned to Miami alone. Hubbard met him on a Friday, and afterwards Onsager went over to the Kursunoglus for dinner. He did not appear at the Center on the Monday nor answer the telephone. On Tuesday morning,

Hubbard went over to the Onsagers' house on Biltmore Drive, expecting it to be open, as Lars liked a swim in his outdoor pool in the mornings. It was locked, but the neighbors turned out to have a spare key. Lars was lying on his back, dressed in shorts for his early morning swim. It appeared to have been a swift and merciful death—his face was that of someone who had fallen asleep.

A service in his memory was held ten days later, on October 15, in the Dwight Memorial Chapel at Yale University, and tributes were paid him by Henry Margenau, Platonia Kirkwood, and Manfred Eigen.

RETROSPECT

Lars Onsager was not altogether of this world, though he had a deep understanding of its fundamental laws. His life was first and foremost a life of the mind; he had little interest in politics or religion and spared little time for academic or public affairs. His political views were conservative; he once said of then-President Nixon: "I think the man is patriotic and, at least, sincere." He was not prepared to dismiss religion—"There might be something to all this"—but his approach to life was generally pragmatic. He wanted to solve concrete problems and was not interested, for example, in the philosophical paradoxes of quantum mechanics.

He was one of those scientists who would have adorned any age; his achievements were the fruits of his own work, carried out in quiet solitude rather than in the hurry and bustle of teams and projects. By his rare but magnificent contributions he silently gave the lie to the corrupting motto "Publish or perish!" and proved that real intellectual progress demands thorough preparation and unremitting attention to detail.

As Behram Kursunoglu wrote two months after Onsager's death: "He will be remembered, always, as a very great man

222   BIOGRAPHICAL MEMOIRS

of science—with profound humanitarian and scientific qualities which deeply enriched the lives and work of those with whom he came into contact . . . , just as they affected and will affect many generations of scientists throughout the world."

WE ARE MUCH INDEBTED to friends and colleagues for their help in providing us with recollections of Lars Onsager and evaluations of his work. We would, however, particularly like to thank David Buckingham, Fritz Böttcher, Robert H. Cole, Leon N. Cooper, Cyril Domb, Richard P. Feynman, Joseph Hubbard, Oliver Penrose, Michael Stephen, and Julian Sturtevant for valuable sidelights on Onsager's life, Benjamin Widom for a critical reading of the manuscript, and the Kline Science Library at Yale University for material assistance in the preparation of the bibliography, which we believe to be essentially complete.[33] We are also particularly indebted to Otto Frisch for his drawing of Onsager reproduced here.

---

[33] For a list compiled by the Kline Science Library of the biographies of Lars Onsager that appeared from 1938 to 1963, see *Biographical Memoirs*, Royal Society (London) 24(1978):470–1.

APPOINTMENTS

1926–1928   Research Assistant, Eidgenössische Technische Hochschule, Zürich, Switzerland
1928   Associate in Chemistry, Johns Hopkins University
1928–1933   Instructor in Chemistry, Brown University
1933–1934   Sterling and Gibbs Fellow, Yale University
1934–1940   Assistant Professor of Chemistry, Yale University
1940–1945   Associate Professor of Chemistry, Yale University
1945–1973   J. Willard Gibbs Professor of Theoretical Chemistry, Yale University
1951–1952   Fulbright Scholar, Cambridge University
1961   Visiting Professor, University of California, San Diego
1967–1968   Visiting Professor, Rockefeller University
1968   Visiting Professor, University of Göttingen
1970   Visiting Professor, University of Leiden
1972–1976   Distinguished University Professor, University of Miami, Coral Gables

DEGREES

1925   Ch.E., Norges Tekniske Hogskole, Trondheim, Norway
1935   Ph.D., Yale University

HONORARY DEGREES

1954   D.Sc., Harvard University
1960   Dr Technicae, Norges Tekniske Hogskole
1962   D.Sc., Brown University
        D.Sc., Rensselaer Polytechnic Institute
        Dr Naturwissenschaften, Rheinisch-Westfälisch Technische Hochschule, Aachen
1968   D.Sc., The University of Chicago
1969   D.Sc., Ohio State University
1970   Sc.D., Cambridge University
1971   D.Sc., Oxford University

MEDALS AND PRIZES

1953   Rumford Gold Medal, American Academy of Arts and Sciences

1958 Lorentz Medal, Royal Netherlands Academy of Sciences
1962 G. N. Lewis Medal, American Chemical Society, California Section
     J. G. Kirkwood Medal, American Chemical Society, New Haven Section
     J. W. Gibbs Medal, American Chemical Society, Chicago Section
1964 T. W. Richards Medal, American Chemical Society, Northeastern Section
1965 P. W. Debye Award in Physical Chemistry, American Chemical Society
1966 Belfer Award in Pure Science, Yeshiva University
1968 Nobel Prize in Chemistry
     President's National Medal of Science

ACADEMIC AFFILIATIONS AND DISTINCTIONS

FELLOW

American Physical Society (1933)
New York Academy of Sciences (1942)
National Academy of Sciences (1947)
American Academy of Arts and Sciences (1953)

MEMBER

American Physical Society (December 1928)
Sigma Xi Fraternity, Brown University Chapter (1929)
Connecticut Academy of Arts and Sciences (1940)
Royal Norwegian Academy of Science (1953)
Royal Swedish Academy of Science (1957)
Norwegian Academy of Technical Science (1958)
Royal Netherlands Academy of Science (1958)
American Philosophical Society (1959)
American Chemical Society (1962)
Deutsche Bunsen Gesellschaft (1969)

FOREIGN MEMBER

Norwegian Academy of Sciences and Letters, Oslo (1938)
Royal Society of Sciences of Uppsala (1963)
Royal Society (1975)

HONORARY MEMBER

Norwegian Chemical Society (1947)

HONORARY FELLOW

Institute of Physics, U. K. (1974)

ASSOCIATE

Neurosciences Research Program, U.S.A.

BIBLIOGRAPHY

1926

Zur Theorie der Electrolyte. I. *Phys. Z.* 27:388–92.

1927

Zur Theorie der Electrolyte. II. *Phys. Z.* 28:277–98.
Report on a revision of the conductivity theory. *Trans. Faraday Soc.* 23:341–49, 356.

1928

Activity coefficients and mass-action law in electrolytes. *J. Phys. Chem.* 32:1461–66.

1929

Simultane irreversible processor. (Abstract). *Beret. 18d. Skand. NatForsk-Møde, Copenhagen*, pp. 440–41.

1931

Reciprocal relations in irreversible processes. I. *Phys. Rev.* 37:405–26.
Reciprocal relations in irreversible processes. II. *Phys. Rev.* 38:2265–279.

1932

With R. M. Fuoss. Irreversible processes in electrolytes. *J. Phys. Chem.* 36:2689–778.
Viscosity and particle shape in colloid solutions. (Abstract). *Phys. Rev.* 40:1028.

1933

Theories of concentrated electrolytes. *Chem. Rev.* 13:73–89.

1934

With N. N. T. Samaras. The surface tension of Debye-Hückel electrolytes. *J. Chem. Phys.* 2:528-36.
Deviations from Ohm's law in weak electrolytes. *J. Chem. Phys.* 2:599–615.

1935

Solutions of the Mathieu equation of period 4π and certain related functions. Ph.D. thesis, Department of Chemistry, Yale University.

1936

Electric moments of molecules in liquids. *J. Am. Chem. Soc.* 58:1486–93.

1938

Initial recombination of ions. *Phys. Rev.* 54:554–7.

1939

Electrostatic interaction of molecules. *J. Phys. Chem.* 43:189–96.

With W. H. Furry and R. Clark Jones. On the theory of isotope separation by thermal diffusion. *Phys. Rev.* 55:1083–95.

Separation of gas (isotope) mixtures by irreversible processes. (Abstract). *Phys. Rev.* 55:1136–37.

With W. W. Watson. Turbulence in convection in gases between concentric vertical cylinders. *Phys. Rev.* 56:474–77.

1940

Separation of isotopes by thermal diffusion. (Abstract). *Phys. Rev.* 57:562.

1942

Anisotropic solutions of colloids. (Abstract). *Phys. Rev.* 62:558.

Crystal statistics. (Abstract). *Phys. Rev.* 62:559.

1944

Crystal statistics. I. A two-dimensional model with an order-disorder transition. *Phys. Rev.* 65:117–49.

1945

Theories and problems of liquid diffusion. *Ann. N.Y. Acad. Sci.* 46:241–65.

The distribution of energy in turbulence. (Abstract). *Phys. Rev.* 68:286.

1947

With B. Kaufman. Transition points. *Rep. Int. Conf. on Fundamental Particles and Low Temperatures, Cambridge, July 1946*, vol. 2, p. 137. London: The Physical Society.

1948

With J. E. Robinson. De Haas-Van Alphen effect in zinc. (Abstract). *Phys. Rev.* 74:1235.

1949

Effects of shape on the interaction of colloidal particles. *Ann. N.Y. Acad. Sci.* 51:627–59.

With B. Kaufman. Crystal statistics. III. Short-range order in a binary Ising lattice. *Phys. Rev.* 76:1244–52.

Statistical hydrodynamics. *Nuovo Cim. Suppl. (9)* 6:279–87; see also 249, 261.

With W. W. Watson and A. Zucker. Apparatus for isotope separation by thermal diffusion. *Rev. Scient. Instrum.* 20:924–27.

1952

Interpretation of the de Haas-Van Alphen effect. *Phil. Mag. (7)* 43:1006–8.

With L. J. Gosting. General theory for the Gouy diffusion method. *J. Am. Chem. Soc.* 74:6066–74.

Kinetic theory and statistical mechanics. Lecture notes of a course of the same title given at Yale University by Lars Onsager, compiled by Don E. Harrison, Jr. Unpublished manuscript in Kline Library, Yale University, New Haven.

1953

With S. Machlup. Fluctuations and irreversible processes. *Phys. Rev.* 91:1505–12.

With S. Machlup. Fluctuations and irreversible processes. II. Systems with kinetic energy. *Phys. Rev.* 91:1512–15.

Diamagnetism in metals. *Proc. Int. Conf. Theoretical Physics, Kyoto and Tokyo, September 1953*, pp. 669–75. Introductory talk [on liquid helium], pp. 877–80. Tokyo: Science Council of Japan.

1955

With R. M. Fuoss. Conductance of strong electrolytes at finite dilutions. *Proc. Natl. Acad. Sci. USA.* 41:274–83.

1956

With O. Penrose. Bose-Einstein condensation and liquid helium. *Phys. Rev.* 104:576–84.

1957

With S. K. Kim. Wien effect in simple strong electrolytes. *J. Phys. Chem.* 61:198–215.

With S. K. Kim. The relaxation effect in mixed strong electrolytes. *J. Phys. Chem.* 61:215–29.

With R. M. Fuoss. Conductance of unassociated electrolytes. *J. Phys. Chem.* 61:668–82.

1958

With R. M. Fuoss. The kinetic term in electrolytic conductance. *J. Phys. Chem.* 62:1339–40.

With J. L. Lebowitz. Low temperature fluctuations. *Proc. Fifth Int. Conf. Low Temperature Physics and Chemistry, Madison, Wisconsin, Aug. 1957*, p. 119. Madison: University of Wisconsin Press.

Many-electron wave function. (Abstract). *Bull. Am. Phys. Soc.*, Series II, 3:146.

1960

With M. Dupuis and R. Mazo. Surface-specific heat of an isotropic solid at low temperatures. *J. Chem. Phys.* 33:1452–61.

With D. R. Whitman, M. Saunders, and H. E. Dubb. Proton magnetic resonance spectrum of propane. *J. Chem. Phys.* 32:67–71.

With M. Dupuis. Electrical properties of ice. *Re. Scu. Int. Fis. "Enrico Fermi," Corso X, Varenna, 1959*, pp. 294–315. Bologna: Nicolà Zanichelli (Supplement to *Nuovo Cimento*).

1961

Magnetic flux through a superconducting ring. *Phys. Rev. Lett.* 7:50.

With R. M. Fuoss. Thermodynamic potentials of symmetrical electrolytes. *Proc. Natl. Acad. Sci. USA* 47:818–25.

Statistical mechanics course. (Lecture notes from L. Onsager's Statistical Mechanics, Yale University, taken by Robert Hill). Unpublished manuscript in Kline Memorial Library, Yale University, New Haven.

1962

With R. M. Fuoss. The conductance of symmetrical electrolytes. I. Potential of total force. *J. Phys. Chem.* 66:1722–26.

The electrical properties of ice. *Vortex* 23:138–41.

With M. Dupuis. The electrical properties of ice. *Electrolytes, Proc. Int. Symp. Trieste, Yugoslavia, 1959*, pp. 27–46. Oxford: Pergamon Press.

1963

With R. M. Fuoss. The conductance of symmetrical electrolytes. II. The relaxation field. *J. Phys. Chem.* 67:621–28.

With R. M. Fuoss. The conductance of symmetrical electrolytes. III. Electrophoresis. *J. Phys. Chem.* 67:628–32.

With L. K. Runnels. Mechanism for self-diffusion in ice. *Proc. Natl. Acad. Sci. USA* 50:208–10.

Helium II. *Proc. Symp. on the many-body problem, Stevens Institute of Technology, Hoboken, New Jersey, January 28–29, 1957*, pp. 457–464. New York: Interscience.

1964

A correction to the Poisson-Boltzmann equation for unsymmetrical electrolytes. *J. Am. Chem. Soc.* 86:3421–23.

With R. M. Fuoss. The conductance of symmetrical electrolytes. IV. Hydrodynamic and osmotic terms in the relaxation field. *J. Phys. Chem.* 68:1–8.

1965

Electrons in liquids. In: *Modern quantum chemistry. Istanbul Lectures 1964*, ed. O. Sinanoglu, pt. 2, pp. 123–28. New York: Academic Press.

Electrons in metals. In: *Modern quantum chemistry. Istanbul Lectures 1964*, ed. O. Sinanoglu, pt. 2, pp. 265–78. New York: Academic Press.

With C. T. Liu. Zur Theorie des Wieneffekts in schwachen Elektrolyten. *Z. Phys. Chem. (Leipzig)* 228:428–32.

With R. M. Fuoss and J. F. Skinner. The conductance of symmetrical electrolytes. V. The conductance equation. *J. Phys. Chem.* 69:2581–94.

1966

With L. Mittag and M. J. Stephen. Integrals in the theory of electron correlations. *Ann. Phys. (Leipzig)* 7. Folge 18:71–77.

1967

Ferroelectricity of ice? *Proc. Symp. on Ferroelectricity, Warren, Michigan, Sept. 1966*, ed. Edward F. Weller, pp. 16–19. Amsterdam: Elsevier.

Thermodynamics and some molecular aspects of biology. In: *The neurosciences. A study program*, eds. G. C. Quarton et al., p. 75. New York: The Rockefeller University Press.

1968

With S. W. Provencher. Relaxation effects in associating electrolytes. *J. Am. Chem. Soc.* 90:3134–40.

1969

The motion of ions: principles and concepts. *Les Prix Nobel en 1968*, pp. 169–82. Stockholm: Norstedt & Söner. Also in *Science* 166:1359–64.

With L. K. Runnels. Diffusion and relaxation phenomena in ice. *J. Chem. Phys.* 50:1089–1103.

Protonic semiconductors. In: *Physics of ice, Proc. 3rd Int. Symp., Munich, 1968*, eds. Nikolaus Riehl et al., pp. 363–68. New York: Plenum Press.

1970

Possible mechanisms of ion transit. Physical principles of biological membranes. In: *Proc. Coral Gables Conf., 1968*, eds. F. Snell et al., p. 137. New York: Gordon and Breach.

1971

The Ising model in two dimensions. In: *Critical phenomena in alloys, magnets and superconductors* (Report on the Battelle Symposium), eds. R. E. Mills et al., pp. 3–12. New York: McGraw-Hill.

1974

Interpretation of dynamic and equilibrium properties of water. In: *Structure of water and aqueous solutions, Proc. Int. Symp. Marburg, 1973*, ed. Werner Luck, pp. 1–7. Weinheim: Verlag Chemie.

(a) Life in the early days, pp. 1–14; (b) with Edmond Drauglis. The effect of wall charge on the capillary rise of electrolytes, pp. 167–200; (c) with Tag Young Moon. Surface specific heat of crystals. I., pp. 227–79. In: *Quantum statistical mechanics in the natural sciences, Coral Gables Conf., 1973*, eds. S. L. Mintz and S. M. Widmayer. New York: Plenum Press.

With A. M. Stewart. Asymptotic forms for luminescent intensity due to donor-acceptor pair recombination. *J. Phys. C.* 7: 645–48.

With Mou-Shan Chen, Jill C. Bonner, and J. F. Nagle. Hopping of ions in ice. *J. Chem. Phys.* 60:405–19.

1975

With J. McCauley, Jr. Electrons and vortex lines in He II. I. Brownian motion theory of capture and escape. *J. Phys. A* 8:203–13.

With J. McCauley, Jr. Electrons and vortex lines in He II. II. Theoretical analysis of capture and release experiments. *J. Phys. A* 8:882–90.

1977

With Shoon K. Kim. The integral representation of the relaxation effects in mixed strong electrolytes in the limiting law region. *J. Phys. Chem.* 81:1211–12.

With Mou-Shan Chen. The generalized conductance equation. *J. Phys. Chem.* 81:2017–21.

With J. B. Hubbard, W. M. van Beek, and M. Mandel. Kinetic polarization deficiency in electrolyte solutions. *Proc. Natl. Acad. Sci. USA* 74:401–4.

With J. Hubbard. Dielectric dispersion and dielectric friction in electrolyte solutions. *J. Chem. Phys.* 67:4850–57.

1978

With David L. Staebler and Sergio Mascarenhas. Electrical effects during condensation and phase transitions of ice. *J. Chem. Phys.* 68:3823–28.

Alexander Petrunkevitch

ALEXANDER PETRUNKEVITCH

December 22, 1875–March 9, 1964

BY G. EVELYN HUTCHINSON[1]

ALEXANDER PETRUNKEVITCH was born on December 22, 1875, in the Ukrainian town of Pliski, near Kiev, the second son of Ivan Illitch Petrunkevitch and his wife, Anna Kandida. Though of aristocratic birth, his father was an important liberal statesman who worked incessantly for a more democratic form of government in Russia. He was a founder of the *Kadet*, or Constitutional Democratic Party, and was elected to the first *Duma*. He served as majority Party Leader in this body, for which service he was rewarded once with exile and once with imprisonment.

His son, Alexander Petrunkevitch, seems to have become attached to the study of natural history as a small boy. Like many another eminent zoologist he was first interested in the Coleoptera. He also developed considerable manual skills as a machinist—perhaps in part from his friendship with a member of the English-born Bromley family, who had started a factory in Russia early in that country's industrial development. He retained his machinist's skill throughout his life.

At the University of Moscow, Petrunkevitch's first publi-

[1] The Academy wishes to express its special thanks to Dr. Jonathan Coddington of the Smithsonian Institution for his editorial help with the preparation of this essay.

cation was a note on the development of the heart in a chrysomelid beetle.[2] His second, on fat absorption by the crop of the cockroach, was received unfavorably at first and only later recognized as a significant contribution to insect physiology.[3]

Petrunkevitch was also much attracted to literature and about the same time published—under the pseudonym Alexandr Jan-Ruban—a Russian translation of Byron's *Manfred*.[4] He used the same pseudonym for two later volumes of poetry[5] and retained his literary interests throughout his life. Much later he repaid his debt to English letters with an English prose translation of the *Lay of the War-ride of Igor*, the oldest important monument of Russian literature,[6] and—in connection with the centenary of Pushkin's death— prose translations of some of the great Russian poet's poems.

His professors in Moscow seem to have been a varied lot, ranging from the alcoholic to the eminent. Among the latter was the great geochemist, V. I. Vernadsky, with whom Petrunkevitch evidently had quite a close connection. He recounted how the two of them once visited a mine together. A high official of the mining company accompanied the distinguished professor from Moscow University and his young friend in the cage, and a mine worker with an anarchistic turn of mind decided to cut the rope suspending the cage and send at least one mining company official to his doom.

[2] "Über die Entwicklung des Herzens bei Agelastica Redt. alni L.," *Zool. Anz.* 31(1898):140–43.

[3] See A. Petrunkevitch, "Zur Physiologie der Verdauung bei Periplaneta orientalis und Blatta germanica." *Zool. Anz.* 32(1899):137–40, and "Die Verdauungsorgane von Periplaneta orientalis und Blatta germanica." *Zool. Jahrb.* 13(1899):171–90.

[4] *Manfred*, by George Gordon, Lord Byron. Translated into Russian from the English by Alexandr Jan-Ruban [Alexander Petrunkovitch]. Moscow, 1898, publisher unknown.

[5] Alexandr Jan-Ruban, *Pesni Liubvi i Pechali* (Songs of Love and Sorrow), Moscow, 1899; and *Doomy i Vpechatlenija* (Thoughts and Impressions, a book of Poems in Russian), Leipzig: Raimund Gerhard, 1900.

[6] Alexander and Wanda Petrunkevitch, "'The Lay of the War-Ride of Igor,' translated from the old-Russian," *Poet Lore* (Summer, 1919):289–303.

Fortunately, the cage tilted obliquely and stuck in the shaft very close to an adit through which its occupants were rescued unharmed. Later in life, Vernadsky's son, the distinguished Russian historian George Vernadsky, was to become a colleague of Petrunkevitch at Yale and, between them, they were instrumental in introducing to America V. I. Vernadsky's ideas about the biosphere.

THE UNIVERSITY OF FREIBURG (1899–1903)

Before proceeding to an advanced degree Petrunkevitch ran afoul of the authorities in a protest against the way students had been treated in the disturbances in Russia in 1899. Finding he would have to escape from the country if he did not wish to be arrested, he left and made his way to Germany to complete his education. Characteristically, he chose to work under August Weismann at the University of Freiburg because the great German zoologist had been violently attacked by Timariazev, professor of plant physiology at Moscow University. So it was that he first came to study and then to admire Weismann's work.

Although Petrunkevitch came to differ with Weismann on many matters of theoretical interpretation, their admiration and affection for each other were mutual, and their friendship continued until just before Weismann's death when the first World War interrupted their correspondence. Long walks and conversations at a time when Weismann was partially blind evidently played a determining role in developing Petrunkevitch's interest in the philosophy of biology.

In 1900 he took his Ph.D. *summa cum laude* and stayed on at Freiburg as *privat Dozent*. Throughout 1902 and 1903 he lectured on cytology and human parasitology. He also had charge of the parasites and spiders in the University collection, the first record of Petrunkevitch as arachnologist.

A certain naïveté and impatience with what seemed foolish conventions showed themselves in his German career. A newly appointed *privat Dozent*, for instance, was expected to pay ceremonial calls at the houses of all 140 members of the faculty. Since this merely involved leaving a card, Petrunkevitch worked out the most efficient route, hired a cab, and set out—only to discover that order of academic precedence, not geographical convenience, should have dictated the way. His mistake caused considerable offense, but despite such misunderstandings he became an effective spokesman for Weismann's students and junior staff, as is evident from his account of an unfortunate situation that developed when the behavior of a lazy, ignorant, and opinionated man began to ruin the reputation of the laboratory.

The Honeybee

Petrunkevitch's most significant scientific work during his Freiburg period was the study he did for his doctoral dissertation, published in 1901, on the cytology and early development of the egg of the honeybee. Although much of the detail recorded in this and in subsequent papers has been superseded by later investigations, Petrunkevitch gave the first statistically adequate cytological demonstration of the truth of Dzierzon's hypothesis that worker and queen bees are developed from fertilized eggs, while drones are developed from unfertilized eggs by parthenogenesis.

Petrunkevitch loved to tell the story of Dickel, an experienced and highly intelligent beekeeper who supplied him with eggs and had his own ideas on bee caste and sex-determination. Doubting what the young investigator could discover by microscopic examination, Dickel sent in the last batch of eggs for investigation with the labels switched. Petrunkevitch discovered the anomalous situation as soon as the eggs were sectioned and went off immediately to confront Dickel. Producing a friend as a witness, the beekeeper smiled sheepishly and admitted that the labels had been switched—

an incident Petrunkevitch recorded briefly in the resulting memoir.

Petrunkevitch's Fixing Fluid

A minor, but nevertheless important, byproduct of this study was the introduction of a modification of Gilson's corrosive sublimate fixing-fluid—a modification that has been widely used as "Petrunkevitch's fluid" in both American and European laboratories. Continental biologists visiting New Haven were sometimes surprised to find themselves in the presence of the almost legendary inventor of this fixative.

It is probable that the mixture was not Petrunkevitch's first attempt in the field; it is certain that he returned again and again to the problems of fixation. Later, in 1943, he obtained remarkable results with a bromophenol-cupric formula, which he believed had finally solved the problem of a "fixing fluid that would leave the tissues soft and at the same time give good nuclear and cytoplasmic fixation."

The fixation process was by no means the only aspect of histological technique that interested him. His work on differential staining at controlled hydrogen ion concentrations did much to interject elementary physical chemistry into histological practice.

While in Weismann's laboratory, Petrunkevitch and George von Guaita completed a morphological study of sound-producing organs in the Orthoptera. This study may well have prepared him for his discovery, over fifty years later, of a biting midge fossilized in amber, the wings of which apparently bore stridulatory organs—a unique occurrence in the Diptera, or two-winged flies.

YALE UNIVERSITY (1910–1964)

In Germany Petrunkevitch met an American, Wanda Hartshorn. They were married in London and came to her home in New Jersey in November 1903. Although he had an appointment for one term at Harvard, he was compelled to relinquish it on account of his wife's ill health. After that he lived as a private scholar until 1910, maintaining a small laboratory in Short Hills, New Jersey, and, for the summers, in South Harpswell, Maine.

He replaced C. H. Eigenmann for a term and was a visiting professor at the University of Indiana in 1905–1906—in retrospect, a very happy time. In 1906 he returned briefly to Russia, believing that his father's life was in danger as the result of the activities of the Black Hundred, a reactionary group backed by certain members of the Imperial Government. From 1909 until sometime in 1911, he held an honorary curatorship at the American Museum of Natural History.

But in 1910, hearing that A. E. Verrill had retired, he applied for a position at Yale. R. G. Harrison, though embarrassed to suggest a rank so grossly inferior to Petrunkevitch's ability and accomplishments, offered him an instructorship and Petrunkevitch accepted. A year later he was appointed assistant professor, and, in 1917, professor.

During the period between coming to America and his appointment at Yale, Petrunkevitch laid the foundations of his deep knowledge of spiders. His first published paper on the group dealt with the optical properties of the eyes of several species and contained estimates of the possible visual activities of such eyes. This was followed by a number of short works on taxonomy, morphology, and behavior, and in 1911—just after he came to Yale—by a catalog of the spiders of the New World. In 1913 he published "A Monograph of the Terrestrial Paleozoic Arachnida of North America" (1913) the first of his many significant paleontological works.

POLITICAL ACTIVIST

From 1917 to 1924, Petrunkevitch was much involved with lecturing on Russia and on the political changes taking place in his homeland. On May 1, 1917, he made an important speech before the Economic Club in New York warning Elihu Root's commission, then about to depart for Russia, that the moderate provisional government the United States supported might easily collapse. Such a collapse would make a separate peace between Russia and Germany probable and free up a great number of German troops to fight on the Western front. On July 4, 1917, he made an address in Center Church, New Haven, on the spirit of freedom.

He was a founder and president of the Federation of Russian Organizations in the United States of America. From 1919 to 1924 he was also president of the Russian Collegiate Institute of New York, set up to assist in the education of Russian refugees. Initially, he taught biology there once a week. In 1921 he made great efforts to ameliorate the position of I. P. Pavlov and seems to have felt that these efforts were not fruitless.

Petrunkevitch was particularly opposed to the United States' recognition of the Bolshevik government in 1924. That same year he became associated with the magazine *Current History* and contributed several articles on the political and social events in Russia and the Baltic states. This association was terminated, however, by a disagreement with the editor, who apparently felt Petrunkevitch was biased against communists.

RESEARCH PUBLICATIONS

Though all this outside work must inevitably have interfered with his research, he published another paleontological monograph—this time on the Tertiary spiders and harvestmen of North America—in 1922, along with a number of small papers.

In 1925–26 he was a visiting professor at the University of Puerto Rico. Though he had to return as the result of his wife's sudden death in New York, he was able to use the results of his work there to prepare a work of more than 500 pages revising the taxonomy of spiders on that island (1929,2; 1930,1,2).

From this time until the end of his life Petrunkevitch published, quietly but continuously, a series of classic works. His *Inquiry into the Natural Classification of Spiders, Based on a Study of Their Internal Anatomy* (1933,1) was the first comparative anatomy for any group of arthropods that could be used in classification. In this publication, Petrunkevitch described all but three of the families of spiders, investigating two of the three missing families in subsequent publications. Some later workers have felt that a few of Petrunkevitch's primary divisions, based on the number of pairs of ostia in the heart, indicate grades rather than clades—to use J. S. Huxley's useful terminology. Despite this minor caveat, all subsequent studies of the higher taxa of spiders have been obliged to take his basic findings into account.

Oligocene Amber Spiders

In 1942, having resumed paleontological study, Petrunkevitch produced the first of four basic papers on the spiders of the Oligocene preserved in Baltic amber (1942,1). These investigations continued long after his retirement from Yale in 1943 and became his greatest interest. In 1958 he summarized his findings in a lengthy paper on amber spiders in European collections (1958,1). At the time this paper went to press, Baltic amber spider fauna that had been properly investigated was referable to thirty-three families of which six were extinct; ninety-six genera of which seventy-eight were extinct; and 160 species, all seemingly extinct. It is, therefore, in its familial composition, an essentially modern fauna, though composed of species that have no longer survived.

After he had completed this work, amber spiders turned up in Mexico from deposits of about the same age as in the Baltic countries. Petrunkevitch's second paper on these Mexican amber spiders was his last work. Unfinished when he died, it was completed by his friend and fellow worker, Harriet Exline, who, unhappily, herself died while the work was in press (1971,1).

Paleozoic Arachnids

In addition to studying amber spiders, Petrunkevitch devoted a great deal of his extraordinarily productive retirement (about one-quarter of his scientific work was published after he became emeritus) to the Paleozoic arachnids. A prolonged trip to European museums in 1949 greatly furthered this project, which led to several monographs and is summarized in his section on fossil arachnids in *Treatise on Invertebrate Paleontology* (1955,1). His work led to an extensive critical evaluation of existing knowledge regarding all the higher taxa of the class and to a new, and greatly improved classification.

Surveying the whole evolutionary panorama presented by the Arachnida, he came to feel that all the major lines were established very early by a macroevolutionary process comparable to what his friend Richard Goldschmidt had postulated for his so-called "hopeful monsters." Even the most dyed-in-the-wool proponent of the more conventional view (such as the present writer) must admit that the fossil record of the Arachnida does suggest a macroevolutionary establishment of major lines early in the evolutionary process. However the record is interpreted, it seems reasonable to find the most primitive group—the scorpions—appearing before all others in the Silurian but extremely queer to find the mites, often regarded as one of the most specialized orders, present as early as the Devonian.

PHILOSOPHER

In addition to evolutionary speculations arising directly from his work, Petrunkevitch had deep philosophic interests, partly from his biological background and partly from his upbringing in a libertarian political tradition. Any form of philosophical determination worried him, and he was continually trying to find a way of reconciling a position that he called "materialistic" with a belief in the freedom of will.

This led him to a position not unlike that of Irving Langmuir in his treatment of an indefinitely large number of small causes producing divergent phenomena. He regarded it as ironical that an early article of his should have been rejected because it was written by a biologist while later the same journal accepted a paper on this subject by Langmuir, an eminent physicist. Actually, of course, the whole intellectual climate had changed.

AWARDS AND HONORS

Petrunkevitch was elected to the National Academy of Sciences in 1954. This event gave him great pleasure but came too late in his life for him to play a significant advisory role.

Among the other societies to which he belonged, the Connecticut Academy of Arts and Scientists, the youngest of the three 18th century learned bodies in the United States, was particularly dear to him. He occupied its presidential chair from 1931 to 1946 and published many of his most important papers in its *Transactions*. As president, he revitalized the ancient institution and made its meetings—followed by what the Academy home secretary, George F. Eaton, called a reresupper—unique intellectual and social occasions of particular value to newly-arrived expatriates, whom he often invited to attend.

Many others will chiefly remember him for "Pete's tea"— the weekly gatherings in his laboratory at 4:30 on Mondays at which all graduate students and faculty members were welcome. He continued holding these teas long after his retirement, almost to the end of his life. It is quite likely that many young experimentalists, attracted first by a break with tea and cookies, later learned to appreciate the tarantulas in Petrunkevitch's vivarium and the beautifully prepared specimens in amber under his binocular microscope. Perhaps these pleasant memories made them friendlier to behavioral, systematic, and evolutionary studies when such matters came under consideration at faculty meetings and on committees for the awarding of grants.

IN PREPARING THIS ACCOUNT I am conscious of the help that I have received from Alexander Petrunkevitch's dear friend and colleague, the late Grace E. Pickford, another invertebrate zoologist with whom he collaborated so beneficially in the later years of his life. I would also like to mention Eugene Kinkaid's general essay, "Arachnologists," in the *New Yorker Magazine* (Part 1 in April 22, 1950, pp. 38–59, and Part 2 in April 29, pp. 37–55).

SELECTED BIBLIOGRAPHY

1901

Die Parthenogenesis bei der Honigbiene. *Naturwiss. Wochenschr.* May 26.

1904

Künstliche Parthenogenese. *Zool. Jahr.*, Supplement 7:1–62.

1911

A synonymic index-catalogue of spiders of North, Central, and South America with all adjacent islands—Greenland, Bermuda, West Indies, Terra del Fuego, Galapagos, etc. *Bull. Am. Mus. Nat. Hist.* 29.

1913

A monograph of the terrestrial palaeozoic arachnida of North America. *Trans. Conn. Acad. Arts Sci.* 18:1–137.

1922

Tertiary spiders and Opilionids of North America. *Trans. Conn. Acad. Arts Sci.* 25:211–79.

1923

On families of spiders. *Ann. N.Y. Acad. Sci.* 29:145–80.

1925

External reproductive organs of the common grass spider, *Agelena naevia* Walckenaer. *J. Morphol. Physiol.* 40:559–73.

1926

Tarantula versus tarantula-hawk: a study in instinct. *J. Exp. Zool.* 45:367–93.
The value of instinct as a taxonomic character in spiders. *Biol. Bull.* (Woods Hole, Mass.) 50:427–32.

1928

Systema Aranearum. *Trans. Conn. Acad. Arts Sci.* 29:1–270.

1929

The spider fauna of Panama and its Central American affiliation. *Am. Nat.* 63:455–69.

The spiders of Porto Rico, part 1. *Trans. Conn. Acad. Arts Sci.* 30: 1–158.

1930

The spiders of Porto Rico, part 2. *Trans. Conn. Acad. Arts Sci.* 30:159–355.

Sex in the eternal triangle of life. *Yale Rev.* 20:107–20.

The spiders of Porto Rico, part 3. *Trans. Conn. Acad. Arts Sci.* 31: 1–191.

1933

An inquiry into the natural classification of spiders, based on a study of their internal anatomy. *Trans. Conn. Acad. Arts Sci.* 31:299–389.

1939

With H. Exline. Catalogue of American spiders. I. Classification of the Araneae with key to suborders and families. List of species suborder Mygalomorpha. *Trans. Conn. Acad. Arts Sci.* 33: 133–338.

1942

A study of amber spiders. *Trans. Conn. Acad. Arts Sci.* 34:119–464.

1943

Some curious effects of salts of metals and other chemicals in fixation. *Anat. Rec.* 86:387–99.

1945

Palaeozoic Arachnida of Illinois. *State of Illinois Scientific Papers* 3: 1–72.

1946

Fossil spiders in the collection of the American Museum of Natural History. *Am. Mus. Novit.* no. 1328, 36 pp.

1949

A study of the structure, classification and relationship of the Palaeozoic Arachnida. *Trans. Conn. Acad. Arts Sci.* 37:69–315.

1950

Baltic amber spiders in the Museum of Comparative Zoology. *Bull. Mus. Comp. Zool. Harv. Coll.* 103:259–337.

1952

Principles of classification as illustrated by studies of Arachnida. *Syst. Zool.* 1:1–19.

1953

Palaeozoic and Mesozoic Arachnida of Europe. *Mem. Geol. Soc. Am.* no. 53, 128 pp.

1955

Arachnida. In: *Treatise on invertebrate paleontology.* pt. P: Arthropoda 2. Raymond C. Moore, ed., pp. 46–162. Kansas City: Geol. Soc. Amer. and Univ. Kansas Press.

Trigonotarbus arnoldi, a new species of fossil arachnid from southern France. *J. Paleontol.* 29:475–77.

1958

Amber spiders in European collections. *Trans. Conn. Acad. Arts Sci.* 41:97–400.

1963

Chiapas amber spiders. In: *Studies of fossiliferous amber arthropods of Chiapas, Mexico,* pp. 1–40. Berkeley: Univ. Calif. Press Publ. Entomol. 31.

1971

Chiapas amber spiders. II. In: *Studies of fossiliferous amber arthropods of Chiapas, Mexico,* completed and edited by Harriet Exline, pp. 1–44. Berkeley: Univ. Calif. Press Publ. Entomol. 63.

Kenneth B. Raper

KENNETH BRYAN RAPER

July 11, 1908–January 15, 1987

BY ROBERT H. BURRIS AND ELDON H. NEWCOMB

S OME ASSOCIATE Kenneth Raper with the penicillia and penicillin, others with the aspergilli; developmental biologists may remember him most for having introduced *Dictyostelium discoideum* as a superb subject for study. His friends and associates will remember Ken not only as an outstanding, versatile scientist but also as an unusually warm human being.

EDUCATION AND EARLY LIFE

Kenneth Bryan Raper was the seventh child and the sixth son of William F. and Julia Crouse Raper. With the arrival of the seventh son, John—also to become a member of the National Academy of Sciences—the family was completed. The farm in Davidson County, North Carolina, provided—with its tobacco fields and small dairy herd—a satisfying, if not affluent, living.

Each of the Raper children was expected to carry his or her share of the chores, the bright-leaf tobacco requiring a great deal of hand labor. The farm also had two deciduous forests of giant oaks, maples, and hickories, and an area of magnificent mature pines, all of which were sacrificed during the Depression.

Social life in Welcome, North Carolina, centered on the local church and school and entailed a good deal of visiting

251

among relatives and friends. The Raper family held membership in the Friedberg Moravian and Mount Olivet Methodist churches, favored primarily because of their proximity, though Mount Olivet had also been the church of Ken's father.

Both churches emphasized music. Ken participated in their vocal groups and conceived a lifelong appreciation for music, though he was not among the Rapers who became proficient on an instrument. His brother John, on the other hand, was talented enough on the trumpet to consider music as a career. Education was of prime importance to the family, and despite limited resources, all the Raper children went to college, six earned M.S. degrees, and three completed the Ph.D.—Arthur in sociology, Ken and John in biology.

Ken enjoyed school, did well, and was moved from the sixth to the eighth grade based on a county-wide entrance examination. Before this move he attended a two-room school in Enterprise, travelling the two miles to school on foot, or in severe weather, by horse-and-buggy. The wooden schoolhouse was heated with wood-burning stoves that served as rallying points before classes started. Classes at the front of the room did recitations while other classes at the back mastered their lessons.

Ken retained pleasant memories of his high school years. He was one of twelve in the first class to graduate from Arcadia High School, to the construction of which the Raper family had donated land, lumber, and labor. The school covered grades eight through eleven, and the pupils studied English, French, Latin, algebra, geometry, civics, and some chemistry—but no biology. Ken particularly enjoyed chemistry experiments and the school library, which included the *Book of Knowledge*. He gained recognition in debating and public speaking and as a senior won a gold medal in declamation. He also enjoyed sports, though he never took part in inter-school competitions.

Kenneth's older brothers and sister had gone to college and he assumed he would also. In the fall of 1925 he enrolled at the University of North Carolina in Chapel Hill, where two brothers still in residence helped to ease the transition. But the family had money enough for only the fall quarter, and the problem of how to accumulate enough for the winter and spring loomed large. Ken earned his meals by waiting on table in the college dining hall. He collected suits for a cleaner, delivered the *Daily Tar Heel*, sold felt pennants at ball games, and personalized pillows as Christmas gifts.

At the university Ken enjoyed his classes in English, American history, and mathematics. Then, during his second semester, he met the botanists W. C. Coker, H. R. Totten, and J. N. Couch, who raised his interest in plants and launched him on his scientific career. He was fascinated by his studies, and his enthusiasm impressed his professors sufficiently for them to offer him a $260-a-year undergraduate assistantship. "I have received no offers since," he wrote late in life, "that pleased me more."

The assistantship allowed him to spend more time in the Botany Department, and Professor Couch gave him space to help in a study of the symbiotic relationship between scale insects and fungi of the genus *Septobasidium*. He always considered it a great privilege to have worked with John Couch. Ken's undergraduate minor was history; later he sometimes wished it had been chemistry.

As a junior Ken Raper took a mycology course from W. C. Coker, who was interested in the water molds, Saprolegniaceae. Ken recovered several genera of water molds from surrounding field and forest areas. His descriptions impressed Coker, who urged him to publish. At the age of twenty, K. B. Raper's first paper appeared in the September 1928 issue of the North Carolina Academy of Sciences's journal, *The Journal of the Elisha Mitchell Scientific Society*.

WASHINGTON, D.C.: THE DEPARTMENT OF AGRICULTURE'S DIVISION OF SOIL MICROBIOLOGY

Before graduating in 1929 Raper took a competitive civil service examination for a position as junior mycologist with the U. S. Department of Agriculture. When Charles Thom, a mycologist with USDA, visited Chapel Hill, he sent word ahead to Couch and Coker that he wanted to meet this Kenneth Raper. Thom was starting a federal Division of Soil Microbiology, and he signed Raper up to come to Washington immediately after graduation. He arrived at Thom's office at the USDA building near the Washington Monument on July 5, 1929. Thereafter the two collaborated closely until Thom's death in 1956.

Although Thom was a crusty character, Raper found working with him at an adjacent desk to be a marvelous experience. Thom was both knowledgeable and willing to share his vast experience of mycology. He also knew almost everyone in the field, and Ken had the opportunity to meet them when they dropped in. Acting on Thom's suggestion, Ken enrolled in evening courses in bacteriology and biology at George Washington University and completed his M.S. degree within two years.

The mycology laboratory was next to the Mall and the Smithsonian museums, and Ken thoroughly enjoyed a quick museum visit at noon and more leisurely tours on weekends. Washington offered many lectures and concerts, and Ken found Rock Creek Park a great place in which to hike. But most of all he remembered Washington as the place where he met and married Louise Montgomery Williams, whom he affectionately characterized many years later as his "beloved companion, counsel, and benevolent critic."

Thom assigned Raper the task of maintaining and becoming familiar with a large collection of molds. In Ken's earlier experience the penicillia and aspergilli had been treated as weeds, but in the Thom collection they were dominant, and he had to develop an appreciation for them.

Thom then suggested that Ken complete his graduate education by studying at Harvard. After receiving a tuition fellowship and the assurance that his position with the Department would be kept open, Raper moved to Harvard in 1933 to work with William H. Weston.

During a brief summer vacation in North Carolina before entering Harvard, Raper had collected some forest leaf-mold while hiking in the Appalachian Mountains. From litter collected at a site in western North Carolina's Craggy Mountains, he isolated a remarkable new species of cellular slime mold belonging to the genus *Dictyostelium*. He realized that a number of the unusual structural and behavioral features exhibited by this species made it especially attractive for experimental work.

HARVARD YEARS (1933–1935)

At Harvard, Ken showed Weston cultures of his new species of *Dictyostelium* and asked whether he could do his thesis work on it. Though Weston was unfamiliar with the organism, he agreed.

Ken named the new species *Dictyostelium discoideum* and described it in an article in the *Journal of Agricultural Research* in 1935. He then began a two-year exploration of the behavior of the new slime mold. In an extensive series of ingenious experiments, he laid the groundwork for the later adoption of this organism as a model system in which the sorts of intercellular communications and controls that operate in multicellular organisms could be investigated on a more primitive, approachable level.

Ken found his years at Harvard both demanding and rewarding. His researches were highly successful and he established many helpful friendships. Like so many others, he found "Cap" Weston to be an excellent teacher and counselor. Ken also discovered that Weston rarely assumed authorship of papers and preferred for students to publish under their names only.

In 1936, armed with his Ph.D., Ken returned to Washington with a promotion from junior to assistant mycologist and a $200-a-year raise. The leveling experiences of the Great Depression are difficult to appreciate today.

PEORIA (1940–1953)

During Ken's absence, Thom had delayed several projects he wished to finish, and Ken once again took up the study of the aspergilli and penicillia. Together they concentrated on the various molds described as species of *Aspergillus glaucus* and *A. nidulans* and clarified the nomenclature and descriptions of the two groups. With the taxonomy of these and several other troublesome groups clarified, they were able some years later to publish their *Manual of the Aspergilli* (1945).

During this period Raper also worked on *D. discoideum* and wrote up his thesis work for publication, papers that, a few years later, sparked great interest in this slime mold.

The thirties in America were marked not only by the Great Depression but also by substantial surpluses of farm products in some parts of the country. Seeking ways to use these surpluses, Congress authorized the construction of four regional USDA research laboratories. The Northern Regional Research Laboratory (NRRL) in Peoria, Illinois, was assigned the task of exploring the fermentation of farm commodities to produce valuable new derivatives, and a large proportion of the USDA fermentation laboratory staff in Washington was transferred to Peoria.

The Thom collection of microorganisms was to serve as the nucleus of a collection at Peoria to be explored for their potential in the production of citric, gluconic, lactic, and itaconic acids. In 1940 Kenneth Raper was asked to organize and supervise the collection.

The Rapers arrived in Peoria before any laboratory equipment had been installed, and the USDA group had to improvise benches before they could continue the work begun in Washington on itaconic acid. In the first recorded case of an attempt to improve the product yield of a mold by mutation, Alexander Hollaender sent them—from Bethesda, Maryland—irradiated cultures of *Aspergillus terreus* whose best mutants gave somewhat increased yields. Ken Raper, however, isolated a strain from Texas soil that surpassed even the mutants.

Penicillin

Within the first year of operation of the Peoria laboratory, its focus shifted to the production of penicillin. At Oxford University in England, Florey and Heatley had been isolating penicillin. In animal and (very limited) human experiments, they had demonstrated spectacular therapeutic success.

In the summer of 1941 the two British researchers came to the United States to enlist aid in improving yields of penicillin, which from surface cultures at that time were about two Oxford units per ml. Not receiving an enthusiastic welcome from the pharmaceutical firms, they turned to the National Academy of Sciences, which sent them to Dr. Thom. Thom suggested the new laboratory at Peoria as having the requisite flexibility and expertise in fermentation technology and the willingness to start studies on penicillin production immediately. Penicillin certainly must have sounded more exciting and challenging than itaconic acid!

At Peoria and across the country the search was on for ways to improve the medium for penicillin production, to produce penicillin in submerged cultures, and to develop more productive strains of the mold. Since only Fleming's strain of *P. notatum* was known at that time to produce penicillin, and it produced it only in surface culture, Raper's laboratory concentrated on finding more productive strains.

This work on penicillin was an unusually successful example of cooperative research. Though the NRRL played the leading role, there was a remarkable sharing of information among industrial laboratories, laboratories at Cold Spring Harbor, the University of Wisconsin, the University of Minnesota, and elsewhere. A newsletter distributed the latest information, and the collaborating laboratories met all three of their goals. Before D-Day, the Allies had an adequate supply of penicillin on hand to treat their casualties.

Growing the Fleming strain in surface culture was very cumbersome, but the strain did not produce penicillin in submerged culture. When NRRL strain 832 (from the Peoria culture collection) was shown to produce some penicillin in submerged culture, a wider search was sparked to find a more effective organism. Cultures from many laboratories were tested in Peoria. But the best strain, NRRL 1951, came from a moldy cantaloupe brought to the laboratory by a Peoria housewife in July 1943.

In subsequent years the press perpetuated many stories—mostly apocryphal—about "Moldy Mary," but it is fact that the housewife's strain of *Penicillium chrysogenum* immediately proved equal to the best surface strains and was superior in submerged culture to NRRL 832, the strain generally adopted in industry. An even better subculture, NRRL 1951-B25, produced around 250 as compared with the earlier 2 units per ml. and was immediately put to industrial use. Before the war ended, X-radiation at the Carnegie Institution in Cold Spring Harbor and testing at the Universities of Minnesota and Wisconsin had given rise to strains producing 1,000 units per ml. in submerged culture, allowing for a drop in price from twenty dollars to three cents (wholesale) per 100,000 units. The pharmaceutical industry later took over efforts to raise yields and brought them to their present levels of some 50,000 units per ml.

UNIVERSITY OF WISCONSIN AT MADISON (1953–1987)

After the war priorities were rearranged at Peoria and a number of investigators, responding to the emerging interest in antibiotics other than penicillin, left for positions in the pharmaceutical industry. In 1946 Ken Raper welcomed an invitation to teach a course in industrial microbiology as a visiting professor in the botany department of the University of Illinois. Though it involved driving to Urbana on Saturday mornings, the students were mostly veterans who worked hard, and Ken enjoyed teaching them.

After retiring in the early forties, Dr. Thom had been appointed collaborator at the NRRL, where he came each year to work. He and Raper completed their book on the aspergilli and, in 1949, published their comprehensive *Manual of the Penicillia*—especially noteworthy, since the success of penicillin had raised the lowly penicillia to an exalted status.

The NRRL culture collection also acquired prominence, as individual researchers and pharmaceutical firms sought new antibiotics. Also the ruling of the patent office that cultures of patented organisms had to be deposited in support of claims caused many of these to be placed in the NRRL collection.

Although officially Ken had no time at Peoria to work on

Dictyostelium, he was able to search for cellular slime molds by routinely scanning the plates that had been seeded with soil for the recovery of penicillia. He then used lyophilization to preserve spores of the slime molds for later examination.

In 1952 Kenneth Raper accepted a joint appointment in bacteriology and botany at the University of Wisconsin and in January 1953 moved to Madison with Louise and their son Charles. He shared a course in industrial microbiology in the Department of Bacteriology and also taught a jointly listed course in mycology. He and Louise promptly became confirmed "Badgers."

Ken Raper found it easy to make the transition to academic life at the University of Wisconsin. He had known E. B. Fred, president of the University, for many years, and had worked closely with a number of the faculty during the years of joint research on penicillin, including J. F. Stauffer, Myron Backus, W. H. Peterson, M. J. Johnson, and Elizabeth McCoy.

Though teaching left him less time for research, Ken enjoyed the freedom to choose his research problems and the stimulus of working with graduate students. He now put his primary research emphasis on the cellular slime molds, which were becoming increasingly prominent in developmental biology. Since his old book on the aspergilli with Thom was by now both out of date and out of print, he undertook to modernize the treatment of the group, especially by incorporating information on the phenomena of heterokaryosis and heterothallism on which he and his colleagues had worked.

As for the cellular slime molds, no contemporary, comprehensive coverage of these organisms had yet been published. Attention had been focused primarily on *D. discoideum,* yet Raper had collected a number of other species that invited detailed examination.

He and his colleagues soon recognized that the Acrasiomycetes were not homogeneous but included two distinct subclasses, the Acrasidae and Dictyostelidae. Both had independent amoeboid cells that aggregated to form fruiting bodies, but the two groups differed in mode of aggregation, nuclear structure, and form of pseudopodia. Although Raper concentrated on the Dictyostelidae, he and his graduate student, Ann Worley Rahn, also examined and described several new members of the Acrasidae. Among these, the species *Fonticula alba* was of particular interest, because it appeared to span the two subclasses in some of its characteristics.

Raper and his colleagues sought to isolate slime molds related as closely as possible to the original strains described in the literature. They placed special emphasis on isolating organisms from soil, the source of many of the species originally described. Collaborators worldwide sent cultures for examination. A number of known species were recovered, while new species were also isolated and described.

Other aspects of dictyostelids examined by Raper and his colleagues included the development of macrocysts, methods for axenic culture of the slime molds, the phenomenon of cell aggregation, and the phototaxis of pseudoplasmodia.

By the time of his official retirement in 1979, Raper felt that he and his students had accumulated enough information to justify a book on the Dictyostelidae. His early "retirement" years were spent in producing *The Dictyostelids*, published in 1984 in collaboration with Ann Worley Rahn. Part I covers the biology of the cellular slime molds; Part II is devoted to the systematics of the dictyostelids.

HONORS AND PUBLIC SERVICE

Kenneth Raper was elected to the National Academy of Sciences in 1949 and was a member of its Council when the Academy met with President Kennedy in celebration of its hundredth anniversary. He served on the NAS Committee on Science and Public Policy and on several committees of the National Research Council, including the executive committee of the Division of Biology and Agriculture, and the Merck and National Science Foundation Postdoctoral Fellowship Boards.

He served on a committee to strengthen the American Type Culture Collection, an assignment that required substantial effort since the ATCC, barely surviving, was housed in different institutions. In 1950 Ken signed a contract on a residence in Washington, D.C., to which the collection was moved. The importance of the American Type Culture Collection has become much more apparent in recent years. Ken Raper was pleased to establish it firmly in Rockville, Maryland, where it continues with a diverse home collection of 40,000 cultures and 70,000 distributed cultures a year.

Kenneth Raper also played a major role in *Biological Abstracts'* struggle to survive, serving for five years as a trustee and one year (1969) as vice president. A survivor of hard times, BIOSIS today publishes a number of abstracts journals and runs computer-operated retrieval services.

For several years Ken was associated with the International Union of Biological Sciences. He served as national chairman from 1962 to 1965 and was a member of the U. S. delegation at four General Assemblies abroad. As an outgrowth of the IUBS experience he was asked to chair the organizing committee for the XI International Botanical Congress held in Seattle in 1969. This involved several years of planning and put him in direct contact with prominent biologists from many countries.

CONCLUSION

Although his early scientific endeavors were not in academia, at the University of Wisconsin Ken taught for many years at the undergraduate and graduate levels. He found teaching both challenging and enjoyable and was particularly fond of laboratory courses, where he could observe the blossoming interest of the students. Supervision of graduate students afforded him the opportunity to watch young investigators develop into productive scholars and lifelong friends.

Ken Raper always found time to participate actively in professional societies. Working as he did at the interface between plants and animals, between eukaryotes and prokaryotes, he interacted with microbiologists, mycologists, and botanists. Ken sometimes thought he might have spread himself too thin, but he also recognized that his interdisciplinary efforts gave him unusual insight as a "naturalist." By any standard, his was an interesting, satisfying and unusually productive career.

Kenneth Raper once listed what he considered to be his seven major contributions to science. These were:

(1) the isolation of better penicillin-producing molds during World War II, culminating in the isolation of NRRL 1951, the parent of virtually all strains of *Penicillium chrysogenum* used in the production of penicillin;

(2) the publication of authoritative books on the aspergilli and the penicillia;

(3) the establishment and initial direction of the Northern Regional Research Laboratory culture collection;

(4) the use of lyophilization to preserve the spores of filamentous fungi and of cellular slime molds;

(5) the discovery of *Dictyostelium discoideum*, a unique cellular slime mold, followed by pioneering investigations on the growth, morphogenesis, and cellular differentiation of this microorganism, which seemingly bridges the gap between the plant and animal kingdoms;

(6) sustained investigations of the cellular slime molds, culminating in publication of *The Dictyostelids* summarizing what is known of the natural history and systematics of the class Acrasiomycetes; and

(7) the help that he was able to give to students and associates in their development of a broader vision of the microbial world.

Kenneth Raper lived a full and happy life. In his later years he was alert and productive until stricken by a heart attack. His death a week after the attack left his friends saddened but appreciative of having been able to share even a small portion of his life. We can only hope that there will be others with his high intelligence, insight, compassion, sense of duty, and zest for life.

THE INFORMATION in this sketch was taken almost entirely from an unpublished autobiography written by Kenneth Raper and submitted to the Academy in July 1986. It is available upon request in the Academy archives.

HONORS AND DISTINCTIONS

DEGREES

1929	A.B.	University of North Carolina, Chapel Hill
1931	A.M.	George Washington University, Washington, D.C.
1935	A.M.	Harvard University, Cambridge, Massachusetts
1936	Ph.D.	Harvard University (Austin Fellow)
1961	D.Sc.	University of North Carolina, Chapel Hill

PROFESSIONAL APPOINTMENTS

1929–1936	Junior mycologist, Bureau of Chemistry and Soils, USDA, Washington, D.C.
1936–1940	Assistant mycologist, Bureau of Plant Industry, USDA, Washington, D.C.
1940–1953	Microbiologist, senior microbiologist, and principal microbiologist, Northern Regional Research Laboratory, USDA, Peoria, Illinois
1946–1953	Visiting professor of botany, University of Illinois, Urbana
1953–1966	Professor of bacteriology and botany, University of Wisconsin, Madison
1966–1979	William Trelease Professor of Bacteriology and Botany, University of Wisconsin, Madison
1979–1987	Professor emeritus, University of Wisconsin, Madison

ACADEMIES AND LEARNED SOCIETIES

1949	National Academy of Sciences; Council, 1961–1964; Committee on Science and Public Policy, 1962–1966
1949	American Academy of Arts and Sciences
1958	American Philosophical Society
1954	Wisconsin Academy of Sciences, Arts and Letters

BOARDS AND COMMITTEES

AMERICAN TYPE CULTURE COLLECTION

1948–1962 Trustee
1952–1955 Chairman, Executive Committee

BIOLOGICAL ABSTRACTS (NOW BIOSCIENCES INFORMATION SERVICE)

1959 Vice president
1964–1969 Trustee
1966–1969 Executive Committee

NATIONAL RESEARCH COUNCIL

1953–1957 Merck Fellowship Board, National Science Foundation
1956–1961 Executive Committee, NRC Division of Biology and Agriculture

NATIONAL SCIENCE FOUNDATION

1961–1964 Selection Committee for Senior Postdoctoral Fellowships
1966–1969 Chairman of Biological Sciences

XITH INTERNATIONAL BOTANICAL CONGRESS (IBC)

1965 U.S. National Committee
1966–1969 Chairman, Executive Committee

INTERNATIONAL UNION OF BIOLOGICAL SCIENCES (IUBS)

1958 Chairman, American Delegation, XIIIth General Assembly, London
1961 American Delegation, XIVth General Assembly, Amsterdam
1964 Chairman, American Delegation, XVth General Assembly, Prague
1967 American Delegation, XVIth General Assembly, Montreux

MEMBERSHIPS

American Association for the Advancement of Science; Council (1970–1975)
American Institute of Biological Sciences

American Society for Microbiologists; Council (1954–1958)
American Society of Naturalists
American Society for Cell Biology
American Academy of Microbiology
Botanical Society of America
Mycological Society of America (charter member); President (1951)
Society for Developmental Biology
Society for General Microbiology (Great Britain)
Society for Industrial Microbiology (charter member); President (1953)

HONORS

1929 Phi Beta Kappa
1936 Sigma Xi
1946 Lasker Award (to Peoria Penicillin Team, NRRL)
1947 USDA Distinguished Service Award (to Peoria Penicillin Team, NRRL)
1957 George Ives Haight Traveling Fellowship for travel in France, Holland, and the United Kingdom
1960 Certificate of Merit, Botanical Society of America
1967 Charles Thom Award, Society for Industrial Microbiology
1981 Distinguished Mycologist Award, Mycological Society of America
1983 Honorary member, American Society for Microbiology
1984 Honorary member, British Mycological Society

UNIVERSITY COMMITTEES AND POSTS,
UNIVERSITY OF WISCONSIN

1959–1960 Cancer Research Committee
1959–1960 Plant Science Colloquium
1960–1962 Secretary, Executive Committee, Faculty Biological Division
1970–1974 Executive Committee, Faculty Biological Division
1959–1965 Research Committee, Graduate School
1970–1971 President, Wisconsin Chapter of Sigma Xi
1971–1975 University Senate
1974–1975 President, Wisconsin Chapter of Phi Beta Kappa
1974–1977 Press Committee
1976–1979 Faculty Rights and Responsibilities Committee

SELECTED BIBLIOGRAPHY

1928

Studies on the frequency of water molds in the soil. *J. Elisha Mitchell Sci. Soc.* 44:133–40.

1932

With C. Thom. The arsenic fungi of Gosio. *Science* 76:548–50.

1935

Dictyostelium discoideum, a new species of slime mold from decaying forest leaves. *J. Agric. Res.* 50:135–47.

1937

Growth and development of *Dictyostelium discoideum* with different bacterial associates. *J. Agric. Res.* 55:289–316.

1940

Pseudoplasmodium formation and organization in *Dictyostelium discoideum*. *J. Elisha Mitchell Sci. Soc.* 56:241–82.

1941

With C. Thom. Interspecific mixtures in the Dictyosteliaceae. *Am. J. Bot.* 28:69–78.

1943

The culture collection of the Northern Regional Research Laboratory. *Chron. Bot.* 7:340–41.

1944

With D. F. Alexander and R. D. Coghill. Penicillin II. Natural variation and penicillin production in *Penicillium notatum* and allied species. *J. Bacteriol.* 48:639–59.

1945

With A. Hollaender and R. D. Coghill. The production and characterization of ultraviolet-induced mutations in *Aspergillus terreus*. I. Production of the mutations. *Am. J. Bot.* 32:160–65.

With D. F. Alexander. Preservation of molds by the lyophil process. *Mycologia* 37:499–525.

With C. Thom. *Manual of the Aspergilli*. Baltimore: Williams & Wilkins. 273 pp.

1949

With C. Thom. *Manual of the Penicillia*. Baltimore: Williams & Wilkins. 878 pp.

1952

A decade of antibiotics in America. *Mycologia* 44:1–61.

1953

With D. I. Fennell. Heterokaryosis in *Aspergillus*. *J. Elisha Mitchell Sci. Soc.* 69:1–29.

1954

With W. B. Cooke. The 1950 foray of the Mycological Society of America. *Mycologia* 46:670–79.

1957

Microbes—man's mighty midgets. *Am. J. Bot.* 44:56–65.

1958

With M. S. Quinlan. *Acytostelium leptosomum*: a unique cellular slime mold with an acellular stalk. *J. Gen. Microbiol.* 18:16–32.

1961

With T. M. Konijn. Cell aggregations in *Dictyostelium discoideum*. *Dev. Biol.* 3:725–56.

1962

With H.-R. Hohl. Nutrition of cellular slime molds. III. Specific growth requirements of *Polysphondylium pallidum*. *J. Bacteriol.* 86:1314–20.

1965

With J. C. Cavender. The Acrasieae in nature. III. Occurrence and distribution in forests of eastern North America. *Am. J. Bot.* 52:302–8.

With D. I. Fennell. *The Genus Aspergillus*. Baltimore: Williams & Wilkins. 686 pp.

1973

With G. W. Erdos and L. K. Vogen. Mating types and macrocyst formation in *Dictyostelium discoideum*. *Proc. Natl. Acad. Sci. USA* 70:1828–30.

The Acrasiomycetes. In: *The fungi*, eds. G. C. Ainsworth, F. K. Sparrow, and A. S. Sussman, vol. IV-B, pp. 9–35. New York: Academic Press.

1978

The penicillin saga remembered. *Am. Soc. Microbiol. News* 44:645–54.

1979

With A. C. Worley and M. Hohl. *Fonticula alba*: a new cellular slime mold (Acrasiomycetes). *Mycologia* 71:746–60.

1984

The dictyostelids. Princeton: Princeton University Press. 453 pp.

FRANCIS W. REICHELDERFER

August 6, 1895–January 26, 1983

BY JEROME NAMIAS[1]

F RANCIS WILTON REICHELDERFER'S career spanned that exciting era when meteorology was transformed from a qualitative to an exact science, from a discipline dependent on rather simple instruments to one employing sophisticated radar, satellites, and high-speed computers. As chief of the U. S. Weather Bureau (now the National Weather Service) from 1938 to 1963, Reichelderfer, who had a keen sense for meteorology's future, played an important role in initiating and maintaining these developments. He was also a sympathetic administrator who helped his staff and soothed the tantrums of more belligerent colleagues. As a government official with many fires to extinguish, he yet managed to get the most out of his staff, both for official tasks and for making contributions to science.

EDUCATION AND EARLY YEARS

Francis Reichelderfer was born in Harlan, Indiana, on August 6, 1895, and died in Washington, D.C., on January 26, 1983. The son of a Methodist minister, he grew up in the Midwest and enjoyed boating and water sports but showed

[1] The Academy wishes to express its special thanks to Dr. Daniel R. Cayan of the Scripps Institution of Oceanography, University of California, San Diego, for his editorial help with the preparation of this essay.

no great interest in meteorology—although he did build an aneroid barometer. He was more interested in chemistry and chemical engineering, and when he went to Northwestern University, he majored in this field, taking a B.S. degree in 1917.

When he graduated, the United States had just entered World War I, which had much to do with his joining the U.S. Naval Reserve Force with the aim of becoming a pilot. He was sent to the ground school at MIT, where he signed up for aerological (meteorological) training—in part because he thought it meant he would soon be off to the front lines in Europe. When he got his commission, however, his name was apparently not English enough for some Allied bureaucrat, and he was sent instead to Nova Scotia to brief anti-submarine patrols on weather phenomena.

At that time the Naval weather service was minuscule, but Reichelderfer sensed that the science of weather forecasting was to become increasingly important, not only for sea maneuvers but also for aircraft, which he saw as the wave of the future in warfare. In December 1917, Assistant Secretary of the Navy Franklin Delano Roosevelt asked Dr. Alexander McAdie, director of Harvard's Blue Hill Meteorological Observatory, to help the Navy by organizing a training program for weather officers. Reichelderfer was selected to take the intense course, which sharpened his interest in meteorology as a science and possible career.

After the Armistice he decided he must have flight training. His request to the Navy was approved, and he was sent to Miami and Pensacola to earn his wings. Shortly afterward he was sent to Lisbon, Portugal, to be meteorologist for the first transatlantic flight of the Navy's NC-4.

In December 1919 he was assigned to the Naval Air Station at Hampton Roads, Virginia, where he got a first taste of the dangers of flying squall lines when Billy Mitchell, a pioneer who would later make aviation history, was forced to land his light observer's plane on the beach. This event impressed Reichelderfer with the frightening responsibility of being a forecaster and the need to improve the science (or art) of weather forecasting. He devoted much of his subsequent life to this, not through working directly on scientific problems, but in initiating and encouraging the development of instrumentation, networks, and international collaboration among the many branches of meteorology.

While at Hampton Roads Reichelderfer analyzed weather maps and studied articles relating to weather and meteorology. Although there were a number of texts on meteorology, little had been written in America on how to construct weather maps or on how to forecast weather. One of the better books at that time was Milham's *Meteorology*,[2] but even this was far from practical. *Weather Forecasting in the United States*, written by top forecasters of the U.S. Weather Bureau, contained hundreds of charts and rules for forecasting, empirically derived and completely lacking in interpretation. Many of the rules seemed contradictory. The book was frustrating to read and, though published in 1916, was studied by few. After just a few years, the book was already a relic, only of historical interest. Today only a handful of meteorologists even know it exists.

THE NORWEGIAN SCHOOL AND NAVY AEROLOGY

It was in this atmosphere that Reichelderfer decided to "learn by doing" and turned to the publications of the Bergen School, directed by the famous Norwegian meteorologists, V. and J. Bjerknes. The first eight-page paper he read— "On the structure of moving cyclones," by J. Bjerknes—ex-

---

[2] Willis I. Milham, *Meteorology: A textbook on the weather, the causes of its changes and weather forecasting for the student and general reader*, New York: Macmillan, 1912. New editions appeared in 1914, 1921, 1925, and several times thereafter.

cited him and many other meteorologists around the world. For the first time weather phenomena—clouds, rainfall, and temperatures—were treated in physical terms and not as exercises in isobaric geometry.

The Bergen school method became known as "air mass and frontal analysis" and viewed fronts as discontinuities separating air masses deployed from polar and tropical source regions. Using the Norwegian method, Reichelderfer analyzed many maps and made forecasts. He also gave reasons for his analyses and later on expanded this work into a more complete report. Now called *The Reichelderfer Papers*, it resides in the headquarters of the American Meteorological Society in Boston. Though never published, this report was studied by many fledgling meteorologists, both in and outside the Navy (1920?,1).

In 1922 Reichelderfer was appointed head of Navy Aerology, where he worked in a corner of the Map and Forecast Room of the U.S. Weather Bureau and was regarded as harmless. Not interfering with the official forecast work of the Weather Bureau, he was content to serve as liaison officer with the Navy and occasionally try out one of his new-fangled ideas. Head of Navy Aerology from 1922 to 1928, Reichelderfer built it into a first-class organization. He developed special training courses for officers and enlisted men who served as observers.

In the mid-1920s, lighter-than-air craft in the form of dirigibles came into vogue, and Reichelderfer quickly saw their importance to meteorology. He convinced his superiors to expand the Navy Aerological Service and to assign him to Lakehurst, New Jersey, where he became chief meteorologist for all lighter-than-air operations. He served as weather officer for the flights of the *Los Angeles*, one of the best-known Navy dirigibles. He also took direct part in free-air ballooning and participated in contests, including the International Balloon Races at Brussels. His flights on the *Los Angeles* were credited as sea duty, important for advancement in the Navy.

During his stint at the Weather Bureau he met Carl-Gustav Rossby, a Swede who worked on many topics, including air mass and frontal analysis and rotating tanks in which fluid motions simulated atmospheric circulations on the rotating earth. They became friends and this friendship was to lead to successful careers for both.

BERGEN, NORWAY (1931)

Reichelderfer, active in air mass and frontal analysis, wanted to go to the source of these ideas in Bergen and finally convinced the Navy to assign him there for several months in 1931. Certain reactionary meteorologists at that time were not encouraging. When he did get to Europe, the meteorologist in charge at Tempelhof Airport in Berlin said, "How could anything important scientifically come out of a tiny, conservative country like Norway?"

In 1928, a few years preceding this trip to Norway, C. G. Rossby—Reichelderfer's old friend from his Weather Bureau days—established the United States' first, full-fledged meteorological department at MIT. Rossby had left Washington upon the completion of his Scandinavian-American fellowship to establish the first airways meteorological network, funded by Harry Guggenheim, on the West Coast. Reichelderfer knew Guggenheim and was able to play an indirect part in the establishment of the MIT department (also funded by Guggenheim) by supporting Rossby (as did many others) as its head. MIT further profited by this friendship in that Reichelderfer arranged for naval officers to be sent there for graduate training in meteorology.

At that time the central problem in meteorological research was air mass and frontal analysis, so it is not surprising that the new curriculum at MIT was heavily slanted in this direction. As new methods of map analysis were taught at the new department, Reichelderfer compared his own analysis and sometimes found disturbing differences. This was part of the reason given to Navy authorities for his study sojourn in Norway.

Shortly after arriving in Bergen, Reichelderfer began to analyze weather maps, first for Europe and later for North America. He got on well with the Bergen group and became good friends with J. Bjerknes, its leader and principal instructor. In a letter to his Navy superiors, Reichelderfer requested a series of North American maps of abnormal meteorological situations, writing:

"There certainly is something fundamental and of value in the new principles vs. the old. It is a chance of a lifetime to develop those as applying to the U.S. and to use them to improve forecast service."

He reanalyzed these problem cases with the help of Bjerknes and other members of the Bergen team, including Tor Bergeron (later a professor at the University of Uppsala), and Sverre Petterssen (who would replace Rossby at MIT).

While at Bergen, Reichelderfer reviewed many scientific papers and became conversant with the new techniques being developed. This work enabled him to write the *Report of Norwegian Methods of Weather Analysis* used by Navy meteorological officers around the world and, coincidentally, by many other progressive meteorologists.

At Bergen Reichelderfer learned that deck experience was required in order to qualify for lieutenant commander. He was, therefore, assigned to the battleship *Oklahoma* for two years. At the end of this tour of duty he returned to Lakehurst and to his role in the rigid airship service.

In 1936 he was, as meteorologist, taking part in flights of the *Hindenburg*, the famous transatlantic dirigible that used hydrogen and suffered a tragic fire. Reichelderfer was lucky not to have been aboard on this trip, or on the fatal flights of the *Akron* and *Shenandoah*. These tragic events signalled the end of the airship as a means of transatlantic travel and the end of Reichelderfer's career in this specialized branch of meteorology. He was then assigned to an aircraft carrier and later, in 1938, to the battleship *Utah*.

CHIEF OF THE U.S. WEATHER BUREAU

In 1938 Willis R. Gregg, head of the Weather Bureau, died suddenly and a new chief had to be selected. One of the people selecting the new head was Robert A. Millikan, president of Caltech. He had met Reichelderfer several times when the latter was sent by the Navy to evaluate a new meteorology department being established at Caltech by Irving P. Krick. Millikan's support, plus the fact that Reichelderfer was well known as one of the top experts in the United States on Norwegian methods, had rendered considerable services to aviation, and was politically acceptable resulted in his appointment as chief of the Weather Bureau.

Becoming chief of the Weather Bureau in 1938 was not exactly an envious assignment, but it was certainly one of the most challenging. I have hinted at the sad state of science at the Weather Bureau at that time, in part because the prevailing notion was that meteorology was largely learned by apprenticeship. Problems of weather forecasting, furthermore, were treated as problems of geometric or pattern recognition. Whereas today even high school students know that upward vertical air motions are largely responsible for clouds and precipitation, at that time some people in top jobs—including many forecasters—did not. Many believed that rainfall came from the mixing of bodies of air with differing temperature and moisture content—an idea that elementary physics easily disproves. Many of Reichelderfer's colleagues ignored and even frowned upon the Bergen school's ideas of air mass and frontal analysis, and if the Norwegian publications were in the excellent Weather Bureau library, it would have taken sleuths to discover them. Their study was not encouraged.

Forced to face this situation, Reichelderfer did so most effectively. First he persuaded C. G. Rossby to take the job as assistant chief (a job Rossby held for two years before returning to academia). Together, Reichelderfer and Rossby instituted many innovations at the Bureau. Perhaps most importantly, they set up a thorough training course with scholarships for Weather Bureau employees, who were then encouraged to take graduate courses and conduct scientific research. In this way they helped create a cadre of young enthusiasts that was to influence the entire course of meteorology in America to a degree never before dreamed of.

World War II brought with it tremendous changes in science and science administration, and the Weather Bureau was no exception. Even before the United States entered the war the military saw the need for meteorological support. Reichelderfer encouraged the universities—at that time mainly MIT and Caltech—to teach forecasting and its applications, and the Army Air Corps and Navy sent more officers to school for advanced training.

Several officers were sent to MIT and Caltech to do research and develop extended forecast techniques. Aided administratively by Reichelderfer and Henry Wallace, Secretary of Commerce and Reichelderfer's superior at the time, Rossby and his colleagues pioneered in this effort. Since Wallace was a famous agriculturalist, he took more than a casual interest in meteorology and was cooperative on many pressing matters. He appreciated scientific work, went out of his way to inquire about new developments in weather forecasting, and suggested new avenues of approach.

Many revolutionary developments were taking place in

atmospheric sensing, including the introduction of radar. Reichelderfer, who saw its meteorological potential early on, asked R. A. Watson-Watt, pioneer in the invention of radar, to help introduce it as a major tool in the Weather Bureau's observational and forecasting program. Radar was most useful in determining winds aloft—information vital to aviation.

At times it appeared that its service to aviation might swallow up the Weather Bureau, but Reichelderfer managed to keep this important branch of meteorology in perspective so that other facets (agriculture, marine meteorology, cloud physics) would not suffer. He served, alongside the heads of the Navy and Air Force, as the civilian member of the Joint Committee on Meteorology, a group that made important decisions on emerging problems.

As an outgrowth of the recommendations of Horace Byers' advisory committee, appointed a few years earlier by Franklin Roosevelt, Reichelderfer established an Air Mass and Frontal Analysis (AMAFA) Center manned by capable Weather Bureau meteorologists, later supplemented by colleagues from the Air Force and Navy. Reichelderfer disbanded Byers' program so as not to interfere with AMAFA's operations and, much to his gratification, the new analysis center soon enjoyed national—and later international—acclaim. After the war the AMAFA Center became a model for weather bureaus all over the world.

Another major accomplishment Reichelderfer helped to bring about during World War II was the preparation of a forty-year series of carefully analyzed weather maps, which extended the Northern Hemisphere surface analyses back to 1899. The project involved scores of specialists and technicians and produced maps of great value to research and forecasting during the war and for decades thereafter.

Passionately interested, Reichelderfer insisted on reviewing all the maps produced, piling them so high on his desk he could hardly be seen. On one occasion a top staff member asked him what he was doing with them. Replying gruffly, "Damn it, I'll show you!" Reichelderfer pulled out some analyses on which he had altered the indicated frontal positions—an example of the "hands on" approach that characterized all his efforts and led to the criticism that he was overly concerned with detail.

Reichelderfer was also criticized for the penury of his budget requests to Congress. He felt a personal responsibility to see that none of the taxpayers' money was wasted and occasionally went so far as to interview young men recommended for promotion from "subprofessional" to the lowest professional grade. On one occasion the Undersecretary of Commerce for Transportation asked if Reichelderfer were a "magician"—he had accomplished so much on such a very small budget.

Reichelderfer's wartime effort also included encouraging some of his key men to lecture at universities and military schools and to serve in research projects at the Pentagon and in the Navy. Some of his people entered the military to serve in the theaters of war; others worked on the home front. While Rossby and Joseph Kaplan directed the selection of thousands of college men to attend the meteorology courses, Reichelderfer helped shape the public policies to get the training program started and keep it maintained. To this day, the elite corps they assembled and trained comprises the major contributors to the science of meteorology.

Cloud Seeding and Rainmaking

After the war, both the Weather Bureau and the universities attracted hundreds, if not thousands, of capable young meteorologists from the military. The cream of the crop applied for positions, and Reichelderfer took an active part in getting funds to hire them. Those with advanced university training enabled the Bureau to introduce new techniques and programs, including numerical (objective) forecasting with the help of high-speed electronic computers, advanced radar, remote sensing by satellite, and studies in cloud physics.

Cloud physics, however, proved disappointing to enthusiasts who thought that seeding clouds with dry ice or silver iodide would increase rainfall appreciably. Reichelderfer, ever the skeptic about claims of rainmaking, had insisted on proof, and his conservative view led to much criticism. Many meteorologists and others, sometimes in high places, thought that he was becoming reactionary and averse to new developments—a depressing turn of events for one who had always been known as progressive.

Reichelderfer insisted that his scientists test cloud seeding and rainmaking efforts to evaluate the extravagant claims made by university researchers and commercial cloud seeders. When his chief science advisor, Harry Wexler, joined him in asking for proof, he too was called a reactionary. Yet both Bureau tests and research elsewhere failed to indicate that cloud seeding—and especially rainmaking—was successful to an economically valuable degree. A couple of decades later, a thorough study of thirty-five rainmaking experiments in different countries showed that only one (in Israel) may have led to positive results. Though studies relating to the physics of clouds contributed to basic scientific knowledge, the ultimate goal of causing precipitation at will was never realized.

Computers and Numerical Weather Forecasting

One of the most successful advances in forecasting came with the introduction of electronic computers for numerical weather forecasting. The idea of numerical forecasting was first proposed by the English meteorologist, L. F. Richardson, in a classic paper of the early 1920s. But without high-speed computers, the necessary data, and correct numerical methods to implement the theory, he was unable to verify his idea.

Reichelderfer had heard of John von Neumann's new use of computers to attack ballistic problems at the Institute for Advanced Study in Princeton, where he had access to ENIAC, the first electronic computer. The two met at a banquet in Washington, and some say Reichelderfer put forward weather forecasting to von Neumann as a likely candidate for machine computation.[3]

It is probable that von Neumann would have proceeded along this path without urging, for in the mid–1940s he and V. K. Zworykin, head of RCA Laboratories and inventor of the electron microscope, came to Washington to brief Weather Bureau officials on new possibilities of numerical forecasting with computers. This was an exciting meeting that fired up all those present, even though the goal sounded remote.

Reichelderfer brought the subject before the Joint Meteorological Committee, which then established a meteorological center at the Institute for Advanced Study with von Neumann as head. Top Weather Bureau, Navy, and Air Force scientists were scheduled to go to Princeton frequently to see how this work was proceeding.

In 1948 Jule G. Charney returned from a year of study

---

[3] This story, credited by many, cannot be entirely authenticated. In his biography of Jule Charney, to appear in *Biographical Memoirs* vol. 66, Norman A. Phillips records that Charney attended a meeting at Princeton's Institute for Advanced Study in August 1946. Von Neumann had convened the meeting on the subject of the application of electronic computers to weather forecasting. "In his conversations with [G.] Platzman," Phillips writes, "Jule suggests that this idea might have come from von Neumann's acquaintance with V. Zworykin at nearby RCA. F. Nebeker, however, points out in his Princeton University [doctoral] thesis that it was [C.-G.] Rossby who suggested to von Neumann that the Institute for Advanced Study should submit a proposal for meteorological funding to the Naval Office of Research and Invention, and that this was done by May 1946." *Editor's note*

in Norway to join the project, bringing with him fresh ideas, enthusiasm, and an ability to work well with von Neumann. Not long after, the team produced the first computer-generated numerical forecast—for weather patterns at about five kilometers and twenty-four hours in advance. Though the computation took ENIAC about twenty-four hours to complete the calculations, this was a real breakthrough and fully justified the Weather Bureau, Air Force, and Navy's support.

John Mauchly, incidentally, one of the inventors of the ENIAC, was himself a meteorologist who dreamed of realizable numerical forecasting. It is also noteworthy that the method for making the first forecast incorporated ideas developed in the Extended Forecast Project by Rossby and his colleagues at MIT.

Following this first success, progress was rapid. In 1954 a joint Numerical Weather Prediction Unit (Weather Bureau, Air Force, and Navy) was established in Washington and obtained a new computer in 1955. George Cressman (later chief of the National Weather Service) was selected as head, and it numbered Joseph Smagorinsky and Phillip Thompson among its top scientists.

Reichelderfer spent a great deal of time and effort seeing to it that this unit got all it needed, including state-of-the-art computers and manpower. In later years the endeavor was to be repeated at many centers around the world. It led, furthermore, to a new, efficient form of research on topics ranging from the climatic effects of rising CO_2 to more objective forecasts covering several days. Meteorological research without high-speed computers is almost unthinkable today.

Satellites, Radiation Sensing, and International Meteorology

Later in Reichelderfer's tenure, the science of meteorology was greatly advanced by the use of satellite photos and radiation sensing. Seeing the potential of the rocket-sounding experiments at White Sands, which returned cloud pictures from aloft, Reichelderfer established a Satellite Meteorology Division outside Washington, D.C. He and Keith Glennan, a NASA administrator, ensured efficient collaboration between the two agencies, and the effort soon became international in scope.

Well before the Sputnik-and-satellite era, Reichelderfer was active in international affairs. He did much of the planning for the World Meteorological Organization (WMO) and in 1951 was elected its first president. He greatly helped worldwide observing and forecasting programs, including the early World Weather Watch pioneered and planned by Harry Wexler and the Russian meteorologist, Bugaev.

In addition to all these activities, Reichelderfer managed the multifaceted operations of the Weather Bureau, whose research had by that time expanded to include prediction of tornadoes, hurricanes, air pollution episodes, stratospheric behavior, advanced aircraft environment, and long range (a month to a season) general weather characteristics.

By 1963 Reichelderfer felt that it was time to step down and let a younger man take over. President Kennedy appointed Robert M. White, now president of the National Academy of Engineering, to succeed him. In his congratulatory letter to White, Reichelderfer wrote:

"It has been my great fortune to be in office during a period of rapid development in the technology of meteorology and its data-gathering facilities and in the capabilities and responsibilities of the Weather Bureau. It has been a period of unusually rewarding personal associations and noteworthy achievements. I do not know of a greater expression of best wishes to you in your new capacity than to desire for you all of the gratification, the rewarding associations, and the loyalties that [it has] been my privilege to enjoy during these many years past; and knowing the Weather

Bureau and its fine men and women as I do, I am confident you will receive no less in the years to come.

With Best Wishes for Every Success,
Cordially, Reich"

HONORS AND AWARDS

Reichelderfer received many honors and was a member or fellow of a number of scientific societies. He was elected to the National Academy in 1945 and was a member of the Philosophical Society. He received the International Meteorological Organization (IMO) Prize in 1964 and later received awards from Chile, Cuba, France, Japan, and Peru.

In 1919, he became a charter member of the American Meteorological Society and was later made a fellow and honorary member; he served as its president in 1941 and 1942. He received the Society's 1964 Cleveland Abbe Award for distinguished service and was given a Special Award in 1972. In the fall of 1982, shortly before his death, the American Meteorological Society voted to establish, in his honor, the Francis W. Reichelderfer Award.

Reichelderfer was also a member of the American Geophysical Union and was elected vice president from 1949 to 1953 and 1959 to 1960. He was president of the Meteorological Section of the American Geophysical Union from 1944 to 1947. Mention has already been made of his election as first president of the World Meteorological Organization, in which post he served from 1951 to 1955. He was a member of the Institute of Aeronautical Sciences and belonged to the Cosmos Club and the Federal Club.

IN CONCLUSION

Reichelderfer is survived by his son, Bruce Allen Reichelderfer, of Roanoke, Virginia. His wife, Beatrice, passed away in 1975. In the two decades following his retirement he kept abreast of meteorological developments both domestic and international and served as a consultant on many issues.

Perhaps the best summing up of his career was that delivered by President John F. Kennedy on the occasion of Reichelderfer's retirement:

"You have held the post of Chief of the Weather Bureau with great distinction under four presidents. . . . As Chief of the Weather Bureau, you presided over the evolution of meteorology and weather forecasting from an art to a science."

A GOOD DEAL OF THE MATERIAL for this memoir comes from personal letters sent to me from time to time by Francis Reichelderfer. These were largely in connection with a report on the history of American meteorology that I presented at a symposium in Philadelphia sponsored by the American Meteorological Society on the occasion of the U.S. bicentennial celebration (*Bulletin of the American Meteorological Society*, vol. 64, no. 7, July 1983). In addition, Patrick Hayes's two papers on Reichelderfer's career (*Weatherwise*, April and August, 1981) were very helpful. Obituaries and articles by George Cressman (*Bulletin of the American Meteorological Society*, 64[4]: April 1983, and 66[11]: November 1985) were also valuable sources.

SELECTED BIBLIOGRAPHY

1920?

Air mass analysis as practiced by the Bergen School. Unpublished mono-graph.

1921

Forecasting thunderstorms by means of static electricity. *Mon. Weather Rev.* 49(March):152–53.

1928

Aeronautics' challenge to weather science. *Pap. Intl. Civ. Aeronaut. Conf., Washington, D.C., 1928.*

1930

Airship meteorology. In: *Aeronautical meteorology*, ed. W. R. Gregg. New York: Ronald Press Company.

1929

Some aerological principles applying to airship design and opera-tion. *Aeronaut. Eng.* (July-Sept.):171–75.

1932

Norwegian methods of weather analysis. U.S. Bureau of Aeronautics, Navy Department. 45 pp.

1939

Recent progress in meteorological service for aviation. *Nat. Aeron-aut.* 17(9):44–45.

1940

The contribution of Wilkes to terrestrial magnetism, gravity, and meteorology. *Proc. Am. Philos. Soc.* 82:583–600.

1941

The how and why of weather knowledge. In: *Department of Agri-culture Yearbook, 1941*, pp. 129–53. Washington, D.C.: Govern-ment Printing Office.
The Weather Bureau—fifty years of progress. *Sci. Mon.* 53:482–85.

1943

Something is being done about the weather. *Dept. Comm.* 31:3–7.

Weather's role in the fight for freedom. U.S. Weather Bureau, Office of the Coordinator of Inter-American Affairs, Press Division, April.

1945

Meteorology and climatology. In: *The American yearbook, 1944*, pp. 764–66.

1946

Remarks on Weather Bureau policy, plans and program. *Bull. Am. Meteorol. Soc.* 27:169–71.

1947

The science of the atmosphere. In: *The scientists speak*, ed. Warren Weaver, pp. 19–23. New York: Boni & Gaer.

1950

The importance of meteorological observations from ocean station vessels. U.S. Weather Bureau. Mimeo.

1952

Physical basis of water supply for the United States. In: *U.S. Congress, House Committee on Interior and Insular Affairs, Physical and Economic Foundation of Natural Resources*, vol. 2, pp. 11–14.

1954

Meteorological services and bad weather flying. *Interavia* 9:220–23.

1957

Hurricanes, tornadoes, and other storms. *Ann. Am. Acad. Polit. Soc. Sci.* 309:23–35.

1959

United States National Hurricane Research Project. *Marine Obs. (London)* 19(186):188–91.

1960

On the role of the IUGG in advancement of geophysics. *Trans. Am. Geophys. Un.* 41(March):1–3.

1961

Meteorological satellite systems in weather research and services. *Aeros. Eng.* 20:22–23, 91–96.

WILLIAM JACOB ROBBINS

February 22, 1890–October 5, 1978

BY FREDERICK KAVANAGH
AND ANNETTE HERVEY[1]

D R. WILLIAM JACOB ROBBINS lived several lives: botanist, teacher, administrator, educator, valued advisor, and avid fisherman.[2] A scientist most of his life, he earned his living as a teacher for twenty-eight years and an administrator for nearly fifty. Yet Robbins kept his separate lives apart so successfully, few who knew him in one role knew of his accomplishments and problems in the others.

A robust man about five-feet-eight inches tall and weighing 175 pounds in his prime, Robbins rarely missed a day of work. During the years he was director of the Garden he lived in a large house in Bronxville and—until he was seventy-three—maintained garden and grounds himself. A man of prodigious energy, he often slept only a few hours a night and in 1949 compained "that he was no longer capable of working more than fourteen to sixteen hours a day without some diversion."[3]

Since Robbins worked discreetly behind the scenes, his

---

[1] A longer version of this essay appeared in the *Bulletin of the Torrey Botanical Club* 108(Jan.–March 1981):95–121.

[2] David R. Goddard, past president of the National Academy of Sciences, wrote: "It is my evaluation that Dr. Robbins played a larger part in the NRC and NAS than any other botanist in the last several decades," in letter to the editor of the *Biographical Memoirs* dated March 10, 1982.

[3] [Mrs. Henry] Steeger, "Our Director," *Garden* 2(September 1949).

influence was much greater than the public record indicates. His extensive correspondence shows he was often consulted on matters of American science and that his judgment of people was consistently sound. An old-fashioned man, he believed that position and power carried with them responsibilities and that people and organizations should live within their means. He believed in hard work, perseverance, and honesty—and that promises and confidences should be kept.

EDUCATION AND EARLY LIFE

Frederick Robbins, William's father, grew up on a farm near Northumberland, Pennsylvania, where Robbinses had lived since 1794. When his son William Jacob was born, Frederick was principal of the high school in North Platte, Nebraska. A year later he took a job as principal of a school in South Williamsport, and the family returned to Pennsylvania. For the next twenty-seven years Frederick Robbins served as high school principal, then Superintendent of Schools, in different Pennsylvania towns, keeping up all the while the skill he had developed in his youth as a cabinet maker.

William remembered his father as a quiet but forceful man whom he revered for his scholarship and rectitude. Another influential man in his life was his Uncle Clint, with whom he spent many summers on the farm as a boy.

Clara Jeanette (Federhof) Robbins, William's mother, was a highly intelligent and gregarious professional journalist. A lifelong Democrat, she remained active in politics all her life. Her son was devoted to her and took care of her and her affairs in her later years.

From 1906 to 1910, William attended Lehigh University in Bethlehem, Pennsylvania. While there he spent a summer on the river taking water samples to be tested for bacterial contamination and found it a marvelous way to make a living.

This experience, coupled with summers spent working on his grandmother's farm, got him interested in biology and impelled him to go on to Cornell University, where he expected to become a plant pathologist on the way to becoming a scientific farmer.

When he got to Cornell in 1911, however, he found that Professor H. H. Whetzel could not accept him in plant pathology for lack of space. Instead, Dr. Lewis Knudsen took him in plant physiology. It was at Cornell that he met both Dr. B. M. Duggar and Liberty Hyde Bailey—both had beneficial influences on his life. Robbins spent the summers of 1912, 1913, and 1914 as Duggar's assistant at the Marine Biological Laboratory in Woods Hole. They apparently got along beautifully, for Duggar was later instrumental in getting Robbins posts at the Alabama Experiment Station and the University of Missouri, and it was he and Bailey who later persuaded Robbins to accept the directorship of the New York Botanical Garden.

Robbins's own education was unusual for a botanist in that he studied—in addition to Greek, physics, and botany—zoology, Latin, and mathematics during his four years at Lehigh University. On the subject of education, he had decided ideas:

"I am, as you know, a plant physiologist," he wrote Harry Kelley in 1960. "My first course was given by a zoologist who gave me a textbook by Genung and a place in which to work. I had no lectures, no instruction and no fellow students. What I did, I did myself and little as it was I think it had much to do with making me a plant physiologist, at least of a sort.

"I never learned that I could think for myself until I was a junior in college. I was a good student and studied the assignments given to me. There was considerable satisfaction in the process, as my teachers were likeable and just and the answers were always in the book or, if not, the teacher had them.

"In my junior year, I was given by the professor of psychology (and education) a major theme to prepare which differed from the usual type since it required an answer to a question; the question, what is art? I discovered to my surprise, and somewhat to my horror, that there was no agreement in the books I read as to what art is. I was forced to make up my own mind, and in the process I learned that I could think, that I could consider a variety of different answers to a question and decide for myself what I believed to be correct. For the first time I was not looking for an answer which was given in the back of the book or in paragraph 6 on page 25 in footnote 5, Chapter 3, or in the pronouncement of one of my revered teachers. I was on my own, using the brains I had by a procedure which had been drilled into me by a long and thorough grounding in mathematics, namely—analyze and define the problem and then seek for its solution.

"I am inclined to believe that there are too many scholarships and fellowships and too few assistantships. I should like to see more use made of assistantships in the small institutions, as this in my opinion would encourage more boys and girls to follow a science career. This leads to my last point, and that is the importance of encouraging women to enter science. There are not enough opportunities and not enough encouragement and rewards for good women scientists.

"All of this is intended to emphasize the benefits to be derived from active participation. There are lectures and lecturers who perform a most useful function in arousing interest and stimulating an individual to pursue a subject. Such lecturers are not common. Nothing in my opinion takes the place of the 'do it yourself' approach."[4]

Christine Chapman Robbins and the Robbins Family

On July 15, 1915, shortly after receiving his Ph.D. from Cornell, Robbins married Christine Faye (Chapman) Robbins, who soon became the most important person in his life. Herself a trained botanist, Christine Robbins was also a gracious hostess and a scholarly scientific biographer. Robbins had complete confidence in her intelligent understanding, and their discussions contributed significantly to his success.

Born November 24, 1889, in Palmer, Massachusetts, Christine Chapman was the second daughter of Harvey

---

[4] W. J. Robbins, in a personal letter to Dr. Harry Kelley of the National Science Foundation, January 26, 1960.

Chapman (1860–1926) and Lydia Caroline Sharpe (1861–1913). John Chapman, the American primitive naturalist known as "Johnny Appleseed," was related to her father through a collateral line. She graduated from Wellesley College and, encouraged by Margaret C. Ferguson, head of Wellesley's Botany Department, entered a Ph.D. program in botany at Cornell. Upon obtaining her M.A. degree, she returned to Wellesley to teach for two years. Then, much to Dr. Ferguson's disappointment, Christine abandoned further education in botany to marry William Robbins.

William and Christine Robbins were true American intellectuals. Superb, careful, and critical workers, both were Phi Beta Kappa as undergraduates, and their common interests in plants, nature, and science continued to bind them—along with family matters, gardening, current affairs, fishing, cooking, and travel—for the rest of their lives. Mrs. Robbins was also an active member of the League of Women Voters for many years.

A member of the Colonial Dames of America, Mrs. Robbins could trace her American ancestry back to the 17th century, while the earliest known American of her husband's line was Daniel Robbins (1765–1864), of New Jersey. In her later years, Christine Robbins became a meticulous genealogical scholar. In addition to preparing comprehensive genealogies of the Robbins and Chapman lines, she wrote book-length biographies of David Hosack (C. Robbins, 1960) and John Torrey (C. Robbins, 1968). As a gift to each son, she and her husband drew up a comprehensive "family bible" that included charts, photographs, and biographies. Christine Robbins died of heart disease February 9, 1974, in New York City.

The oldest Robbins son, Frederick, entered the Army Medical Corps during World War II after two years at the University of Missouri Medical School. He completed his medical studies at Harvard, and—with John E. Enders—succeeded in growing poliomyelitis virus in tissue culture. In 1954, Enders, Robbins, and Thomas Weller received the Nobel Prize in Physiology or Medicine. Frederick became professor of pediatrics and later dean of Case Western Reserve University Medical School. In 1980 he went to Washington, D.C., to become president of the Institute of Medicine. He was elected to the National Academy of Sciences in 1972.

William Clinton Robbins graduated from Cornell Medical School and served in the Navy. He became an internist in private practice in New York City and clinical associate professor of medicine and associate attending physician at the New York Hospital-Cornell Medical Center.

Daniel Robbins attended Columbia University and also served in the Navy. After earning an M.S. in engineering he went on to become vice president of engineering for the Itek Corporation's Graphic Equipment Division in Rochester, New York.

THE INTERIM YEARS: 1916–1919

In February 1916 the Robbins family moved to Alabama, where William had accepted a post as professor and chairman of the Botany Department and plant physiologist for the Agricultural Experiment Station. Arriving in Auburn with very little money, they rented a house for $25 a month. The cash book Mrs. Robbins kept from February to August, when Frederick was born, makes interesting reading. But if the position at Auburn offered only a small increase in salary (it paid $2,000 a year), it offered the more important opportunity for Robbins to make his own, independent decisions.

A year later, however, Mrs. Robbins's father fell ill, and the couple moved to Springfield, Massachusetts, to be near him. From August 1917 to July 1918, Robbins managed Chapman & Brooks, the family's wholesale hardware business, discovering through a mathematical analysis of the business that a trusted employee had been stealing from the company.

The Springfield episode ended when Robbins, an ardent patriot, enlisted in the Army in 1918. A second lieutenant in the Sanitary Corps, he was sent to Yale to study bacteriology, but the war ended before he could be sent abroad.

THE UNIVERSITY OF MISSOURI (1919–1938)

After a stint of a few months in Washington, D.C., where Robbins was a soil biochemist with the U.S. Department of Agriculture, he accepted a post as professor and chairman of the Department of Botany at the University of Missouri. In September 1919 the family moved to Columbia, Missouri. With a beginning salary of $2,400 a year, Robbins was expected to teach all courses in botany and only after 1924 was able to shift the beginning courses to Dr. H. W. Rickett.

Rather unusually for his time, Dr. Robbins liked and respected women as scientists. He himself had many female graduate students and assistants and in 1936 persuaded Dr. Barbara McClintock to come to the University of Missouri. She stayed six years working on the genetics of corn, and he gave her fine work the same due he gave to that of his male colleagues.

When Robbins moved to the University in 1919, his administrative duties were limited to the usual hiring of staff and selection of students for graduate study. When he returned there from Europe in 1930, he added the responsibilities of dean of the Graduate School and—during Walter Williams' absence in 1933–1934—of acting president of the University.

In 1935, Franklin Roosevelt established the Works Progress Administration (WPA), which made funds available for new building and improvements. Robbins was immediately ready with the University of Missouri's construction plans, and, under his direction, the University was able to complete its library, several classroom buildings, a small research building on the shores of Lake Lefevre, and many badly needed improvements.

Yet Robbins managed to live strictly within his means. He did not spend money he did not have and deficits, under his management, did not occur. Imbued with the idea that authority meant acting in the best interests of the organization, he was also ready when necessary to give corrective interviews, change his subordinates' jobs, and let staff go. He tried not to let his personal opinions influence his judgment and withstood personal rebuffs with indifference. He did not compromise on certain matters of personal behavior, and some considered him "stuffy." Yet his sound fiscal policies gave stability to the institutions he managed, and if his efforts were not universally appreciated, he managed to instill unflagging loyalty in those who worked with him most closely— H. W. Rickett, E. E. Naylor, W. E. Maneval, and C. M. Tucker.

Highly intelligent, well educated and organized, Robbins enjoyed his work and worked hard. He always found time for reading—*The New York Times*, magazines, and books—if not for social activities. During the four months before moving to New York, he was able to finish a substantial part of his pioneering work on the growth of excised roots and the vitamin requirements of fungi.

THE NEW YORK BOTANICAL GARDEN (1938–1958)

Cleaning House

When they visited England's Kew Gardens in 1888, Dr. and Mrs. Nathaniel Lord Britton were so impressed they decided, on their return home, to establish a Botanical Garden in New York. The Garden, managed by the private, nonprofit corporation they began, is also a public institution supervised by the City Parks Department. The city owns the 250-acre public park complete with renowned rose and rock gardens and magnificent display houses; the corporation owns the contents.

As a scientific institution, the Garden in its early years was best known for its taxonomic work and some outstanding research in plant physiology. A leading mycological journal and several taxonomic publications were also edited there. Until 1930 Dr. Britton was the Garden's nominal director (though he invariably left New York during the winter months), but it had been operating under acting directors for years when Robbins arrived to take over on March 1, 1938.

Robbins quickly learned that his new job was more challenging and onerous than that at the University of Missouri. The senior staff consisted of Dr. Fred J. Seaver (mycology), Dr. Arlow B. Stout (compatibility in higher plants), Dr. B. O. Dodge (a plant pathologist who, in 1928, had done the ground-breaking work with *Neurospora* in microbial genetics), Dr. Henry Allan Gleason (head curator and chief taxonomist of the higher plants), and Dr. John Hendley Barnhart (the librarian, who obtained prized books for the Garden even if it meant buying them himself).

Dr. Britton had wanted the Garden to function as the Botanical Department of Columbia University, but this was not to be. As head of the Columbia department, Robert A. Harper also held a seat on the Board of Managers of the New York Botanical Garden, and when the two men were at loggerheads, relations between the institutions cooled. When Harper retired, Robbins was able to establish a program with Columbia and with Fordham University (whose campus adjoins the Garden) whereby graduate students could receive degrees for work at the Garden. The funds he obtained encouraged students, more of whom chose the taxonomy of the higher plants than any other botanical discipline.

Neglected administratively for many years, the institution's staff was depleted yet contained many in need of superannuation. It had no policy for retirement, few young people, and no long-term goals. Over the next several years, Dr. Robbins strove to change this condition of institutional anarchy.

Keeping the administrative structure he found in place, he used scientific production as his only yardstick, retaining many whom others would have fired on grounds of age or behavior. If someone was a bad administrator but otherwise useful, Robbins either did the administrative work himself or assigned it to others.

He dealt even-handedly with all facets of the Garden. He established a two-year training course for professional gardeners, who were badly needed to staff the private gardens in the area. He gave the study of South American flora (a long-term interest of taxonomists) a great boost by bringing in Bassett Maguire as its head. He promoted horticultural activity, through flower shows and prizewinning displays. As financial capabilities permitted, he increased and improved the Garden's plantings.

To alleviate the plight of the city employees who worked a seven-day week operating the power plant in the winter, he asked the Parks Department every year for more men, and, in 1945 he got them. City employees were becoming unionized at about that time. Although Dr. Robbins was opposed to unionization, he negotiated the Garden's first contract with its union employees. Because he could not tolerate dishonesty and expected employees at all levels to earn their pay, he was unpopular with some, but a member of the first union negotiating committee said that the committee trusted whatever Robbins said.

In addition to dealing with the Garden's staff, employees, and Board of Managers, Robbins immediately established friendly working relations with Columbia University, Com-

missioner of Parks Robert Moses, Mayor LaGuardia, the
president of the Borough of the Bronx, Fordham University,
the WPA, and the local horticultural societies. One of his first
acts was to revive the moribund Women's Advisory Council,
which he then used effectively to improve the Garden, even
persuading the Board of Managers to elect women to its
ranks.

During Robbins's tenure, the Garden had two presidents
of the Board of Managers—Joseph S. Swan and Charles B.
Harding, both ardent gardeners and both partners in the
investment banking firm, Smith, Barney, & Co. Dr. Robbins
and the two presidents became close personal friends, and
he kept them informed of his actions and anything that
might affect the welfare of the Garden. He often sought the
advice of Harding, in particular, whose business and social
contacts provided potential sources of funding for the Garden. Dr. Robbins's infectious enthusiasm for the New York
Botanical Garden untied many a private purse string, and
the team of Swan, Harding, and Robbins proved highly successful as fund raisers. They were equally effective in dealing
with Parks Department Commissioner Robert Moses, without
whose support and permission no substantial changes could
be made in the Garden's buildings and grounds.

With the money they raised and 180 WPA workers,
Robbins was able to reconstruct the fifteen display houses of
Range 1, so deteriorated from neglect they had to be replaced from the ground up. (This was recently done again
with private funds.) WPA workers also built propagating
houses and manure pits, a rock garden, a bridge, and roads
inside the Garden. They did extensive repairs on the Museum Building and cleaned the bronze statue in front of its
patina. He had WPA workers mount the million herbarium
specimens that had accumulated over the previous forty
years and was even able to get a fence built around the Gar-

den. He then began to raise money to support the scientific functions of the Garden staff and each year tried to get more money from the City for custodial and maintenance work.

As if this were not enough, Dr. Robbins also strove to raise money for the National Arboretum in Washington, D. C., on whose advisory council he served. Pointing out the Europeans' superior record regarding support for botanical gardens, he wrote:

". . . Kew, for example, which has an area about the same as the New York Botanical Garden and an annual attendance of approximately the same as ours, maintains forty-five uniformed policemen and 100 gardeners and assistants. This compares to our half-dozen elderly guards and thirty-six gardeners and assistants. A comparison with the National Arboretum would, of course, be [even more] striking."[5]

Harding Research Laboratory

When Robbins arrived at the Garden he found no laboratory for plant physiology. On the ground floor of the museum building where the carpentry shop had been he brought in water, gas, and electricity; purchased a sterilizer and water-distiller; installed a hood; and constructed a transfer room where dirt, dust, and spores were filtered from the air. He converted display cabinets into constant-temperature incubators for growing fungi and roots, and when he was finished, he had the first laboratory of its type in the United States.

By the fall of 1938, he had recruited Drs. Mary B. Schmitt and Frederick Kavanagh from Missouri and five WPA workers for the lab. He selected many high quality scientists for the Garden, including John Wurdack and Richard Cowan as graduate students in taxonomy, Bassett Maguire as the ex-

[5] William J. Robbins, "The Palms: An Appreciation," *Bull. Fairchild Trop. Gard.*, (1954):7–11, and "The Palms," *J. N.Y. Bot. Gard.* 4(1954):83–84.

pert on South American plants, P. P. Pirone to succeed B. O. Dodge as plant pathologist, Clark Rogerson as mycologist, T. H. Everett and Louis Politias as horticulturists, H. W. Rickett as bibliographer, Elizabeth Hall as librarian, and Marjorie Anchel as the lab's principal chemist. The six laboratories Robbins eventually had fitted out in the museum's east basement saw a good deal of first-class research in plant physiology, mycology, virology, and biochemistry related to plants.

Then in the early 1950s, Robbins obtained substantial private funds to construct a separate research laboratory. Finished on October 24, 1956, it was later named the Charles B. Harding Laboratory in commemoration of Harding's thirty years of devoted and effective service to the Garden, Robbins having refused to have it named after himself.

The official working day for the scientific staff was nine to five, but Dr. Robbins was usually in the laboratory before eight. Promptly at nine he went up to his office to meet with the five or six heads of operating departments. After the meeting, he addressed the same courteous attention to letters from Commissioner of Parks Moses as to those from children asking about plants. Few days passed without at least one visitor, and there was always something to be planned or something to be negotiated with the Parks Department.

Every day Robbins spent at least an hour in the lab and walked around the Garden, observing what was done and what needed doing. He discussed problems and progress with each staff member at least once a month. Fund raising often spilled over into the evenings, and he and Mrs. Robbins had a heavy official social schedule. The record shows he spent more time and effort on Garden affairs than on his own research, which, however, continued very productively.

As director of the New York Botanical Garden and Laboratory until his retirement in 1958, Robbins carefully selected its staff from the fields of mycology, tissue culture, plant physiology, and chemotaxonomy, as well as the more traditional botanic disciplines of bio-and organic chemistry. He obtained the long-term grants that insure the stability necessary for extended scientific work and created an atmosphere congenial to interdisciplinary research of a kind all too rare in academic settings.

After his retirement the Robbins spirit continued, even among Garden staff who had never worked with him. This continuity contributed greatly to the lab's scientific success. Today scientists all over the world recognize the contributions of the laboratory Robbins established and ran, and whose principal investigators were supported by the National Institutes of Health for forty-two years.[6]

FAIRCHILD TROPICAL GARDEN, FLORIDA

William J. Robbins was one of the first persons Col. Robert H. Montgomery consulted when planning the Fairchild Tropical Garden. Montgomery, inspired by David Fairchild's *Exploring for Plants*, dedicated the Fairchild Tropical Garden in March 1938 so that others might see and study the finest collection of tropical plants possible.[7]

Dr. Robbins served on the Fairchild Garden's Board of Trustees from 1948 to 1962 and as its president from 1962 to 1969. After Montgomery's death in 1953, his voice on the advisory committee became even more influential: "Dr. Robbins proved to be a mentor who could provide both inspiration and practical advice, for there was hardly any area

[6] NIH supported research in the Harding Laboratory for twenty years under Robbins's direction and twenty-two after his retirement. The New York Botanical Garden has now established different goals, however, and the research laboratory is being phased out.

[7] Lucita H. Wait, *The Fairchild Tropical Garden—The First Ten Years*, New York: Ronald Press, 1948.

in which he lacked experience, as a teacher, researcher, administrator. . . ."[8]

He was most influential in strengthening the Fairchild Garden's scientific research program. In 1959, for example, when Col. Montgomery's widow, Mrs. Alvin R. Jennings, began the Montgomery Foundation, Robbins suggested that it devote its resources to research in tropical botany and horticulture. On May 5–7, 1960, Dr. Robbins chaired the National Academy of Sciences' Conference on Tropical Botany at the Fairchild Garden, attended by thirty-five of the world's outstanding botanists and funded by the National Science Foundation.

In 1966, the NSF approved a grant of $153,000 to build and equip a major research facility at the Montgomery Foundation on property leased from the Fairchild Tropical Garden. Dedicated March 8, 1967, the tile-roofed William J. Robbins Plant Science Building houses a herbarium and reference library, plus facilities for investigations on the anatomy, physiology, and genetics of plants.

RESEARCH

"The research of Dr. W. J. Robbins covered a long period chronologically and was channeled in several distinct lines involving both the higher and the lower plants. He was the American pioneer in plant tissue culture and published a method of transferring root tips through several generations in 1922. This achievement undoubtedly stimulated research by others leading to successful continuous cultures. His later studies with tomato root tips showed that they synthesize both biotin and pyridoxin in the presence of thiamin. He was particularly interested in vitamin relationships to plants at this period and began to study these and other growth factors in relation to the lower plants such as *Euglena* and many fungi, particularly those of dermatological interest and the wood rotting basidiomycetes. He was able to demonstrate that ferulic acid and several fatty

---

[8] N. Smiley, "William J. Robbins: Indomitable Scientist," *Fairchild Trop. Gard. Bull.* 33(October, 1978):28–31.

acids were growth factors for a *Polyporus*. The scope of studies was broadened to involve also environmental factors of light and temperature. Many antibiotic substances were discovered not only from fungi but also from higher plants such as *Cassia*.

". . . One long continued interest, which he pursued vigorously during his long retirement, was in the phenomenon of topophysis exhibited by some plants or the striking dimorphism exhibited by some plants—both in the gymnosperms and angiosperms as they progress from the juvenile state to maturity, and [in] the capacity to form seeds. He showed that hormones could influence these changes when he caused mature English ivy to produce juvenile-type growths by repeated sprayings with gibberellin. He also used tissue culture methods to study this phenomenon. His evaluation of the importance of this phenomenon in horticulture [has been] justified, since reversions to juvenile growth are being used to start successful tissue cultures of certain woody plants.

"He maintained a parallel interest in the chemical and environmental factors involved in the reproductive cycles of fungi. Some notable discoveries regarding the life cycles of fungi were made in his laboratory and also by other staff at the Garden."[9]

Over the years his methodical attack enabled him to isolate the essential mineral or organic nutrients required for most fungi, except morels, filling in many gaps in the knowledge of the physiology of the lower plants.

Root Tips

Interested throughout his life in the growth and development of plants, Robbins's interest was piqued by Jacques Loeb's observation that a hormone produced by the leaf of Bryophyllum conditioned the development of roots in the leaf notches. In 1917 Robbins suggested that Loeb's hormone might be sugar because the root lacked chlorophyll and was unable to synthesize its own carbohydrates. To test this hypothesis he compared the growth of excised root tips from

[9] Vernon Stoutemeyer, personal communication, 1980.

corn, peas, and cotton—the seeds at hand—in a mineral salts solution with that of root tips in mineral salts and sugar.

He found that glucose, though essential to growth, was not the whole story. Successive subcultures from roots grown in the solution containing glucose soon stopped growing. Corn roots would grow through two subcultures but not in a third. Something besides sugar, therefore, was needed to permit continued growth of corn roots. When Robbins sent his findings to Loeb, he wrote back encouraging him to continue his research, but the work was interrupted in the summer of 1917 when Robbins moved to Massachusetts to run his ailing father-in-law's hardware company.

Coming to the University of Missouri in 1919, Robbins resumed his work on the cultivation of excised roots. He worked alone or with Dr. Willis E. Maneval, an excellent technician who taught bacteriology, mycology, and beginning plant pathology. (In 1928–1929, when P. R. White was in the department, it was Maneval who taught him sterile techniques.) Robbins published the 1917 work in the first of the 1922 papers. In the second 1922 article he published work done with yeast extract added to the medium. He made this additon knowing the extract to contain vitamine—which increased growth in animals, bacteria, and yeast[10]—and found that medium containing yeast extract was capable of supporting unlimited growth of tomato roots.

About 1921, Robbins sent the results of the 1917 work with peas, corn, and cotton—all important agricultural products in Alabama—to Professor Gottlieb F. J. Haberlandt, the eminent German plant physiologist. Reply to the letter came in 1922 in the form of a publication by one of Haberlandt's

[10] Only vitamine was known in 1917, the vitamin complex not yet having been dissected. The yeast extract Robbins used in his experiments contained thiamine, pantothenic acid, nicotinic acid, biotin, pyridoxine, and PABA. The most important ingredient for excised roots was thiamine, isolated in 1933.

students, Walter Kotte. Kotte had grown beans, corn, and cotton root tips with the same results as Robbins. The Robbins letter was not cited.

Robbins's root work seemed to reach a dead end in 1923, and he switched his attention to other subjects. Aside from one paper in 1924,[11] he did not deal with excised root tips again until 1934, following P. R. White's publications on the cultivation of tomato roots in a mineral solution containing yeast extract and sucrose.

At that time Robbins obtained a small amount of vitamin B_1 (thiamine), newly isolated in crystalline form, from R. R. Williams and showed that it would substitute for yeast extract in permitting unlimited growth of excised tomato roots. Thiamine had been established as an animal vitamin but not as one for plants. Robbins's experiments with tomato roots and fungi supported the idea that all life required thiamine. (James Bonner was also working in this field, and the two were in constant touch keeping each other apprised of progress.)

Robbins's last publication, with Mary Stebbins, on the growth of excised tomato roots, came out in 1949. The roots were in the 144th passage, the last 131 of which had been maintained in a solution limited to mineral salts, cane sugar, and thiamine or thiazole for more than twenty years.

pH

Though Robbins had relatively little time for research from 1926 to 1935—concentrating instead on teaching, administration, his European sojourn, and writing the textbook of botany he published with H. W. Rickett in 1929—he did address the problem of hydrogen ion (pH) concentration. In

---

[11] W. J. Robbins and W. E. Maneval, "Effects of light on growth of excised root tips under sterile conditions," *Bot. Gaz.* 78(1924):424–32.

the early 1920s, the importance of pH concentration to the toxicity of acidic and basic dyes, the action of acidic and basic drugs, the staining reaction of dyes, and the solubility of proteins was just beginning to be appreciated. Buying a Clark & Lubs hydrogen electrode apparatus for measuring the hydrogen ion concentration of solutions, Robbins measured isoelectric points of many plant tissues and showed its importance to absorption and toxicity. His last publication in this field was in 1935, on the effect of dyes in yeast fermentation as influenced by hydrogen ion concentration.

Fungi (1935–1945)

In the decade from 1935 to 1945, Robbins's lab was primarily given over to the study of the effect of B-vitamins upon the growth and fruiting of fungi and the germination of fungal spores. During World War II, Robbins began a screening program for antibiotics produced by *Basidiomycetes*, a fungal group not previously surveyed. The first group of these wood-destroying fungi (obtained from Ross Davidson and Frances Lombard, USDA) showed promise, and he attempted to obtain as many isolates of wood-destroying basidiomycetes as possible. Annette Hervey developed the techniques for screening the fungi and, after reporting on the first 500 cultures in 1947, continued with additional isolates that eventually totalled over 3000 cultures. In the first decade of effort, the researchers isolated more than a dozen new antibiotic substances and published forty-four papers.

Robbins's mycological and chemical studies—done collaboratively with Frederick Kavanagh, Marjorie Anchel, Alma Barksdale, Trevor McMorris, M. S. R. Nair, and Susan T. Carey and supported by NIH—showed fungi metabolites to be of interest far beyond their antibiotic activity. To date some fifty of the new compounds have been discovered with antibacterial, antifungal, antitumor, antileukemic, and cardiotonic activities. Many had novel structures, and Robbins's lab was the first to isolate from fungi members of such classes of compounds as monoterpenes, sesquiterpenes, and a monoterpene with the structure of an alkaloid. Robbins's lab was also first in isolating, determining the structures of, and synthesizing steroidal fungal sex hormones. The lab's nutritional studies identified active substances in natural preparations to improve the growth of certain fungi in a "complete" medium, and in 1947, supported by a grant from the National Foundation of Infantile Paralysis, it initiated a six-year program to screen actinomycetes for antiviral activity.

Shortly after *Euglena gracilis* var, *bacillaris* was shown to exhibit a quantitative growth response to crystalline antipernicious anemia factor (Vitamin B_{12}), Robbins started to search for its primary source in nature. He found major sources of Vitamin B_{12} in bacteria, actinomycetes, and blue-green algae—but not green algae and higher plants.

Intrigued by challenging and difficult problems, he spent time trying to cause *Morchella esculenta* to fruit. Encouraging his associates on this quest, he told them repeatedly how delicious morels were sautéed in butter. This was followed by the promise of a champagne party to celebrate success, but *Morchella*, unfortunately, refused to cooperate.

In 1963 at the Cosmos Club in Washington, Robbins had a casual conversation with Dr. Neal Weber (who had received an NRC Fellowship in 1934 when Robbins was chairman of its National Fellowship Board in the Biological Sciences) that led to a project to identify the fungi that leaf-cutting ants cultivated as food in underground "gardens." Thirty-six isolates collected by Weber were preserved at the Harding Laboratory, one of which fruited in culture and was identified by the Garden's Clark T. Rogerson as a species of *Lepiota*. From it, Robbins's lab isolated and elucidated the structures of two metabolites with antileukemic activity.

Robbins's laboratory technique was impeccable. Many experiments required chemically clean and bacteriologically sterile glassware, and he invariably used distilled or redistilled water. The importance of this was illustrated by the case of the bacteriologist who used deionized water—thinking it equivalent to distilled water—and failed to confirm Robbins and Hervey's 1944 report of *Pythiomorpha gonapodyides'* high manganese requirement.

The Rockefeller University

After Robbins retired from the New York Botanical Garden, he began a laboratory at the Rockefeller University, where he embarked on new research whose uncertainty would have daunted a younger researcher. But they were fun, and at his age, he decided, he had nothing to lose.

For many years Robbins had been fascinated by the sharp physiological and morphological differences separating the juvenile and adult stages of *Hedera helix*, and the fact that gibberellic acid applied to adult *Hedera* caused reversion to the juvenile form. With leisure to study *Hedera helix*, he tracked the growth rate of calluses in adult and juvenile plants, finding that callus from the latter always grew faster. Juvenile callus maintained its differences from adult callus through fifty-four passages extending over a period of about six years. He also studied the development of plants from leaf discs of variegated *Coleus* as related to patterns of leaf chlorosis.

In 1965, Robbins's essay on topophysis[12] won the American Philosophical Society's Lewis Prize and revived interest in the subject. Topophysis—important to nurserymen—is the phenomenon that occurs when the part used to propa-

[12] W. J. Robbins, "Topophysis, a problem in somatic inheritance," *Proc. Am. Philos. Soc.* 108(1964):395–403.

gate a plant determines the plant's morphology and physiology.

Robbins's most popular later publication was the note he and Annette Hervey wrote on the toxicity of distilled water stored in "inert" polyethylene bottles (1974). They had used excised roots of *Bryophyllum calycium* (sensitive to material leached from the plastic) as a test subject, making the span of Robbins's work with excised roots more than sixty years. Of the thirteen research papers published from his Rockefeller laboratory, ten were on some aspect of tissue culture of plant parts or topophysis and three were about growth factors for higher fungi.

"He succeeded—where so few do," said an admiring Maclyn McCarty in 1980, "in maintaining a lifelong commitment to laboratory research even after becoming a senior statesman of science."[13]

EDUCATOR AND TEACHER

Dr. Robbins was an outstanding teacher with a great fund of knowledge and lucid style. He taught undergraduates at Lehigh, Cornell, Auburn Polytechnic Institute, and Missouri and graduate students at Missouri and Columbia, keeping their interest by asking questions and interjecting stories, many of them humorous.

At Missouri he gave three five-hour courses in plant physiology. This meant three one-hour lectures each week and two two-hour laboratories. Sitting at his table in front of the room, he talked and smoked his pipe, covering the material in unhurried detail. Beginning with no textbook, he used his magnificent collection of reprints to keep his lectures current. Though material he taught bored him, students never detected that it did. As for the plant physiology laboratory,

[13] Maclyn McCarty, *Memorials of the Century Association*, New York, 1980, pp. 304–6.

he trusted the competence of his graduate assistants and rarely appeared.

He himself supervised relatively few graduate students. During the Depression years of 1930 to 1937, the number of graduate students was limited by University funds available to pay them. What with research funds limited to several hundred dollars a year and the military drain of World War II, few students were available. Robbins never sought to dominate those he did supervise, but rather kept in close touch with their work in the laboratory while allowing them to use their own judgment.

His own laboratories were relaxed places to work. Never in competition with anyone else, he felt free to devote the time required to do a complete job. He spent hours writing up observations so that when he went back to them later the information was there. His notes fill many bound laboratory notebooks.

Botany (New York: D. Van Nostrand Company, 1929–1939), the textbook Robbins wrote with Harold W. Rickett, sold very well and went through three editions in ten years. For the first edition, Robbins wrote on taxonomy, morphology, anatomy, and evolution; Rickett on physiology parts. The manuscript was then worked into a book by the authors and the teaching staff.

During his two years abroad from 1928 to 1930, Robbins visited botanists in every country of Europe except Greece, Spain, and Portugal, evaluating research projects proposed for Rockefeller Foundation grants and interviewing scientists—including one Polish couple, studying coprophilous fungi, with whom his only common language was Latin! Given his own rigorous standards, he was shocked by what he found:

"One of the most important things which a teacher or investigator must do is to familiarize himself with the literature in his special field and related fields. Some years ago I spent two years with the European office of the Rockefeller Foundation. I was astonished to find that many of the outstanding European biologists depended very largely on reprints sent them by their colleagues and very little on abstract journals or the journals themselves. In many instances, I found notable gaps in the acquaintance of outstanding men with publications in their field." [14]

As dean of the Graduate School at Missouri, Robbins supported graduate studies in all fields. Of the opinion that work done in education did not deserve a Ph.D., however, and that granting it would degrade the quality of that degree, he opposed a Ph.D. program in education. He was equally certain that the state legislature would not finance both a University and a four-year medical school adequately so that, if a medical school were established, the University would suffer. (The University had, at that time, an excellent two-year program in medicine whose graduates—including Robbins's son Frederick—went on to complete their studies at excellent four-year schools elsewhere.) Using a standard bureaucratic technique, he appointed a committee to study these matters. It was never able to reach a decision, and nothing was done until he left in 1938. [15]

From 1931 to 1937 Dr. Robbins served as chairman of the National Fellowship Board in the Biological Sciences, a National Research Council committee that granted NRC postdoctoral fellowships supported by Rockefeller Foundation grants. These were given in the fields of agriculture, anthropology, botany, forestry, psychology, and zoology. In the first fourteen years of its existence (1923–1937), the Board considered 1,414 new applicants, of whom 398 became NRC fellows and went on to be America's most productive biological scientists. At the end of his service as chairman, Robbins

[14] W. J. Robbins, letter to Dr. Carl G. Hartman, 1948.
[15] Shortly after Robbins left Missouri a Ph.D. program was established in education. The University obtained a four-year medical school after World War II.

made a detailed analysis of the sources of fellows' undergraduate training, finding that their undergraduate degrees
came from 158 colleges and universities in the U.S. and Canada. Many of these institutions had enrollments of 500 students or less; schools with enrollments of less than 3,000 accounted for about half the fellows; while some large schools
counted no fellows among their graduates.[16]

After World War II, certain influential people in the National Academy of Sciences wanted to give most federal funding for education to the East coast universities and the University of California at Berkeley. Knowing that many good
people were educated in schools without great reputations
throughout the country, Dr. Robbins opposed this. His proposal to allocate at least twenty-five percent of the funds to
lesser known schools was defeated, with serious consequences
for research in universities—as is now becoming evident.

Writing in 1935, he summarized his strong views regarding research as a crucial part of scientific training:

"I conceive research as an attempt to answer questions or to solve problems by a method which involves three steps: first, the definition, analysis
and comprehension of the problem; second, a search for the solutions or
answers; third, the testing of the solutions by reasoning, by experimentation if possible, and by checking the proposed solutions against the knowledge we now have.

"The highest type of research is that kind the results of which increase
the sum total of human knowledge, add new knowledge to that which we
have. In the minds of many this alone should be regarded as research. I
prefer, however, to consider as research every attempt to answer a question
or to solve a problem by the method indicated above, whether it reveals
knowledge as yet unknown to the world at large or whether it merely adds
to the knowledge an individual may have.

"It is my firm conviction that the chief business of education is the
development in the student of the power to solve problems. I am con-

---

[16] W. J. Robbins, "National research fellowships in the biological sciences," *Science*
86(1937):429–34.

vinced, also, that this power cannot be given by *ad hoc* or particulate training, by supplying the students with ready-made solutions, by training them in techniques or skills. Not only because we cannot foresee the problem an individual will meet, the questions which will be presented to him, but because there are too many problems in life for which to supply an individual with ready-made solutions and because new times bring new problems. For these new problems, solutions must be found and new solutions for the old problems devised."[17]

FISHERMAN: QUARTET CAMP, MAINE

Dr. Robbins became an expert fly-fisherman as a boy and continued the sport throughout his life. During the 1930s the Robbins family spent their summers in the Rocky Mountains, Michigan, and Canada, backpacking in to find good trout streams and lakes. On these outings Robbins had fresh fish for breakfast every morning, for Mrs. Robbins dearly loved to eat the fish he so enjoyed catching.

From his late sixties and over the next dozen years, Dr. Robbins cured his annual attack of "spring fever" with a fishing trip to Quartet Camp in Maine. In addition to the spectacular flora and fauna of the deep woods in early spring, the camp offered a unique group of distinguished older men addicted by the thrill of fishing for landlocked salmon just after ice-out in April. These included the president of MIT, Dr. Karl T. Compton; the pioneer aeronautical engineer, Dr. Jerome C. Hunsaker; the famed aviator, Lt. Gen. James Doolittle; Vice-Admiral Emory Land; the noted cardiologist, Dr. Paul Dudley White; and Senator Ralph Flanders of Vermont—most of whom Dr. Robbins survived.

For two weeks, six or eight fishermen and an equal number of guides, cooks, and boatmen gathered at the camp. Its remoteness on Grand Lake, with no road, no electricity, no

---

[17] W. J. Robbins, "The graduate school and research." *Gamma Alpha Rec.* 25(1935):79–84.

telephone, appealed to Robbins, who liked to hear loons call at night; sight deer, osprey, and eagles; and tell fish stories.[18]

LAST DAYS

Robbins smoked cigars, cigarettes, and a pipe during much of his adult life and in 1957 could not walk a block without having to stop three or four times because of pains in his chest. On January 1, 1958, after a heart specialist had diagnosed cardiac insufficiency, he resigned as director of the New York Botanical Garden, put his affairs in order, and prepared to die at any time. Then Mrs. Robbins suggested he stop smoking cigarettes, which he did, and his anginal pain cleared.[19] As his health improved and he realized death was not imminent, he took on many administrative assignments and established his own laboratory at the Rockefeller University.

The last few years of Robbins's life were made difficult by his wife's lingering illness and her death in 1974, as well as his own cataract operations and increasing deafness. When he could no longer hear conversations even with a hearing aid, he stopped going to meetings and conferences.

Dr. Robbins walked the quarter-mile between his apartment and the Rockefeller University every day, but in 1976 his legs began to give him problems and his physician told him to stop smoking entirely. He went home, put away his pipes, gave away his tobacco and cigars and—breaking a habit of sixty years' standing at the age of eighty-six—never smoked again. Still, the circulation in his legs did not improve. On October 1, 1978, he suffered a massive stroke. He died on October 5 at the New York Hospital, having worked

---

[18] Personal communication from J. Hunsaker, Jr., to Annette Hervey, February 22, 1979.

[19] W. J. Robbins in a taped interview with C. R. Long, *N.Y. Bot. Garden Oral Hist. Prog.*, July 20, 1973.

the day before in the laboratory as usual. All his bills were current. His ashes are buried beside his wife's in Montoursville, Pennsylvania.

HONORS AND DISTINCTIONS

In 1941 Dr. Robbins was elected to membership in the American Philosophical Society, the oldest and one of the most distinguished learned societies in America, started by Benjamin Franklin in 1743. He was its president from 1956 to 1959 and was executive officer in 1960 when the Society's million-dollar Benjamin Franklin Library was completed. David R. Goddard published a biographical memoir of Robbins in the Society's *Yearbook* in 1980.[20]

Elected to the National Academy of Sciences in 1940, he was its treasurer from 1948 until 1960. At the request of General MacArthur, he and five other Academy members formed a Scientific Advisory Commission to Japan in 1947 to evaluate Japanese scientific activities and suggest future directions. According to Dr. Robbins the Commission's real mission was to reestablish contact with Japanese scientists, which they did.

Robbins was also a member and director of the Boyce Thompson Institute for Plant Research, Inc., for twenty-nine years and a member of its Executive Committee for twenty-four years. In 1973, the Institute passed a resolution honoring him that stated:

". . . His consistently offered wise counsels . . . on matters both large and small and has been an inspiration to its managing director and scientists."

He was a trustee of the Rockefeller University from 1956 to 1965. Upon establishing his laboratory at the University, he

---

[20] David R. Goddard, *Yearb. Amer. Philos. Soc.*, 1980, pp. 100–1.

became Trustee Emeritus, avoiding thereby even the appearance of conflict of interest.

A life member of the Torrey Botanical Club, Robbins was elected president in 1943 and served on the nominating, program, grants, and endowment committees. His good advice helped the Club's treasurer to increase the return on the endowment funds from one to five percent and more, and he often advised the Council and the officers of the Club unofficially. He was a guest speaker on several occasions and published frequently in the *Bulletin*.

MAN AND SCIENTIST

Dr. Robbins believed in authority and respected the requests of those in positions of responsibility. Living this way himself, he expected others to. Though he did not always agree with the Board of Managers at the Garden, he lived under their control, even turning down requests from the U.S. State Department because of their objections. He was, however, a steadying influence on the Board. Once, when several women of the advisory council were offended by a supervisor's abusive language, he smoothed the situation over by creating a non-supervisory post for the man rather than firing him.

Many who criticized Robbins for a certain managerial and social rigidity did not realize that he was upholding standards of a managerial Board not always in agreement with those of the community. He also had no administrative assistant in the early days and could not do everything requested of him. Staff members trying to obtain funds for their own activities resented his apparent unresponsiveness, though they often benefited by becoming more self-reliant as fund-raisers. Robbins had a well-developed sense of humor and in his younger days played practical jokes and was a great tease.

Those who thought him stuffy never realized that his delightful humor could be so dry as to be dusty!

While at the University of Missouri it was Dr. Robbins's practice to go through Lefevre Hall upon his return from summer vacation shaking hands and talking with the permanent support staff, including the two Negro janitors. For a white man to shake hands publicly with a Negro in Columbia, Missouri, in 1932 was very unusual, but Robbins treated everyone with the same courtesy.

Despite his stringent standards for himself, he had an extraordinary tolerance for error and incompetence in the people who worked for him. He rarely lost his temper, and when he did the outburst was brief. He respected opinions even when they differed radically from his own—a kind of forbearance that is considered a handicap in an administrator today.

To Robbins, the most exciting thing in life was to identify a problem in nature and attempt to solve it. He was happiest when he was in the laboratory, yet he spent most of his time in administration, leaving little time to do what he liked best. After refusing many full-time administrative positions (including the presidencies of several large universities) he took the job at the New York Botanical Garden in the expectation of having more time in the laboratory. In reality, he had no more time for research there than he had had at Missouri.

Yet he enjoyed position and power and often accepted calls upon his time he could have avoided. He valued his own satisfaction and the private opinions of his peers more than public acclaim and was therefore unwilling to have the Garden's research laboratory named after himself. He guarded his good scientific name jealously, reacting vigorously to any fancied or real attempts to obtain unauthorized benefit from association with him. Working ever to the exacting standards of the inner man, he delayed publishing his pioneering work on growth of excised plant roots for six years.

His high principles caused him on at least one occasion to refuse a large increase in salary offered to him by the Board of Managers of the Garden. Although he and his family certainly could have used the money, he felt that an increase for him alone would cause too great a disparity between his salary and that of others at the Garden.

He was one of those rare persons who can project to the future, be it nine months or nine years, and see the consequences of an action taken or avoided today. Spending much of his life with people for whom the future meant next week, he yet obtained their support for his programs by giving thoughtful answers to their questions. He never rushed into projects without first considering their effect upon both the people and the institution.

Finding research important to the welfare of man fun, he preferred to spend his Sunday mornings working in his yard or in his laboratory rather than in church. He professed not to understand preachers, whose sermons made no sense, yet had little patience with those who questioned the value of laboratory work because less than one percent of it was of value. "It may be one-tenth of one percent," Robbins wrote, "But the one-tenth . . . is what has brought us from the darkness and barrenness of the scholasticism of the middle ages."[21] Alone of all the presidential portraits at the American Philosophical Society, Robbins's shows him in a laboratory coat.

Dr. Robbins was a true conservative in the best sense of the word—in matters personal, financial, administrative, political, and scientific:

"Science is democratic, not autocratic, for in science no man's word is taken as law," he wrote with some urgency in the dark years preceding World War II. "Any discovery he makes, any statement given as truth, must be

---

[21] Geoffrey T. Hellman, "A square deal among the fungi," *New Yorker* (July 19, 1947).

susceptible of confirmation by others. As Sir Thomas Brown says, 'The mortallest enemy unto knowledge and that which hath done the greatest execution unto truth has been a preemptory adhesion unto Authority.'

"Liberty, equality, and fraternity are as necessary attributes of science as they are those of the political philosophy of republican France. Life, liberty, and the pursuit of happiness are conditioned as much by the progress of science as they are by the continuance of our democratic form of government.

"So I would say to the politicians and to the statesman—cherish science, it yields large profits and exemplifies the principles you profess. To the layman—embrace science, it offers you freedom, equality, and fraternity. To the scientists—guard science, lest those who do not understand cripple it with strictures which mutilate its body and destroy its soul."[22]

DOCUMENTS PERTAINING to Robbins's years at the Rockefeller University and the New York Botanical Garden are in the latter's archives along with a twenty-nine-page transcript of his contribution to the Columbia University oral history program. Those from his years at the University of Missouri are in the American Philosophical Society and National Academy of Sciences archives. We were unable to locate reports made to the Rockefeller Foundation for 1928 to 1930. The authors obtained other materials from Dr. Robbins during our long association with him (forty-six and thirty-six years, respectively) as teacher, employer, and friend. In addition his son, William C. Robbins, M.D., supplied biographical information about his father, mother, and grandfather. J. Hunsaker, Jr., furnished the information about the fishing at the Quartet Camp. James Bonner and Vernon Stoutemeyer made evaluations of Dr. Robbins as a botanist and as a friend. Marjorie Anchel provided information about the chemical programs and gave the manuscript a critical reading. Harold Rickett and Carol Woodward read a version of the manuscript and made editorial and factual corrections. We thank these and the others who contributed to this publication. Bernice Winkler, Dr. Robbins's secretary who stayed on at the Harding Research Laboratory after his retirement, deserves special thanks for the assistance she provided.

[22] W. J. Robbins, "Science and Scientists," *Proc. Missouri Acad. Sci.* 3(1937):43–49.

SERVICE TO THE NATIONAL ACADEMY OF SCIENCES AND THE NATIONAL RESEARCH COUNCIL[23]

1976	Member Emeritus of the National Academy of Sciences
1962–1965	Chairman, Advisory Committee on Research to National Park Service
May 1960	Organizer, Conference on Tropical Botany.
1948–1960	NAS Treasurer
1949–1960	Committee on Chemicals
1941–1960	Executive Board of the NRC (Committee on Policies, 1941–1946; Committee on Exhibits, 1945–1947; Acting Chairman, Committee on Insect Control, 1945–1946)
1953	Committee on Publications of the Academy
1948–1951	Atomic Energy Commission Postdoctoral Fellowship Board in the Biological and Agricultural Sciences
1948–1955	Advisory Board on Quartermaster Research and Development
1946–1948	Committee on Quartermaster Problems
1946–1949	Chairman, Subcommittee on Germicides, Insecticides, and Biologicals
1945–1949	Panel on Botany (Chairman, 1946–1948)
June 1947	NAS Scientific Advisory Mission to Japan
1944–1947	Chairman, NAS Botany Section
1940–1945	NAS Committee on National Science Fund, (Chairman, Board of Directors, 1941–1945)
1941	NAS Finance Committee
1940	Member, National Academy of Sciences
1931–1937	Chairman, NRC Fellowship Board in the Biological Sciences

[23] We are indebted to Janice Goldblum of the National Academy Archives for this list, which she included in a letter to David R. Goddard on February 15, 1979. We have omitted references to Dr. Robbins's service on temporary, Council, and award committees. *Editor*

SELECTED BIBLIOGRAPHY[24]

1922

Cultivation of excised root tips and stem tips under sterile conditions. *Bot. Gaz. Chicago* 73:376–90.

Effect of autolyzed yeast and peptone on growth of excised corn root tips in the dark. *Bot. Gaz. Chicago* 74:59–79.

1926

The isoelectric point for plant tissue and its importance in absorption and toxicity. *Univ. Mo. Stud.* 1:1–60.

1935

The graduate school and research. *Gamma Alpha Record* 26:79–84.

1936

With E. Kobs. Hydrogen-ion concentrations and the toxicity of basic and acid dyes to fungi. *Am. J. Bot.* 23:133–39.

1937

With M. A. Bartley. Vitamin B_1 and the growth of excised tomato roots. *Science* 85:246–47.

With F. Kavanagh. Intermediates of vitamin B_1 and growth of *Phycomyces*. *Proc. Natl. Acad. Sci. USA* 23:499–502.

Science and scientists. *Proc. Mo. Acad. Sci.* 3:43–49.

National Research fellowships in the biological sciences. *Science* 86:429–34.

---

[24] A more complete bibliography appears in the *Bull. Torrey Bot. Club* 108(Jan.-March 1981):116–121. Regarding Robbins's published works, Frederick Kavanagh writes: "In a scientific career spanning sixty-two years, Dr. Robbins published at least one scientific article in fifty-six [of them]. He did non-scientific work in seven years. He published in at least seven areas of botany. I have titles of 206 scientific publications. He had twenty-four co-authors. He wrote at least forty popular articles. . . . [His] longest period of collaboration was [with] Annette Hervey, who [worked with him] on thirty-three [joint] publications. She was much more than a collaborator. To do justice to her would take many pages. I [myself] had . . . twenty-three publications with Dr. R," personal communication to the *Biographical Memoirs*, September 24, 1990.

1938

With M. B. Schmidt. Growth of excised roots of the tomato. *Bot. Gaz. Chicago* 99:671–728.

1939

With H. W. Rickett. *Botany*. 3rd ed. New York: D. Van Nostrand Company.
Growth substances and gametic reproduction by *Phycomyces*. *Bot. Gaz. Chicago* 101:428–49.

1942

With V. Kavanagh. Vitamin deficiencies of the filamentous fungi. *Bot. Rev.* 8:411–71.
With V. Kavanagh and F. Kavanagh. Growth substances and dormancy of spores of *Phycomyces*. *Bot. Gaz. Chicago* 104:224–42.

1944

With F. Kavanagh. Temperature, thiamine and growth of *Phycomyces*. *Bull. Torrey Bot. Club* 71:1–10.
With A. Hervey. Response of *Pythiomorpha gonapodyides* to manganese. *Bull. Torrey Bot. Club* 71:258–66.

1945

With M. B. Schmidt. Effect of cotton on the germination of *Phycomyces* spores. *Bull. Torrey Bot. Club* 72:76–85.

1948

With F. Kavanagh and A. Hervey. Synergism between some antibacterial substances. *Bull. Torrey Bot. Club* 75:502–11.

1949

Some factors limiting growth. *Growth Symp.* 9:177–86.

1957

The influence of Jacques Loeb on the development of plant tissue culture. *Bull. Jard. Bot. Bruxelles* (Jubilee vol.) 27:189–97.
Gibberellic acid and the reversal of adult *Hedera* to a juvenile state. *Am. J. Bot.* 44:743–46.

1958

The plains and the prairies. In: *A prairie reserve. Univ. Mo. Bull.* (Handb. 5) 60:9–17.

1960

Further observations on juvenile and adult *Hedera. Am. J. Bot.* 47:485–91.

1962

Bernard Ogilvie Dodge, 1872–1960. In: *Biographical Memoirs*, vol. 36, pp. 85–124. New York: Columbia University Press for the National Academy of Sciences.

1964

Topophysis, a problem in somatic inheritance. *Proc. Am. Philos. Soc.* 108:395–403.

1974

With A. Hervey. Toxicity of water stored in polyethylene bottles. *Bull. Torrey Bot. Club* 101:287–91.

1978

With A. Hervey. Development of plants from leaf discs of variegated *Coleus* and its relation to patterns of leaf chlorosis. *In Vitro* 14:294–300.

With A. Hervey. Auxin, cytokinin, and growth of excised roots of *Bryophyllum calycinum. Am. J. Bot.* 65:1132–34.

G. G. Simpson

GEORGE GAYLORD SIMPSON

June 16, 1902–October 6, 1984

BY EVERETT C. OLSON[1]

G EORGE GAYLORD SIMPSON's passing in 1984 brought
an era in vertebrate paleontology to an end. Along with
Edward Drinker Cope, Henry Fairfield Osborn, and Alfred
Sherwood Romer, Simpson ranks among the great paleontologists of our time. The intellects of several generations of
students were shaped by either following or rejecting his elegant analyses and interpretations of evolution and the history
of life.

Although the "Simpson Era" had its roots in the 1920s
and 1930s, it seemed to emerge fully formed and without
precedent with the publication of *Tempo and Mode in Evolution*
(delayed until 1944 by World War II), following belatedly on
the heels of *Quantitative Zoology* (1939), which Simpson had
written with Anne Roe. Both books left researchers in a variety of fields pondering and often revising, conceptual bases

[1] Although I had earlier written a memorial to George Gaylord Simpson for the
Geological Society of America, I agreed to prepare a more intimate and more personal essay for the National Academy of Sciences *Biographical Memoirs*. The more
objective accounts of his life include the essay mentioned above (*Memorial Series*,
Geological Society of America, 1985) and the essay by Bobb Schaeffer and Malcolm
McKenna (*News Bulletin*, Society of Vertebrate Paleontology, no. 1933, 1985). Simpson's autobiography, *Concession to the Improbable* (New Haven: Yale University Press,
1978) and his book, *This View of Life: The world of an evolutionist* (New York: Harcourt,
Brace and Company, 1964) provide a more comprehensive view of his life and
thoughts.

of evolutionary analysis. The consistent empiricism of *Tempo and Mode* proved so pervasive that terms such as "tempo" and "mode"—and derivatives "pattern" and "process"—continue today to be key words in evolutionary treatises throughout molecular, organismic, and ecological biology.

After the war, the "Synthetic Theory of Evolution" espoused by Simpson created an excitement throughout paleobiology that waned somewhat in the mid-1950s, only to resurface in the 1960s and persist to the present. The debate among paleobiologists has often approached an intensity reminiscent of that following Darwin's publication of *The Origin of the Species* in 1859, including even a new breed of so-called "scientific" creationists.

AS I KNEW HIM

When I first met George Simpson at the American Museum of Natural History in 1935, he was thirty-three years old and already well established as a scholar and scientist, due in no small part to his two monumental works on Mesozoic mammals of the United States (his Ph.D. thesis at Yale) and of Europe, based on the natural history collections of the British Museum. Between 1925 and 1935 he had published some sixty scientific papers, some quite extensive, and all important.

Even then he was to many of us an enigmatic character whom, rumor had it, Walter Granger and Henry Osborn kept sequestered behind closed doors so that the workings of his genius would not be interrupted by trivia. George, who began as an assistant curator of vertebrate paleontology at the American Museum, did not see it that way at all, for though his was a crucial and demanding task, it was not particularly high on the scientific scale. But if truth in this case proved more prosaic than fancy, fancy more often than not won out.

In those early years, I—who was very young, along with

many others who were not—found myself awed and tongue-tied in his presence. This reticence in turn affected George, who, misunderstanding it, acted withdrawn and taciturn, confirming our expectations. I felt he deemed us not quite up to his advanced level of reason and knowledge—a fact that was certainly true but was not, I believe, a correct assessment of his reactions. Looking back this now seems very mixed, but it certainly seemed real at the time and continued to affect George's relations with others for years to come.

A remedy of sorts—the very dry martini—gradually made its effects felt. This beverage was then the favorite of the vertebrate people, and sufficient martinis did much to dispel our mutual shyness. Martinis and serious scientific discussion did not blend well, but this probably did not matter to George, who felt at all times that informal discourse was not profitable for discussing ideas of any import.

When I met George in 1935 he was just thirty-three, yet he had already formulated the roots of *Tempo and Mode*, his ideas of biogeography, and his views on life and evolution.[2] Today the early to mid-thirties are the normal time of life for attainment of the Ph.D. in geology and biology, and some years as a "post-doc" often follow. With much more to learn and the funds available to support it, graduate study now moves at a leisurely pace in sharp contrast to the poverty-stricken years of the 1930s and the hurry-to-finish psychology of the prewar and war years. But even then real eminence at so young an age was rare in the natural sciences. In 1935, with the ink of my own Ph.D. still wet, George's early prominence did not puzzle me. Later it did, and by talking with George and reading what he had written, I came to realize how the complex of phenomena of his life had created the man I met then and would come to know well thereafter.

---

[2] These concepts are presented and discussed in *This View of Life*, cited in note 1 above, and in *The Meaning of Evolution* (New Haven: Yale University Press, 1949).

A BIT OF FAMILY HISTORY

It seems to have gone something like this. Until he went to college at the age of sixteen, George spent most of his years with his family in Denver, Colorado. An exceptionally bright youngster but frail and small, he learned to accept being the "eccentric," the "smart kid," and became the unwilling but docile recipient of taunts and jibes from the "tough guys" of the street. His family supported him fully, and their careful handling of his persistent ailments, which were to plague him throughout his life, engendered a love for his father and mother that lasted the full span of their lives.

Strongly Presbyterian, the family attended church three times on Sunday and once mid-week. George became a Church member and was later, with some difficulty, "deconverted." The dogma of formal religion, he explained to me, did not hold up under his questioning, which led in time to personal and social problems. Yet in a contrary way, the same dogma had much to do with developing his ideas regarding the nature of truth and reality—the scientific philosophy that would permeate his scientific work. As he wrote in his autobiography, his discovery of the "rather silly distinction between dogma and reality" was a starting point for intellectual growth.

His school years, interrupted by periods of bad health and intermittent hard times, went by rapidly. The obligatory piano lessons failed, but those on the flute "took." A puckishness and sense of whimsy carried him through the hard times then and throughout his life, bubbling up in his writings when things were good.[3]

---

[3] This sense of humor came through in many charming ways in his *Letters* (Berkeley: University of California, 1987) and shows up in the offhand comments, vignettes of how he saw himself, and verses which are interspersed throughout his fascinating autobiography. They surfaced now and again as well in his scientific work, as, for

After some time at the University of Colorado (1918–1922), George grasped at an opportunity to attend Yale University. There he studied with Professor Richard Swann Lull, gaining his Ph.D. with the strong support of a superb geology faculty, including such professors as Charles Schuchert and Carl O. Dunbar.

In 1923, while his graduate work was in progress, he married Lydia Pedroja, and from this marriage issued four daughters (Helen, Patricia Gaylord ["Gay," deceased], Joan, and Elizabeth). George loved each dearly, but the marriage ran amuck. During his time of study on the Mesozoic mammals of Europe (1926–1927), Lydia refused even to come to London for a visit. The maintenance of separate residences in southern Europe and London stretched their modest resources, and George worked in London essentially at a poverty level. The whole affair was devastating to him and ended in formal separation in 1930 and divorce in 1938.

The British work completed in 1927, George returned to the United States. As so often seems to have happened to him, frictions (inadvertent or otherwise) had developed at Yale, and he went instead to the American Museum of Natural History. He remained at the Museum, with his star steadily rising, until 1959. It was then to Harvard and the Museum of Comparative Zoology, where, as Alexander Agassiz Professor, he worked with an outstanding group that included Bryan Patterson, Ernst Mayr, and Alfred S. Romer. After this productive but not always happy time (1959–1967) fraught with misunderstandings, he moved to the University of Arizona in Tucson, where he remained contentedly for the rest of his career.

In 1938 George married Anne Roe, whom he had known

example, in the comedic cartoons he used to illustrate some of his biogeographic essays and in the incomparable, *Attending Marvels: A Patagonian Journal* (New York: MacMillan, 1934).

from childhood. She was a noted psychologist and had a great and good influence on him. They proceeded together through the mazes of academia, lived tranquil summers in their New Mexican summer place, made many contributions to their own fields and—working together—jointly to the fields of biometrics, evolution, and behavior. This gentle little coda to the autobiographical notes George deposited with the National Academy of Sciences in 1975 expresses something of their perfect harmony:

"Now, at 4:30 P.M. on Sunday, this tenth day of August, 1975, I leave my study to go play duets with Anne for half an hour, drink some martinis, discuss plans for a trip to Indonesia, and read a murder mystery before going to bed."[4]

This short passage, which shows so well their quiet love and mutuality, also reveals the George Simpson others too rarely saw.

THE EXPLORATORY SCIENTIST

By this time, in the 1970s, Simpson had been showered with honors, medals, honorary degrees from prestigious universities around the world, and membership in many professional organizations at home and abroad. Among these was the signal honor of election to the National Academy of Sciences in 1941. Though quiet about these honors, I know he was immensely proud of them, for they attested to the general acceptance of his work.

There were—and still are—those who disagree with one or another of his methods or conclusions, or even disparage the results of his work and the "bandwagon" effect engendered by his early successes. From time to time George answered his critics in writing, both published and in letters.

[4] This unpublished autobiographical sketch is now in the archives of the National Academy of Sciences in Washington, D.C., and is available upon request.

Because he was hurt by certain criticisms, feeling a gulf of misunderstanding and animosity, his responses were direct and his comments far from gentle.

George's scientific work formed a pyramid, each field he investigated providing a base for advances toward new horizons. Several short reports and two monographs on Mesozoic mammals, one based on his studies at Yale (1928) and one on those at the British Museum (1929), culminated the first phase of his work. While setting the stage for continuing investigations of primitive mammals, it also led to the evolutionary studies that would occupy the next fifteen years of his life.

The Biogeography of the Americas

Beginning in the late 1920s, Simpson extended his interest in primitive mammals to include early Cenozoic mammals of the western United States and South America. The Crazy Mountain Basin of Montana and the San Juan Basin of New Mexico—with their broad exposures of early Tertiary, mammal-bearing beds—were rich targets for his North American work. Though the collections of the U.S. National Museum (now the National Museum of Natural History) provided a wealth of fossils for study, paleontological tradition demanded that the real heart of the work be in the field.

In the basin regions of Montana and New Mexico, Simpson followed his predecessors—walking endlessly over the dry badlands with their stacked layers of rock, "prospecting" for fossils, collecting specimens, and studying the sediments and depositional patterns of the formations. They all sought to understand the life of those remote times—how the preserving beds had been deposited and the environments in which the ancient plants and animals had lived. These studies continued through much of Simpson's life, and the results are preserved in long series of reports, ranging from short papers and essays to book-length descriptions of the life of the early Tertiary in the northern hemisphere.

The San Juan Basin charmed George from the time he first visited it in the 1920s. Beginning in 1947 George and Anne spent their summers and one winter in their cabin-home, Los Piñavetes, near Cuba, New Mexico. Only years later, when neither George's nor Anne's health permitted such isolation, did they give up this way of life they both loved. It was at Los Piñavetes that George wrote his contemplative works about the nature of evolution and the meaning of life.

When Simpson started his scientific career, it had long been known that the mammals of South America evolved in "splendid isolation" during the first two thirds of the Cenozoic era. The carnivores were predominantly marsupials; the herbivores were placentals—including some that had remarkable counterparts of northern-hemisphere mammals; and others that were strangely different, such as the great sloths and armadillos, grouped as edentates. Intrigued by the similarities and differences of the evolutionary pathways of mammals of the north and south during this long time of isolation, Simpson undertook field and museum studies in South America parallel to those he had done on the early Tertiary of western North America.

To carry this work out during the financially lean years of the early 1930s he organized and supervised the Scarritt Expeditions, generously supported by Horace Scarritt. From 1930 to 1931 and 1933 to 1934, Simpson and a young colleague, Coleman Williams (with the aid of many Argentinians) spent long hours in museums and collecting in the Patagonian region of Argentina.

There were many problems to be solved. Two overly-enthusiastic Argentinian patriots, Carlos and Florentine Amgeghino, had claimed that material they had found (and mistakenly dated as more ancient than it was) proved that the ancient beds of South America contained the sources for all mammalian evolution. The evolutionary parallelisms and divergences among mammals evolving separately in South America, North America, and Europe cried out for critical analysis. The biogeographic problems were baffling. The question remained as to why the mixing of the northern and southern faunas began only in the Miocene, first as a trickle and then in successive waves. Then, too, the rodent and primate groups annoyingly did not fit usual concepts of biogeographic arrangement.

Any parallel study of North and South American faunas had to deal with problems of adaptive evolution and differential rates of change in separate regions. It had to address the "mundane" task of taxonomic assignments and more difficult decisions concerning phylogenetic relationships within and between the faunas of the two continents. To this was added the major question of the Americas' biogeographic and continental relationships during the Cenozoic. George attacked these problems with seemingly boundless energy, soon making the leap from the particular to the general to lay the foundation for his most significant theoretical contributions.

The early Tertiary's animal, plant, and land distributions proved particularly puzzling to paleontologists of the early 20th century, who were secure in the "knowledge" that continents were, and always had been, fixed in their positions. The few maverick proponents of continental drift—followers of Alfred Wegener—were generally dismissed as dreamers, and Simpson cast his own biogeographic explanations within a framework of continental fixity. In the 1960s and 1970s, tangible evidence of continental movement was found to support the theory of plate tectonics. This created a revolution in geology and paleontology, and many new, and more meaningful, interpretations emerged.

Yet, within the concept of continental immobility, many

of Simpson's proposals have proved continuously fruitful—such as "island hopping," "rafting," and that Antarctica was a land corridor from South America to Australia. Island biogeography, which has played a seminal role in ecological and evolutionary biology, owes much to his stimulus. When the fixed-continent theory was finally broken, Simpson neither jumped hastily on the bandwagon nor adamantly held to the older view. Studying the emerging evidence, he was able to reject what was inappropriate in his earlier theories and accommodate new information in his explanations.

Theories of Evolution

Simpson's great curiosity about what the fossil record revealed of the ways and means of evolution and his interest in evolutionary ideas formed a backdrop to all his studies. He became a student not only of evolution but of the history of the development of evolutionary ideas as epitomized in his essays on such luminaries as Lamarck, Darwin, and Butler (1941) and his books probing the significance of evolution to humankind: *The Meaning of Evolution* (1949), and *This View of Life* (1964).

When he began his studies, evolution had by no means fully emerged from the anti-Darwinian determinism of the early 1900s or the "Neo-Lamarckism" that espoused the "inheritance of acquired characters." Yet Columbia University's outstanding school of genetics—and, in particular, Theodosius Dobzhansky—had a lasting influence on Simpson, who also greatly admired the studies of J. B. S. Haldane, Ronald Fisher, and Sewall Wright.

Columbia University maintained close ties with the American Museum, and in 1945 Simpson became a professor there. Unlike most of his paleontological colleagues, he recognized the importance of genetics in evolutionary studies. As he had with statistics, probability, and numerous languages, he set out to master the field. Rumor has it that, abetted by his colleagues at the American Museum, he shut himself up for a year and "learned" genetics—though, as a Texas rancher said to me after I had told him a yarn, "It's a good listening story."

Whatever the truth may be, the results of his studies showed in his *Tempo and Mode,* which, among other things, proved to the satisfaction of many that the data of paleontology and the emerging data from genetics were compatible. Recognizing the strong empirical evidence of the congruency, Simpson took the next crucial step of examining the fossil record for solutions to problems of evolution. He saw there rates of change so slow as to be almost nonexistent and so rapid they produced the appearance of major "gaps" in lineages.

To explain extremely rapid evolutionary change he developed the idea of "Quantum Evolution," combining Wright's theories of genetic drift and passage across "nonadaptive zones" with the general tenets of phyletic evolution. Yet this theory proved not fully satisfactory, and he softened his position in *The Major Features of Evolution* (1953), in which he discussed such problems as the long-term trends in evolution, systematics and classification, equilibrium and disequilibrium, and extinctions.

As an alternative to gradualism, a part of many of Simpson's concepts, Eldridge and Gould suggested their hypothesis of "punctuated equilibria."[5] The ensuing controversy produced various hypotheses regarding selection in populations of organisms, with punctuated equilibria, in particular, developing far beyond its initial formulation. In this way Simpson's provocative work stimulated intense study of the

---

[5] Niles Eldridge and Stephen Jay Gould, "Punctuated Equilibria: An Alternative to Phyletic Gradualism," in *Models in Paleobiology,* J. M. Thomas, ed. (San Francisco: Schopf, Freeman and Company, 1972).

fossil and living biological record, even down to the molecular and genetic levels, for evidence of ontogenetic events. It is this sort of stimulation that makes so much of his work of signal importance.

Simpson maintained a deep conviction that evolution worked through populations, not individuals, and that quantitative analyses—with probabilistic statements concerning intra-and interpopulations parameters—were indispensable for understanding evolutionary processes. He was, of course, not alone in this, although he was somewhat lonely among paleontologists in the early and mid–1940s. Others working in a variety of fields were espousing similar concepts—among them, Julian Huxley in evolutionary biology, Ronald Fisher in genetics and eugenics, Ernst Mayr in ornithology, C. H. Waddington in genetics and embryology, and G. Ledyard Stebbins in botany—and the Synthetic Theory of Evolution developed rapidly.

Taxonomy

In the course of his empirical work in museums and the field, George became keenly aware that a hierarchical organization of organisms based on evolutionary relationships was necessary to the orderly study of evolution and biogeography. He became a superb systematist, publishing landmark monographs on mammalian classification and theories of systematics. Two of his best known—both the most followed and the most controversial—are *Principles of Classification and the Classification of Mammals* (1945) and *Principles of Animal Classification* (1961). Mammalian classifications have, of course, been revised, by Simpson and by others, and changes are continuing.

It was Simpson's work in taxonomy and systematic theory that gave rise to the greatest controversies. In 1966 an English translation made Willi Hennig's phylogenetic systematics, originally published in German, more widely known among American and British systematists. Old theories were analyzed, recast, and encoded into what has become known as "cladistics." This new approach to animal and plant distribution, coming of age at a time when the theories of plate tectonics and continental drift were reshaping our ideas of the history of the world, created great conflict among systematic zoologists and vicariance biogeographers.

George's work, as the most lucid exposition of the "old and outmoded" evolutionary systematics, was bitterly attacked in the areas to which he had contributed so much. For the most part he remained silent, although hardly unaware. About a year before his death he casually referred to some members of the institution that had become the U.S. stronghold of cladistics and vicariance biogeography as "the American Museum mafia."

Fieldwork

A crucial aspect of Simpson's career, often overlooked given his extraordinary productivity, was his empiricism: He found his substance in museum collections and in samples he himself gathered in the field.

He was an avid and able field geologist and paleontologist. This time-consuming part of a paleontologist's life is the *sine qua non* of a historian of ancient life depending on the fossil record for his understanding of evolution. Understanding requires walking the rock exposures where fossils come to the surface, digging, collecting and carefully documenting fossils as they appear. Although never completely well, year after year Simpson went where the work was to be done and spent exhausting days and long nights in camps under difficult conditions. Like most true paleontologists, he loved it.

This phase of his work ended only when an unfortunate accident occurred far up the Amazon River in Brazil. Fatal to anyone less stubborn, it left Simpson with a severely impaired leg and put an end to his field trips. From the journals he kept of his ventures into wild, out-of-the-way places, Simpson produced two fascinating accounts of the life of a field paleontologist: *Attending Marvels: A Patagonian Journal* (1934) and *Splendid Isolation* (1980), an account of the lands, peoples, customs, and development of life in ancient times in South America. His equally extensive studies of other areas of the world, particularly western North America, are mostly found in his technical reports.

HISTORIAN AND EDUCATOR

Many scientists follow narrow pathways of research during their careers, seldom being drawn off into byways by problems that crop up and pique their interest. Others are perennial gadflies, lacking any discernible course. Simpson was neither, but continually sought broader meaning in several main lines of study that remained dominant throughout his life. His restless mind frequently carried him off in other directions—at times into byways that led to productive research.

Penguins, for instance, seem far from primitive mammals, his first love, but their unusual morphologies, behaviors, and distributions posed irresistible evolutionary and social problems that led Simpson to study them intensely over a number of years. Horses, one of the prime keys to evolution in the fossil world (as *Drosophila* has been to neobiology), inevitably became a target of his evolutionary interests. He even went beyond his evolutionary interest to study horses in modern times and as a factor in human history.

George's strong bent for history made him interested in those people whose ideas and deeds had opened new vistas in his own field. One of his first books, *Attending Marvels: A Patagonian Journal* (1934) and one of his last, *Discoverers of the*

Lost World (1984), discuss explorers past and present with a sensitivity and humor that often failed to emerge in personal discussions. In his lucid writing, exemplified in *Discoverers*, he paints pictures in which the founders of South American paleontology come alive in a style found only in the best biographies.

Another direction in Simpson's career that is often overlooked was his role in education. Though more effective in print than in personal interactions, George did have a few graduate students under his direction at Columbia and Harvard and taught classes at this level. His scientific papers and books were used widely in advanced graduate classes and seminars. In 1945–1946, the Department of Anthropology and the Paleozoology Program at The University of Chicago sponsored a year-long seminar centered on his *Tempo and Mode in Evolution.*

Yet his greatest direct influence on education was perhaps his *Life: An Introduction to Biology* (1957), written in conjunction with C. S. Pittendrigh and L. H. Tiffany. Designed for less advanced students, the text was widely used in secondary schools and in beginning college courses.

Aside from Simpson's main interests, little things often stirred his curiosity enough to produce a short essay. While at the American Museum of Natural History, he wrote from time to time for the semi-popular magazine, *Natural History*. A sampling includes such items as "Horses and History" (1936), "How to Misconstruct a Mastodon" (1936), "How dost thou portray the simburh?—Animal Art through the Ages" (1941), and "The Meek Inherit the Earth" (1941). He contributed somewhat more technical pieces on subjects well away from his field to the American Museum's *Novitiates*, including: "Large Pleistocene Felines" (no. 1136, 1936) and "Some Carib Indian Mammal Names" (no. 1114, 1941). These short trips into strange areas, declining somewhat after the mid-1950s, continued throughout his life, often in a more philosophical vein (as reflected in his collected essays, *This View of Life* [1965], and the many ruminitive digressions sprinkled throughout his autobiography, *A Concession to the Improbable* [1978]).

THE SOCIETY OF VERTEBRATE PALEONTOLOGY

The Society of Vertebrate Paleontology came into being informally in 1940 through the efforts of George Simpson and Alfred S. Romer and was very important to both of them. With some help from others, it was fledged and nurtured in a meeting—technically a session of the Vertebrate Section of the Paleontological Society—at the Museum of Comparative Zoology at Harvard. The first formal meeting was in 1941, at which time permanent officers were nominated and later elected. There has been some confusion about who did what, what is fiction and what fact. Feelings were hurt, but whatever the truth, a small scientific society emerged and has thrived and grown ever since.

For a number of years its original purpose, to serve as an informal forum for the exchange of ideas without formal papers or a scientific journal, was served by annual gatherings of thirty to forty persons. The open meetings, freedom of discussion, and evening "bull sessions" over a toddy or two were grand, and news of activities was carried (as it is today) in a *News Bulletin*. But, as size increased, this could not last. Limited time eventually led to a format of formal papers with restricted discussions. Evenings, however, have remained informal, and after a smoker and a banquet, the Society's sessions generally revert to the older, more boisterous times.

George and Al Romer missed the older days; George began attending fewer meetings, while Al remained to fight change. All of us "old timers" rued the passing and were staunch in our gratitude to the founders who had had the

foresight to see the need for cementing vertebrate paleontologists into a coherent group. Today the Society of Vertebrate Paleontology has spread around the world, the *News
Bulletin* carries items from foreign regions, and scientific articles appear in the Society journal.

Field conferences in the summer, usually with a relatively
limited participation, were affairs to be remembered, and as
usual George was at the heart of many of them. Evenings and
sometimes all night "off-hours meetings" have been described as boisterous by those who are inclined to be mild.
Sometimes they were, in fact, rather wild (of course in a
gentlemanly and gentlewomanly way).

One of these trips was held in the Permian and Paleocene
of New Mexico and for a night we stayed at the beloved summer home of Anne and George, Las Piñavetes. The creek
was the water supply for a nearby village and George, eyeing
the few children in the party, announced sternly over the P.A.
system mounted on a truck, "Do not urinate in the creek!"
"The pompous ass!" someone near me said in disgust, for
George had managed to turn his real concern for the villag-
ers into a reprimand.

As evening came on, the tensions of the days waned.
Tents, cots, and blankets came out and bottles appeared like
magic. These field conferences brought us together and became the grist for anecdotes for years to come.

FRIENDS AND COLLEAGUES

George Simpson was acquainted with colleagues in the
physical and biological sciences around the world. He was
royally received wherever he went and consistently acclaimed
for his scientific acumen and accomplishments. Too often, as
he himself said, he was asked to give lectures—something he
disliked and was only moderately good at. For all of his interchanges with scientists in many countries, his work re-

mained very largely his own, influenced by the cultures he visited in only the subtlest ways. Among his some 500 publications (not counting reviews), only a few were coauthored and these mostly books. Notable were his joint publications with Anne Roe, *Quantitative Zoology* (1939) and *Behavior and Evolution* (1958).

His insights into evolutionary processes, of course, benefitted through interchanges with his intellectual associates— among them Walter Granger, W. K. Gregory, W. D. Matthews, Theodosius Dobzhansky, Ernst Mayr, and Glenn Jepsen. But he depended more on books and the fossil record than on conversation, and the written word was his favorite medium of communication.

Theodosius Dobzhansky was not only a respected and inspirational colleague of Simpson but a revered friend, both during the years at Columbia and later, when their paths diverged. In my judgment his two closest friends among paleontologists were Bryan Patterson, at Harvard in his later years, and Paul O. McGrew, of the University of Wyoming. Both, like George, were students of fossil mammals.

Bryan was a free-spirited man who knew well the blythe spirit that underlay Simpson's public surface reserve. The two could tangle over serious matters in their scientific work but disagreed only about trivia in their friendship. Bryan, for example, persisted in calling him "G. G.," which George did not like, though I doubt he ever told "Pat" that it irked him.

Paul McGrew was a hardy extrovert, serious in his science but enthusiastically devoted to having a good time, whether at Jack-Straws or climbing mountains. Magnificently complementary, he and George were very fond of each other.

My relationship to George was somewhat different, for our paths crossed in science only in broader theoretical areas and we never worked together for any extended time. Yet my dealings with him were probably not atypical and are perhaps worth a bit of space.

In the informal autobiographical sketch he submitted to the Academy,[6] George wrote of Will Rogers' famous "I never met a man I didn't like":

"I do not believe that I have ever truly hated anyone, but I have despised some and disliked more. I have truly loved a few and liked an enormous number."

So he saw himself. My own experiences with him over the years lead me to temper this a bit, for our relationship vacillated between these categories—never quite reaching "despised" nor, perhaps, "loved," but teeter-tottering somewhere in between. Off and on, it went something like this.

Soon after I received an aggrieved, excoriating letter from George about a remark I had made (recorded on a garbled tape of a session on the "Emergence of Synthetic Theory of Evolution," sponsored by Ernst Mayr), I was asked to give a talk about George along with one by Stephen Jay Gould at a medal presentation. I think George had misunderstood something I said about philosophy and soft science. I accepted the invitation but then had the thought that this might be offensive. I called George to ask if he did or did not want me to give the talk. "But Ole," came back the astonished answer, "you are one of my dearest friends!" I gave the talk.

IN CONCLUSION

This was the George Simpson I had come to know since 1935. I admired his quiet wit, his sharp mind and penetrating intelligence, and I was often a bit awed in his presence. Yet at times awe would melt into affection, as when Anne and George, with just a few hours stopover between trains in Chicago, would call and say "How about coming down to the Palmer House bar for a drink or two?" My wife and I often

---

[6] See note 4 above.

did. At such times with martinis and black coffee, barriers disappeared and there were no closer friends.

In this informal memoir to George Simpson, I have striven to show that, under his greatness and richly deserved position of honor was a very true friend—sometimes shy and sensitive, and sometimes directly cutting. His difficult childhood, bad health, and rapid education broken by long absences perhaps benefitted him later by saving him from the desire to cloak himself in classroom orthodoxy. His on-and-off church experiences, his chance to go to Yale, his first marriage and divorce, his happy marriage to Anne, his four daughters, and the "mishaps" that brought him to the American Museum are all part of what Simpson came to be.

Certainly none of the "greats" of their time are easy to know. Barrages of criticism (too often by critics who have misunderstood a cherished idea) may dim the subject's luster, but they also serve to validate stature—lesser lights do not become "whipping posts." The greats' susceptibility to anecdotes further shapes their public image, for stories repeated and "improved" as they go too often explain much and distort more. I have added my voice to the storytellers, not only to speak of the greatness, but also to show something of the fallible man behind the mask.

SELECTED BIBLIOGRAPHY

1928

Catalogue of the Mesozoic mammalia in the geological department of the British Museum (Natural History). London: British Museum (Natural History).

1929

American Mesozoic mammals. Memoir of the Peabody Museum, Yale. No. 3, pt. 1.

1934

Attending marvels: a Patagonian journal. New York: Macmillan Co.

1937

The Fort Union of the Crazy Mountain field, Montana and its mammalian faunas. U.S. National Museum Bulletin 169. 287 pp.

1939

With A. Roe. *Quantitative zoology, numerical concepts and methods in the study of recent and fossil animals*. New York and London: McGraw-Hill.

1940

Mammals and land bridges. *J. Wash. Acad. Sci.* 30:137–63.

1942

The beginnings of vertebrate paleontology in North America. *Proc. Am. Philos. Soc.* 86:130–88.

1943

Mammals and the nature of continents. *Am. J. Sci.* 241:1–31.

1944

Tempo and mode in evolution. New York: Columbia University Press.

1945

The principles of classification and classification of mammals. *Am. Mus. Nat. Hist. Bull.* 85:1–350.

1946

Fossil penguins. *Am. Mus. Nat. Hist. Bull.* 87:100.

1947

Holarctic mammalian faunas and continental relationships during the Cenozoic. *Am. Mus. Nat. Hist. Bull.* 88:613–88.

1948

The beginnings of the age of mammals in South America. *Am. Mus. Nat. Hist. Bull.* 91:1–232.

1949

The meaning of evolution. New Haven and London: Yale University Press.

1951

Horses. New York: Oxford University Press.

1953

Life of the past. New Haven and London: Yale University Press.
The major features of evolution. New York: Columbia University Press.
Evolution and geography: Condon Lectures. Eugene: Oregon State Dept. of Higher Education.

1958

Behavior and evolution. In: *Behavior and evolution,* eds. A. Roe and G. G. Simpson, pp. 507–35. New Haven: Yale University Press.

1959

Anatomy and morphology. Classification and evolution 1859 and 1959. *Proc. Am. Philos. Soc.* 103:286–306.

1961

Principles of animal taxonomy. New York: Columbia University Press.
Lamarck, Darwin, and Butler: three approaches to evolution. *Am. Scholar* 30:238–49.

1964

This view of life. The world of an evolutionist. New York: Harcourt, Brace and World, Inc.

1965

The geography of evolution. Collected essays. New York and Philadelphia: Chilton Books.

1980

Splendid isolation. The curious history of the South American mammals. New Haven and London: Yale University Press.

1984

Discoverers of the lost world. New Haven and London: Yale University Press.

Owen H. Wangensteen

OWEN HARDING WANGENSTEEN

September 21, 1898–January 13, 1981

BY MAURICE B. VISSCHER[1]

THOUGH MANY PHYSICIANS attain excellence as clinicians and a much smaller number as research scientists, few—like Owen Harding Wangensteen—can claim preeminence in both. His insatiable curiosity, questioning mind, boundless energy, unselfishness, and uncommon human sympathy made him uniquely suited to a career in academic medicine—and specifically, in surgery. As a researcher he made substantial contributions to current knowledge about the causes of appendicitis, clarified problems concerning intestinal obstructions at various levels of the bowel, and provided important insight into the mechanism of peptic ulcer formation and the control of gastric secretion.

EDUCATION AND EARLY LIFE

Owen Harding Wangensteen was born September 21, 1898, in Lake Park, Minnesota. He attended public schools and received all of his earned degrees from the University of Minnesota: A.B. in 1919, M.D. in 1922, Ph.D. in 1925. His academic competence was recognized early, particularly by Elias Potter Lyon, dean of the Medical School, and by William

[1] The Academy wishes to express its special thanks to Rudi Schmid of the Schools of Medicine and Pharmacology, University of California, San Francisco, for his editorial help in the preparation of this manuscript.

J. Mayo. His rise in local academic status was meteoric, and by the age of thirty-two he was surgeon-in-chief of University of Minnesota Hospitals.

After years spent studying the deleterious effects of increased internal viscus pressure in the stomach and intestines, Wangensteen eventually concluded that a number of conditions, most often requiring surgical intervention, were, in fact, caused by excess pressure from the accumulation of gastric and intestinal secretions in an atonic intestine. To establish (against conventional wisdom) that the pathophysiological mechanism was elevated intraviscus pressure, which caused irreversible damage by obstructing capillary blood flow to the intestinal mucosa, Wangensteen and his students devised a number of ingenious animal experiments. The results of these studies led to the construction and eventual world-wide adoption of the Wangensteen suction technique and the so-called "Wangensteen tube," which has become an indispensable surgical instrument.

In 1944 I estimated that this procedure had saved some 100,000 lives; I would now put that number closer to a million. So well known was the Wangensteen technique to the public that, in 1951, Ogden Nash could quip:

> May I find my final rest in
> Owen Wangensteen's intestine,
> Knowing that his masterly suction
> Will assure my resurruction.

As a comprehensive general surgeon, Wangensteen also had a deep interest in cancer. Many of the lower bowel obstructions he studied so intensively were due to malignancy of the rectum or colon. He began, consequently, to concentrate on methods for the management of cancer. He initiated a Cancer Detection Center in his Surgical Department at the

University of Minnesota to discover malignancies early, before symptoms became clinically obvious and metastases had occurred. It was his hope that surgical removal of cancers at an early stage would result in a higher rate of long-term survival. He instituted a so-called "second look" program, designed particularly for patients with cancer of the colon who had lymph node metastases, and found that when recurrent metastases were removed a year after the initial operation, the five-year survival rate was significantly improved.

SURGEON-IN-CHIEF, UNIVERSITY OF MINNESOTA HOSPITALS (1930–1967)

In 1930 Owen Wangensteen was appointed surgeon-in-chief of University of Minnesota Hospitals, a post he would hold for the next thirty-seven years. Almost immediately his graduate program in surgery achieved a remarkable popularity, and for those aspiring to a career in academic surgery, appointment as a house officer in his department remained a coveted prize throughout his tenure as surgeon-in-chief. Designed in accordance with Wangensteen's belief that physiology and animal research were essential preparations for clinical surgery, the Minnesota graduate program became the prototype and model of a modern, scientifically oriented academic department of surgery.

Greatly assisted in his graduate teaching by the University of Minnesota's pioneering graduate medical program—a program that had made possible his own research and clinical career—Wangensteen never forgot the debt to his *alma mater*. His last publishing effort (the editing of which was completed by his widow, Sarah Davidson Wangensteen) was a collection of essays by the students and colleagues of Elias Potter Lyon, former dean of the University of Minnesota Medical School.[2]

[2] *Elias Potter Lyon: Minnesota's leader in medical education*, Owen Wangensteen, ed. (St. Louis: Warren H. Green, 1981).

In the 1930s when Wangensteen took over Minnesota's Department of Surgery, all residents in clinical departments were also required to register as students in the University's general graduate school and to choose a field of basic science pertinent to medicine as their minor field of study. Wangensteen's clinical residents, consequently, spent a significant amount of time and effort in the basic sciences. (I happened to choose physiology, a discipline Owen Wangensteen favored as being most appropriate for prospective academic surgeons.)

Since Wangensteen himself participated in the training of many of his surgical students, I had the opportunity to become familiar with both his scientific work and his educational philosophy. He encouraged his students to develop their own fields of scientific research and surgical expertise. Though not himself a cardiovascular surgeon, for example, he encouraged several members of his department to choose this specialty, several of whom later became innovators in all aspects of open-heart surgery—including cardiac transplantation.

In 1939 he founded the country-wide Society for University Surgeons, where surgeons, particularly young surgeons still in training, could present and discuss research results. This organization enabled these young scientists to get to know their peers in other institutions and to learn about their research interests. An outgrowth of Wangensteen's philosophy of extended graduate education, this national organization helped strengthen the scientific base of clinical surgery throughout the country and, indeed, the world.

In addition to his almost super-human energy and dedication, Wangensteen's extraordinary humanity also deserves special mention. From his early years as head of Minnesota's Department of Surgery he was concerned with the welfare of the patients who came to him rather than with the effect of high-risk patients on his operative mortality statistics. He always did what was possible for his patients without regard to the obvious risks—a point of view that often embroiled him in controversies and disputes. In fact, at one point in his career, his dean, Richard Scammon, recommended to Lotus Delta Coffman, president of the University, that Wangensteen be demoted. Had it not been for Elias Potter Lyon, who was solidly behind him, and for William J. Mayo's writing Coffman he would resign as a Regent of the University if Wangensteen were demoted, it is likely that humanity would have been deprived of Owen Harding Wangensteen's contributions to science and society and this memoir would never have been written.

I have personal reasons for knowing just how much Wangensteen put the patient's welfare first, for—some twenty-five years ago—doctors at a world-renowned clinic diagnosed my aunt as having cholecystitis but, in view of her advanced age and general frailty, declined to operate on her. My aunt then consulted Dr. Wangensteen, who confirmed the diagnosis and the risk but added that, if she wanted to take that risk, he would do the operation. She took it and subsequently enjoyed another eight years of pain-free life.

Owen Wangensteen was equally selfless and forward-thinking with regard to his personal gain from private practice, as is shown by two policies he devised to insure the viability and health of the surgical research and graduate studies programs under his direction. First, he set a limit on the amount of personal income he would accept from his own practice and turned over any excess to a University Surgical Research Fund. Second, he sent his more affluent private patients a letter saying he preferred not to bill for his services, requesting instead that they send a contribution to the Fund in an amount they themselves deemed appropriate. This resulted in many annual gifts to the Fund, which supported graduate students' surgical research long before Federal funds became available for such purposes.

Wangensteen's obvious lack of interest in private fortune impressed many and obtained a number of large private donations, not only to the Department of Surgery, but also to Minnesota's entire medical enterprise. His own unselfishness, therefore, significantly contributed to the building of a private support base for medical research and teaching at the University of Minnesota.

Scientific endeavor is, of course, greatly affected by the temper of the times, and during the 1960s and 1970s American science was well—even lavishly—supported by both public and private funds. But with the current drastic reduction of public support, interest on the part of the private sector is of even greater importance to the health and vigor of science. The substantial financial benefits Owen Wangensteen's selfless devotion to surgical research brought to his institution and his department show how much a single individual can influence private philanthropy.

WANGENSTEEN AS MEDICAL HISTORIAN

In the final chapter of his career, Wangensteen turned increasingly to a longstanding interest: medical history. Forty years earlier he had written of the importance of maintaining a knowledge of past triumphs in medical research. More recently, he devoted much of his time to developing Minnesota's Medical History Department and the historical library he had built almost single-handedly.

He also collaborated with his wife on a 785-page reference book on the evolution of surgical practice, *The Rise of Surgery—from Empiric Craft to Scientific Discipline*, which appeared in 1978, three years before his death. The Wangensteens spent years visiting medical history collections at home and abroad, including the National Library of Medicine in Bethesda, the libraries of royal colleges and university medical schools in London, Paris, Budapest, Montpellier, Vienna, Edinburgh, Glasgow, and Leeds. With 137 pages of notes and sixty-four of author and subject indices, the volume is a monumental and indispensable work.

As a medical historian, Owen Wangensteen had the great advantage of having been himself a participant in many areas of clinical practice and research. Having a strong bent for scholarly reading, he acquired the knowledge necessary to put together a comprehensive treatise on the emergence of surgery from primitive empiricism to the utilization of modern scientific and technological advances.

HONORS, AWARDS, AND SERVICE TO SCIENCE

Owen Wangensteen's unique talents and gifts were recognized early and often by his peers, and he received numerous honors at home and abroad. Elected to the National Academy of Sciences in 1966, he was also an honorary Fellow of the Royal College of Surgeons of England, Scotland, and Ireland; an honorary member of the Hellenic Surgical Society, the Norwegian Academy of Sciences, the French National Academy of Medicine, the Argentine Surgical Society, the Société Internationale de Chirurgie, the International Academy of History of Medicine, and a corresponding member of the German Surgical Congress. He received, among others, the Samuel D. Gross Award and Medal of the Philadelphia Academy of Surgery in 1935, the John Scott Award and Medal in 1941, the Alvarenza Prize in 1949, the Distinguished Service Award of the University of Minnesota in 1960, the Passano Award in 1961, the Lannelongue Medal of the French Academy of Surgery in 1968, the Distinguished Service Award of the American Medical Association in 1968, and the Scientific Achievement Award of the American Surgical Association in 1976. He received several honorary doctorates from American and foreign universities, including the University of Buffalo, The University of Chicago, St. Olaf College, Temple University, the University of Paris (Sorbonne), Hamline University, Marquette University, and the University of Athens.

He also served as president of a number of medical organizations, including the Minnesota Medical Foundation (1948–1954), the Halsted Surgical Society (1957–1959), the American College of Surgeons (1959), and the American Surgical Association (1969). He was named Outstanding Minnesotan by the Governor's Committee in 1969. He was made a Regents' Professor, the highest honor that can be given to a member of the faculty of the University of Minnesota.

He is survived by his widow, Sarah A. Davidson Wangensteen, and three children by his long-deceased first wife, Helen: Mary H. Wangensteen Brink, Owen G., and Stephen L. Wangensteen. Stephen Wangensteen has followed in his father's footsteps to become an academic surgeon. Sarah Wangensteen, co-author of *The Rise of Surgery*, is a professional medical editor.

SELECTED BIBLIOGRAPHY

1928

With G. W. Waldron. Studies in intestinal obstruction. IV. Strangulation obstruction: A comparison of the toxicity of the intestine and other tissues autolyzed in vivo and vitro. *Arch. Surg. (Chicago)* 17:430–39.

1929

The blood supply of the thyroid gland with special reference to the vascular system of the cretin goiter. *Surg. Gynecol. Obstet.* 48:613–28.

1930

With H. H. Cooke. Have the adrenal glands a specific detoxifying function in intestinal obstruction? *Proc. Soc. Exp. Biol. Med.* 27:959–61.

1936

The mechanism of the vermiform appendix: A potential "closed-loop." *Surg. Gynecol. Obstet.* 62:1020–22.

1945

F. Kolouch et al. III. Mechanism of stomal ulcer is related to length of afferent duodenojejunal loop. *Proc. Soc. Exp. Biol. Med.* 58:275–80.

1946

I. D. Baronofsky et al. Vagotomy fails to protect against histamine-provoked ulcer. *Proc. Soc. Exp. Biol. Med.* 62:114–18.

1948

With C. W. Lillehei and J. L. Dixon. The relation of anemia and hemorrhagic shock to experimental ulcer production. *Proc. Soc. Exp. Biol. Med.* 68:125–28.

1949

With R. L. Varco and I. D. Baronofsky. The technique of surgical division of patent ductus arteriosus. *Surg. Gynecol. Obstet.* 88:62–68.

1951

With F. L. Raffucci. Tolerance of dogs to occlusion of entire afferent vascular inflow to the liver. *Surg. Forum* 1:191–95.

With R. W. Toon and F. S. Cross. Effect of inhaled cigarette smoke on the production of peptic ulcer in dogs. *Proc. Soc. Exp. Biol. Med.* 77:866-69.

1954

With A. P. Thal and W. D. Kelly. The effect of transplantation of the stomach to the lower jejunum with preservation of the vagal innervation. *Surg. Forum* 5:294–300.

1958

E. G. Yonehiro et al. Detection of minute gastrointestinal bleeding utilizing radioactive iron, Fe^{59}. *Proc. Soc. Exp. Biol. Med.* 98:339–41.

S. B. Day et al. The development of interarterial intercoronary anastomoses by an arteriovenous fistula between the pulmonary artery and left atrium. *Proc. Soc. Exp. Biol. Med.* 98:561–63.

1960

A. Castenada et al. Antral hyperfunction following portacaval shunt. *Surg. Forum* 11(3):349–51.

1961

J. A. Williams et al. Composition and source of secretion from lymphoid aggregation in the rabbit gut. *Br. J. Exp. Pathol.* 42:153–57.

D. M. Nicoloff et al. Effect of cortisone on gastric secretion in adrenalectomized dogs. *J. Am. Med. Assoc.* 178:1005–7.

O. H. Wangensteen et al. The effect of pitressin on portal hemodynamics. *Physiologist* 4:87.

1962

With H. Sosin, E. F. Bernstein, and E. T. Peter. The effect of serotonin and histamine on gastric blood flow. *Physiologist* 5:214.

D. M. Nicoloff et al. The effect of liver arterialization following portacaval shunt. *Am. J. Dig. Dis.* 7:1034–38.

1963

A. S. Leonard et al. The influence of the hypothalamus on gastric hydrochloric acid secretion. *J. Am. Med. Assoc.* 183:1016–18.

1964

J. P. Delaney et al. The effect of portacaval shunting on upper gastrointestinal blood flow. *J. Am. Med. Assoc. Forum.*

With J. P. Delaney, R. L. Goodale, Jr., and J. Cheng et al. Effects of pitressin on mesenteric capillary blood flow. *Physiologist* 7(3):115.

1968

With J. E. Molina, W. P. Ritchie, Jr., and R. F. Edlich. Role of the vagus nerve in the release of antral gastrin in the dog. *Surgery* 63(3):467–74.

1970

R. Gonzalez et al. Rapid control of massive hepatic hemorrhage by laser radiation. *Surg. Gynecol. Obstet.* 130:199–200.

1978

University selection criteria for future surgical leaders. *Ann. Surg.* 188(1):114–19.

HENRY STEPHENS WASHINGTON

January 15, 1867–January 7, 1934

BY CHARLES MILTON

The National Academy of Sciences memorializes its members in a series of Biographical Memoirs *written by colleagues from their personal knowledge of and esteem for dear departed friends. Strangely, no Academy memorial exists in commemoration of Henry Stephens Washington, one of its most eminent members, whose name and work to this day—full fifty-five years since his death—are known and honored by geologists throughout the world. Aware of this, Dr. Elizabeth J. Sherman, editor of the* Biographical Memoir *series, searched for an author to write an appropriate memoir, realizing that it might be difficult, if not impossible, to find anyone now living who, besides having a vivid memory of seeing and hearing the great man, had also devoted many long hours to arduous study of his works. Yet I am one such—perhaps the only one who still remains—and so accepted the task despite the special difficulties posed by there being none whose memories I could share.*

At first I did not know that so many had hastened to record, in words of moving eloquence, their admiration and even awe of a most extraordinary man. It then became clear to me that any conventional memoir of Washington belatedly written today would be untimely and incongruous. Better instead a summary, assembled from the many scattered sources, giving the known facts of his life. These I have duly listed and annotated, along with references to his many publications; the extensive citations from contemporary memorials and

367

*tributes; available portraits; and lastly, appraisal by a recognized
authority of the lasting significance of Washington's greatest achievement, the CIPW systematization of igneous rock taxonomy.*

*It is in pondering the lives and deeds of great men that we, too—
to some degree at least—may approach greatness and thereby enlarge
our own lesser lives. Henry Stephens Washington was indeed such a
great man.*

HENRY STEPHENS WASHINGTON was born in Newark,
New Jersey, on January 15, 1867, the son of George and
Eleanor Phoebe (Stephens) Washington and descendant in
the collateral line from the family of George Washington. He
died after several years of illness in his New York City home
on January 7, 1934.

Washington's boyhood years were spent on the family
homestead estate in Locust, New Jersey, where his father
acted as his chief teacher. The family was wealthy, and "he
was the product of a cultured home with plenty of servants"
(Clark, 1978). When Washington was twelve years of age, an
old smokehouse on the estate was remodeled into a chemical
laboratory, and a year later the boy was making quantitative
analyses.

After attending private schools and preparing for college
under tutors, he entered Yale College at fifteen. There he
received his first academic training under J. D. Dana, E. S.
Dana, G. J. Brush, S. L. Penfield, and H. L. Wells. After graduating in 1886 with an A.B. and special honors in natural
science, he held the Silliman Fellowship in physics and was
assistant in physics until he took the A.M. degree in 1888. In
his first paper (with W. F. Hillebrand in 1888), he described
the crystallography of rare copper arsenates from Utah. He
then spent four years in extensive travel in the West Indies,
Europe, Egypt, Algeria, and Asia Minor. He acquired an unusual knowledge of languages—not only German, French,
and Italian, all of which he could write and speak fluently—

but also modern Greek, Spanish, and Portuguese, even Arabic and Turkish.

During the winter semesters of 1891–92 and 1892–93 he studied under F. Zirkel and C. H. Credner at the University of Leipzig, where he took the Ph.D. degree with highest honors in 1893. His dissertation, *The Volcanoes of the Kula Basin in Lydia*, was published in New York in 1894.

Later that year he married Martha Rose Beckwith, and for the next two years they lived alternately in Navesink, New Jersey and Venice, Italy. He had also joined the American School of Classical Studies at Athens, taking part in and conducting archeological excavations (some of which he funded) at several Greek sites. The results of this work, done with his brother Charles at Phlius in 1892, were published many years later in the *American Journal of Archaeology* (1923).

IGNEOUS ROCK NOMENCLATURE AND CLASSIFICATION

In 1895 he returned to Yale, where he made rock analyses for Professor L. V. Pirsson, equipped his own New Jersey laboratory where he would work for the next ten years, and assisted Professor E. S. Dana in mineralogy. In 1897 he began analyzing a suite of rocks collected in Norway and comparing it with a suite from Essex County, Massachusetts. Finding rocks of practically the same mineralogical and chemical composition occurring in connection with magmas of quite diverse characters, he urged (in 1898) the need for systematization of igneous rock nomenclature and classification.

CROSS, IDDINGS, PIRSSON, AND WASHINGTON: THE CIPW NORM[1]

J. P. Iddings and Whitman Cross had been working on the same problem and they met with Washington and Pirsson

---

[1] The description of the CIPW norm that follows was contributed to this memoir by Felix Chayes.

in 1899. For three years the four worked together, producing in the end the first systematic, quantitative, chemico-mineralogical classification of igneous rocks.

His part in this project was certainly one of Washington's most significant and enduring contributions to the science of geology: transforming the "coordinates" of an igneous rock composition—the list of essential oxide amounts reported in the bulk analysis—into the chemical coordinates now known as the "CIPW norm." The new variables were clearly intended as proxies for mineral compositions. Each has the simplified, "end member" composition of the anhydrous mineral whose name is abbreviated to form the symbol. (The only exceptions to this rule are the rarely encountered alkali-silicates, which have only formula names, and for which, incidentally, mineral analogues are either unknown or vanishingly rare.)

The ingenious schedule of calculation that determines which of perhaps as many as a dozen of the thirty possible components are present in the norm of a particular analysis, and in what amounts, is one of the signal triumphs of the golden age of American petrography. Washington's actual role in the development of the system is not easily assessed, for its creation was one of the earliest and most successful examples of collaboration in our science, and none of the authors (W. Cross, J. P. Iddings, L. V. Pirsson, and H. S. Washington) ever said publicly which of them was responsible for any particular aspect of the system.

They described their new system in a series of articles in the *Journal of Geology*, reproduced in book form in 1902 under the editorship of Cross. (It is curious that, although the four authors continued scientific activity for many years and remained close friends, there is no further record that they ever published jointly again.)

From the original articles it is clear that—in the minds of

its authors—normative calculation was important primarily as a taxonomic device. The relative amounts of several subsets of the normative components, or "standard minerals," formed the basis for an elaborate "quantitative classification of igneous rocks."

This classification was used extensively by Iddings and Washington in their own further work. Indeed, it controls the structure both of Iddings' magnificent petrological treatise, *Igneous Rocks* (2 vols., 1909–1913), and of Washington's monumental *Chemical Analyses of Igneous Rocks* (USGS Professional Paper 99, 1903)—a quarto volume of some 600 pages containing the analyses essential to the CIPW project and discussions of numerous additional analyses as well. Perceiving the need for a textbook of instruction in the methods of rock analysis, Washington published a manual in 1904 that, with its three later editions, established standard analytical procedures in laboratories all over the world.

Yet during the first third of the century, the CIPW classification system was used rather gingerly, never achieving the general acceptance accorded a number of its contemporary competitors. This was perhaps because its basic parameters were chemical rather than petrological or mineralogical, and chemical analyses were both expensive and rare. Petrologists were also discouraged by the formidable complexity of a system that included specific suffixes to denote classes, orders, rangs, grads, subclasses, suborders, subrangs, and pigeonholes. Today, though sometimes mentioned in theoretical discussions of taxonomy, it is hardly ever used in the practical classification of igneous rocks.

What survives—and thrives—of the CIPW system is the norm calculation itself. Generations of petrologists have discovered that the rules governing it neatly exploit an extraordinary familiarity with the mineral assemblages actually encountered in the commoner igneous rocks, and in many of the relatively rare ones as well. Despite the oversimplified definitions of the "standard minerals" and their anhydrous character, the norm often provides a characterization of rock composition more immediately meaningful than the oxide vector. And even when qualitative agreement (or compatibility) of normative model assemblages is less than optimal, there is usually something to be learned from the discrepancy. Finally, in a development none of the authors could have anticipated, the norm proved invaluable in the critical business of characterizing the components and defining the "systems" studied in the phase equilibrium experimentation that was to begin in the next decade and would for so long remain central to experimental petrology.

At this time Washington and seven other earth scientists were also planning the research program for the Carnegie Institution of Washington's soon-to-be-established Geophysical Laboratory. He spent five months in 1905 collecting igneous rocks in the Mediterranean region, and in 1906 the Carnegie Institution published a 199-page volume of his petrologic studies of the Roman comagmatic volcanic region. In other publications his studies covered rocks from Liberia, Greece, Norway, Turkey, Germany, and America.

THE DARK YEARS (1906–1912)

"One day disaster struck him. He came home from a trip to find that his wife had left him, taking most of his money with her. This almost wrecked his career. There followed a period of bewilderment and despair. He floundered like a rudderless ship. Finally, he had to face reality: for the first time in his life, he had to get a job." (Martin, 1953)

The preceding "period of intense activity . . . now gave place . . . to a six-year period of uncertainty and anxiety during which Washington traveled, and used his laboratory intermittently . . ." (Merwin, 1952). Then, "when [financial] reverses came, he grudgingly gave part of his time to consulting work as a mining geologist, and in this connection he maintained an office in New York from 1906 to 1912" (Lewis, 1935), though still finding time to serve—from 1909 until 1914—on the Board of Managers of the New Jersey Geological Survey.[2]

GEOPHYSICAL LABORATORY OF THE CARNEGIE INSTITUTION OF WASHINGTON

Only in 1912, when he joined the staff of the Carnegie Institution of Washington's Geophysical Laboratory, could he once more devote himself wholly to research. Yet, even during the preceding sad interlude of his life,

". . . under the less rigid laboratory routine, Washington gave thought to problems of a more general type; the distribution of the elements in igneous rocks, submarine volcanic eruptions, and . . . mineral nomenclature; and in spite of interruptions, his analytical and petrographic work yielded nearly a dozen papers." (Merwin, 1962)

A year or two after joining the Geophysical Laboratory staff his (childless) marriage was ended with divorce. For the rest of his life he remained unmarried and worked continuously with the Geophysical Laboratory.

In 1914—with Arthur L. Day, director of the Geophysical Laboratory--he visited the active volcanoes of the Mediterranean. The analytical work he did there and throughout the world resulted in papers on igneous rocks from Sardinia, Pantelleria, Brazil, Colorado, India, Rockall, and Stromboli, in which he presented views on several chemical and mineralogical relationships. In 1917 he began giving his attention to sources and production of potassium salts. In 1919, while at the American Embassy in Rome, he served as an American

[2] *Who Was Who in America* (Chicago: Marquis Who's Who, Inc., 1968).

delegate to the International Geodetic and Geophysical Union's organizational meeting in Belgium.

The following January, once again home in Washington, D.C., he addressed the Arts Club regarding recent archaeological activity in Rome, published *Ave Roma immortalis*—an affectionate poetic tribute to Italy, and began preparing the report on the excavations he had conducted at Phlius nearly thirty years earlier. "His interest in archaeology was permanent, and he repeatedly applied chemical and petrographical methods to the study of its special problems" (Whitman Cross, 1936).

"That spring [of 1918], during the organization of the American Geophysical Union, he was made chairman for volcanology . . . a few weeks later he sailed for Honolulu as delegate to the First Pan-Pacific Scientific Conference, where he presented two papers on volcanoes and one on ocean currents. While in the Hawaiian Islands he and several of his many friends collected volcanic rocks from numerous localities for his future studies. At the final dinner, part of the entertainment was a poem by Washington, 'Pele[3] to the Pan-Pacific'. . . ." (Merwin, 1952)

During the war years (1918–19), Washington served as chemical associate and scientific attaché at the American Embassy in Rome.

From 1920 to 1924, he collected—from the vast literature accessible in the library of the United States Geological Survey—a great number of new igneous rock analyses, whose good quality reflected the two decades in which his 1904 *Manual*, and its later editions, had instructed the world's analysts in proper procedures of rock analysis. In 1917, *Chemical Analyses of Igneous Rocks published from 1884 to 1913, inclusive, with a critical discussion of the character and use of analyses* appeared as *USGS Professional Paper 99*—a massive quarto

---

[3] Pele is the Hawaiian goddess of volcanoes. *Editor's note.*

volume of 1,201 pages, containing 8,600 analyses, "all of them superior." (Cross, 1936)

"In 1922 he became vice-president of the Geological Society of America, and also of the Section of Volcanology of the International Geophysical Union . . . in 1924 he was President of the Mineralogical Society of America, and from 1926 to 1929 Chairman of the American Geophysical Union. . . . With the preparation, in 1930, of the fourth edition of his book on methods of chemical analysis came failing health through the remaining three years of his life, during which he wrote little. . . ." (Merwin, 1952)

In the forty-five years—1887 to 1932—of Washington's active professional life, he produced 169 publications (some four each year), practically all substantial contributions to archaeology, regional and descriptive petrology, geochemistry and geophysics, and mineralogy. Many of these, in their respective fields, are of major significance and enduring value.

HONORS AND SERVICE TO THE SCIENTIFIC COMMUNITY

Much honored throughout his life, Washington ". . . was happy in the recognition accorded his work by fellow-workers at home and abroad, as indicated by official positions and honorary memberships to which he was elected. He was a member of the National Academy of Sciences from 1921, the Geological Society of America (vice-president, 1922), Mineralogical Society (president, 1924), American Philosophical Society, American Geophysical Union (chairman, 1926–1929), International Geophysical Union (vice-president, 1922), the Académie de France, and the Washington Academy of Sciences. He was a cavalier of Italy's Order of the Crown, a foreign correspondent of the Geological Society of London and of the Sociedad Española de Historia Natural, a foreign member of the Academia dei Lincei, Società Geologica Italiana, the Modena, Norway and Turin

Academies, and an honorary member of England's Mineralogical Society. (Information taken from Fenner, 1934.)

WASHINGTON THE SCIENTIST
AS HIS CONTEMPORARIES SAW HIM

H. S. Washington's long scientific career brought him much acclaim from his scientific peers, whose assessments, excerpted here, can best give an idea of the importance and scope of his work:

"When one considers the complexity of the earth's crust, it may be concluded that anything beyond an intelligent guess as to the composition of the crust lies beyond the power of the human mind. And yet here are two men who not only gave us the composition, but gave it to three significant figures! Let us see what manner of men they were, and how they managed to analyze so huge a mass as the earth.

"Frank Wigglesworth Clarke was chief chemist of the U.S. Geological Survey from 1883 until shortly before his death in 1931. Henry Stephens Washington (1867–1934) can only be described as a 'freelance' chemist. He was over 50 before he ever worked for a salary.

"Clarke was the pioneer in the great project of analyzing the earth's crust. He published his first estimate of the composition of the crust as early as 1889. Washington published his first estimate in 1903. . . . In 1908 Clarke published his great treatise, *The Data of Geochemistry*. This went through five editions and remains to this date the Geological Survey's all time 'bestseller.' . . . In 1920, Washington and Clarke collaborated on a revision of their estimates. It is thus evident that the project occupied a good portion of the professional careers of both men. . . . It is interesting to compare these various estimates. . . . It is astonishing how little these values changed through the years despite the accumulation of new data.

"It has been said that Washington and Clarke were mere compilers of other people's data. . . . On the contrary, their careers illustrate beautifully the proper idea of compilation. They did not compile data merely for the convenience of others, as do the makers of handbooks. Rather, they compiled data in order to learn the story the data had to tell. They were creative compilers. . . .

"In his writings, Washington revealed an idealism about quantitative analysis that transcends even the idealism of Stas or Richards. . . . 'The balance and weights should therefore be regarded with a feeling akin to reverence, and the balance case looked upon, so to speak, as a sanctum sanctorum.' . . .

"These two men established an enduring record in the greatest analysis of all time." (Martin, 1953)

WASHINGTON THE MAN
AS HIS CONTEMPORARIES SAW HIM

Such were his achievements, but what of the man himself? For this, we must, once more, turn to the recollections of those who knew him:

"One of the most eminent and picturesque personalities in American science . . . always intensely interested in many intellectual fields . . . he possessed a remarkable store of knowledge regarding ancient peoples, their origins and mode of life and their monuments, inscriptions and art. He was widely read, had a very retentive memory, and there were very few topics on which he was not able to converse with much more than superficial knowledge. His familiarity extended to such varied subjects as botany, philology, literature, the development of social customs, and [the] culinary art. . . .

"Washington took much delight in associating with congenial friends, and was one of the most active members of the Cosmos Club of Washington. In more public assemblages his features and bearing were of a character to make him an outstanding figure. His was a many-sided and exceptional personality, in many ways almost unique. His contributions to science are of lasting value." (Fenner, 1952)

"*Professional Paper 99* . . . is known to every geologist in the world. To those of Washington's acquaintances unfamiliar with the more earnest side of his character—the amount of patient investigation and even drudgery to which he was willing to devote himself in this work is almost unbelievable." (Fenner, 1934)

"With a finely formed head surmounted by a thick mass of wavy white hair, large luminous brown eyes, a Roman nose and full red lips enmeshed in a dense curly white beard, Dr. Henry S. Washington . . . is a picturesque, distinguished, and attractive-looking man. He is as interesting as he looks . . . he is friendly and democratic . . . but never familiar. Learned, he is

never pedantic. He is delightful in conversation for he is an attentive lis-
tener, never argumentative, and when he differs, though definite, he is
never autocratic or apostolic. . . . He is filled with the joy of living. His
favorite sports are golf and billiards. He is fond of music and can strum
an instrument. He enjoys poetry, and on occasion can compose a smooth-
flowing, subtle sonnet. . . . With a gift of tongues . . . his reading ranges
. . . all printed matter except gossip and scandal about which he is completely incurious. Curiously . . . though he has . . . had adventures galore,
he is not anecdotally inclined, though most interesting when he is drawn
out." (Munroe, 1925, cited by Merwin, 1952)

"Washington's magnetic personality was enriched by his brilliant intellect, broad culture, and his genuine interest in and knowledge of an
astounding range of topics, not only in the physical and natural sciences,
but in literature, history, music, art, archaeology, ethnology, and philology.
Following the intense seriousness of his research and his writing he found
relaxation in the lighter mood, and his lively wit and keen sense of humor
were a constant source of delight to those who had the privilege of knowing him." (Lewis, 1935)

"He was hospitable and generous . . . and was popular in many circles.
A cigar was his constant companion, and he handed one to whomever he
met. It was playfully suggested that tobacco-ash accounted for the high
percentages of potash in his analyses." (Spencer, 1936)

Much of Washington's nonprofessional life centered
around the Cosmos Club in Washington, where he found
among its distinguished members many congenial friends.
Commemorating its centenary in 1978, the Club produced
*The Cosmos Club of Washington, a Centennial History, 1878–
1978*, edited by Wilcomb E. Washburn, in which pages 291–
93, by Austin H. Clark, are devoted to Henry Stephens
Washington:

"Henry Stephens Washington (1867–1934)—Harry to a few close
friends—used to describe himself as the enemy of every wife in
Washington. One of the most learned and versatile, and at the same time
most jolly and companionable, of our Club members, he was the friend of
everyone, old and young. For he had something in common with all. He

belonged to that coterie of scholars, now almost extinct, with an interest in everything . . . the product of cultured homes with plenty of servants and no distracting radios or television sets, and thus able to devote all their time to their special intellectual pursuits.

"He was convivial and highly gregarious . . . an enthusiastic devotee of bridge, billiards, and cowboy pool, a cheerful partner or adversary at any game. Their fondness for his company often led them to spend their evenings at the Club when they should have been at home with their wives.

"Harry was moderately good at all games, but he did not take them too seriously. He played for relaxation, with a complete absence of that grim tenseness that characterizes so many players. He did not seem to care whether he won or lost, which made him popular with some, much less popular with others. I can still hear his cheerful 'Sorry, partner' when he lost a game of bridge. His partner was sorry, too, but not cheerfully sorry.

"Conversationally, he was at home on almost any subject.

". . . the Club gave a reception to a group of foreigners which included the President of Haiti, a very large, very stately, and very courteous man. Most of the Club members did not seem to know he was in the room. Seeing the situation, Harry introduced himself, and the two had a long and cordial conversation in French.

"Although a rather extreme conservative in his views of society, Harry was perfectly willing to concede to others the right of having other ideas. I especially remember one evening after a dinner given by Cleveland Moffett, spent mostly in a lively though entirely friendly discussion of the merits and demerits of Socialism with that enthusiastic advocate of Socialism, Charles E. Russell.

"Although Harry Washington was so well known and so well liked by the Club members, most of them regarded him as a bit of a mystery, for his really intimate friends were few and he was very reserved about his personal affairs. The city clerk of Newark, New Jersey, where he was born, writes me that there seems to be no record of his birth in the Bureau of Vital Statistics. . . ." (Clark, 1978)

REFERENCES

1933

Edward B. Mathews. "Memorial to J. P. Iddings." *Bull. Geol. Soc. Amer.* 44:4–6.[4]

1934

S. Kozu. *J. Japan. Assoc. Min. Petr. Econ. Geol.* 12:41–44. With two portraits.
———. *Nature* 133:557–8.
C. N. Fenner. "Henry Stephens Washington." *Science*, New Series 79:47–48. Bibliography (89 titles). Portrait.
L. J. Spencer. *Quart. J. Geol. Soc. London* 90:xlix-l; *Mineral. Mag.*, 304–5.
J. Volney Lewis. Memorial of Henry Stephens Washington. *Amer. Mineral.* 28:178–84. Portrait.

1935

Obituary notice. Report of the Board of Management, Century Assoc.[5]

1936

Tom F. W. Barth. Henry Stephens Washington. *Mineralog. Petrogr. Mitt.* 47:371–2.

1936

W. Cross. Washington, Henry Stephens. *Dict. Am. Biog.* 19:527–8.[6]

---

[4] Mathews devotes two pages to the history of the CIPW System of igneous rock classification and Washington's participation therein.

[5] This eight-line note suggests that Washington was a member of the Century Association (or Club), but the author could find no record of this elsewhere.

[6] In addition to the printed biographical accounts cited here, Cross lists *Yale University Obituary Record* (1934) and *Washington Post* (January 8, 1934). He also refers to a memoir he was preparing for the National Academy of Sciences's *Biographical Memoirs*, which was never completed.

1952

Herbert E. Merwin. Memorial to Henry Stephens Washington. *Proc. Geolog. Soc. Amer.* Annual Report 1951, pp. 165–173. Bibliography (189 titles).[7]

1953

Albert R. Martin. The Great Analysis. *Journal of Chemical Education* 30:566–68. Portraits of Washington and Clarke. Reprinted from *The Capital Chemist* 3(1953):92.[8]

1968

Henry Stephens Washington. In: *Who Was Who in America*. Chicago: Marquis Who's Who, Inc.

[7] With fourteen biographical references and a portrait, this is perhaps the most detailed memoir of Washington.

[8] Frank Clarke was chief chemist of the U.S. Geological Survey from 1883 to 1931, author of *Data of Geochemistry*, and a most unusual scientist and human being. Martin is the only author who refers to the cause of Washington's unhappy period from 1906 to 1912.

SELECTED BIBLIOGRAPHY

1891

Discovery of a temple of archaic plan (Plataia). *Am. J. Arch.* 7(1891):1b.

1894

The volcanoes of the Kula Basin in Lydia (Ph.D. diss., University of Leipzig). New York: Drummond. 67 pp.

1902

With W. Cross, J. P. Iddings, and L. V. Pirsson. A quantitative chemico-mineralogical classification and nomenclature of igneous rocks. *J. Geol.* 10:555–690.

1906

The Roman comagmatic region. *Carnegie Inst. Washington Publ. 57.* 199 pp.

1913

The volcanoes and rocks of Pantelleria. *J. Geol.* 21:653–70; 22:16–27.

1915

The correlation of potassium and magnesium, sodium and iron, in igneous rocks. *Proc. Natl. Acad. Sci. USA* 1:574–8.

1916

An apparent correspondence between the chemistry of igneous rocks and of organic metabolism. *Proc. Natl. Acad. Sci. USA* 2:623–6.

1917

Chemical analyses of igneous rocks, published from 1884 to 1913, inclusive, with a critical discussion of the character and use of analyses: a revision and expansion of *Professional Paper 14. U.S. Geol. Surv., Prof. Pap. 99.* 1201 pp.

1919

Manual of the chemical analysis of rocks. 3rd ed. New York: John Wiley & Sons.

1920

The chemistry of the earth's crust. *J. Franklin Inst.* 190: 757–815.

1923

The density of the earth as calculated from the densities of Mauna Kea and Halekala. *J. Washington Acad. Sci.* 13:453–6.

Remarks on the study of sedimentation by artificial precipitation. *Nat. Res. Council (U.S.) Rept. Comm. on Sedimentation,* pp. 66–8.

1924

Report of the section of volcanology. *Bull. Nat. Res. Council (U.S.)* 41.

With F. W. Clarke. The composition of the earth's crust. *U.S. Geol. Survey Prof. Pap. 127.*

1925

How petrography can aid stone producers. *Explosives Eng.* 3: 331–3.

1926

Review of B. K. de Prorok. *Digging for lost African gods.* New York: G. P. Putnam's Sons, 1926. *Art Archaeol.* 22:103–4.

The eruption of Santorini in 1925. *J. Washington Acad. Sci.* 16:1–7.

1927

Abstract of F. Zambonini and G. Carobbi. A chemical study of the yellow incrustation on the Vesuvian lava of 1631. *Am. Mineral.* 12:1–10.

1928

Europe's volcanoes. *Sci. News Lett.* 13:215–6.

Review of J. Jakob. *Anleitung zur chemischen Gesteinsanalyse,* Berlin. *J. Am. Chem. Soc.* 51:955–6.

1929

The rock suites of the Pacific and the Atlantic ocean basins. *Science* 69:554–5.

1930

The analysis of rocks. New York: John Wiley & Sons.
The earliest recorded rock analysis. *J. Maryland Acad. Sci.* 1: 253–4.

1932

Review of A. N. Winchell. *A descriptive petrography of the igneous rocks,* vol. 1. *Introduction, textures, classification, and glossary.* Chicago. *J. Geol.* 40:182–5.

1939

The crust of the Earth and its relation to the interior. Reprinted in *Physics of the Earth V. Internal constitution of the Earth,* ed. B. Gutenberg, pp. 91–123. New York: McGraw-Hill.

1951

With L. H. Adams. The chemical and petrological nature of the earth's crust. Reprinted in *Physics of the Earth V. Internal constitution of the Earth,* 2nd ed., B. Gutenberg, pp. 81–106. New York: McGraw-Hill.

Post Scriptum

*On October 4, 1990, while this manuscript was in press, its au-
thor, Charles Milton, died. He was 94 and so eloquent geologist
Brian Skinner was once moved to write to him: "Perhaps you would
have been a professional storyteller had not mineralogy claimed you
first. It would have been mineralogy's loss. . . ."[9] Dr. Milton's correspondence with the editor of the* Biographical Memoirs *includes
much of interest—not only to geologists (many of whom are mentioned therein)—but to all who treasure elegance of style or have
considered the nature and purpose of biography. We are, therefore,
reproducing these letters in their entirety for our readers' information
and pleasure. Their quality honors the memory of the splendid author
who wrote them. Editor's Note*

On April 7, 1989, I wrote to Charles Milton (still to be
found, at 93, in his office at the U.S. Geological Survey) and
invited him to prepare a memoir of Henry Stephens
Washington. Dr. Milton replied immediately and at length:

Dear Dr. Sherman:[10]

When I read your letter of April 7, my first reaction was amazement.
For, incredible as it may seem to you, this last month or two Henry S.
Washington has been very much in my thoughts, and I have wanted to
know a good deal more of his life and work than I do now, and wondered
how to obtain such information. And then out of the blue sky, came your
letter, offering me just that!

Let me explain: For a long time I have been worrying, myself and

---

[9] In a letter from Brian J. Skinner to Charles Milton, dated August 16, 1988,
regarding Milton's historical review of the Oldoinyo Lengai "natrocarbonate lava"
and the account of his long association with Hans Eugster. A copy of this essay is
now in the possession of the National Academy of Sciences archives.

[10] Dr. Milton wrote all his letters to the Academy on a computer, with the type
extending to the extreme edges of the page. The letters printed here are unedited
and include his somewhat idiosyncratic style of punctuation.

other people, about PSEUDOLEUCITE; a mineral which, early in this century, and following his studies of volcanic leucite-bearing lavas in Italy, Washington first identified and named; and ever since, pseudoleucite has become established in petrologic science; notably in studies of Arkansas igneous geology, with which I have long been concerned; e.g. and most recently, Flohr and Ross, 1989. For many years I have hoped that someone would take a very close look at pseudoleucite and its history, seeing that I did not have the data to do it myself. So for that reason alone, were there no other, I would be inclined to give very serious consideration to the pro's and con's of your offer.

Some of the pros: I have vivid memories of Henry S. Washington. I saw him, a towering eminence, at G.S.A. meetings, in years long past; only I may yet remain, with such memories. And many, many were the days when I—and countless students more—pored over his monumental CIPW System of igneous rock classification. From Professor W. S. Bayley (a hundred years ago, he was the first Johns Hopkins geology Ph.D.) did I come to know of the rocks of the earth, and of Henry S. Washington. It is incumbent on us, a pious duty, to record chronicles of the great of our times, for instruction and inspiration of those who will come, when we are gone.

Cons: I am a very old man and know from experience that you propose for me no simple or easy task. And with present commitments, it may well be a year before I could commit myself to steady work on the project, and well take another year, for completion. The odds on being alive, *compos mentis et corpore sano*, at 95, are dubious. . . .

So; if you still wish to consider me for the job, we should meet and discuss it further, with the understanding that it would be next year before I could really get to work on it.

You will understand my natural curiosity as to how you thought of me; we have never met before; and a modest and reclusive disposition has preserved me from public notice. It is however possible that your colleague and my good friend Bill Benson drew your attention to me. If such be the case, please tell him that on the occasion of the Hans Eugster Memorial Symposium in Baltimore last year, I compiled a review of the history of the Oldoinyo Lengai Natrocarbonatite Lava in Tanzania; in which, he figures most creditably indeed. Copies will be available, for anyone interested at the International Geological Congress Alkalic Rock and Carbonatite Symposium in Washington this summer; and I shall send him a copy.

One other possibility is my friend Felix Chayes, former president of the Mineralogical Society of America, and leading authority on chemical igneous rock classification and the Washington-Cross-Iddings-Pirsson (CIPW) System.

If neither of these, could you tell me who?

And one final thought: surely among the obituaries and Memorial pages of many learned journals, there should already be ample recording of the career and accomplishments of a scientist of such great renown as Henry S. Washington? If not, it would indeed be a sad commentary on the evanescence of human fame, that not so long after his death, only some obscure scrivener could be found, to take note, that a great man once lived.

Upon receiving the information that Michael Fleischer, of the National Museum of Natural History, had suggested him as a possible author along with offprints of the memoirs of A. F. Buddington (volume 57) and James Gilluly (volume 56), Dr. Milton immediately replied:[11]

Your letter of April 18 with its most interesting enclosures has given me great pleasure. The impressive picture of Henry S. Washington is just as I remember seeing him; and the accompanying correspondence and his colleagues' memoirs tell me much about him personally that I could not otherwise have known. This material at first glance appears ample for compiling an article such as the two of Arthur ("Bud") Buddington and James ("Jim") Gilluly, two splendid men whom I have known more than just casually: Professor Buddington most helpfully critically reviewed one of my first beginner's publications; and Jim Gilluly some 50 years ago nominated me for G.S.A. Fellow.

And the authors of these memoirs: Harold ("Hal") L. James, senior geologist, U.S.G.S.; and Thomas ("Tom") B. Nolan, former director, U.S.G.S., to whom I owe more than I can ever repay; this was alluded to in a memoir written last year on the occasion of the Johns Hopkins Symposium honoring the memory of a very great geologist, Hans Eugster. (In that memoir, also gratefully acknowledged, by name, is the help at a critical juncture of my life, of National Science Foundation Bill Benson and Dick Ray. Mike Fleischer also had a significant, if unrecorded, part in the tale .... And so it was Mike ("my best friend and implacable critic"), and not Bill Benson or Felix Chayes, who gave you my name. Well, I'll be seeing him at the Museum and will thank him accordingly.

[11] Letter of April 21, 1989.

Strange how your more or less random selection "from a vast majority," of these two memoirs, has evoked this surge of memory . . . there
comes to mind the old Arabian tale, wherein Shaharazad tells of the trav-
eler in the desert, throwing aside pits from his frugal date repast; and
suddenly the sky darkened and from it appeared a monstrous *jinni*, scim-
itar drawn, crying "O vile wretch, prepare to die, for with that stone so
cruelly cast, thou did'st slay my beloved only son!" Whereby, we are instructed, that only Allah, the All-Knowing, knows all of what we do . . .
and, perhaps more to the point here, what we are—or were.

For Henry Stephens Washington has now been dead fifty-five years,
and all who knew him, are gone too; and I may be the only one living who
knew him, even distantly. What then can we now know of him? We have
some contemporary biographic material, and an impressive bibliography
of over 150 books and papers, all solid contributions to science, many
outstanding, even classics, in their day. Obviously he was immensely capable and productive; and furthermore, well endowed with social graces:
a *bon vivant*, and fluent in ten languages, ancient and modern.

His long-time colleague at the Geophysical Laboratory, C. N. Fenner,
a well-known geologist, and Austin H. Clark, fellow-member of the (all-
male) Cosmos Club[12] have written most of what we know of him. Fenner,
in four typed, double-spaced pages, describes him, justly, as "one of the
most eminent and picturesque personalities in American science," and "he
took much delight in associating with congenial friends . . . a many-sided
and exceptional personality, in many ways almost unique." Clark, in three
printed pages, emphasizes his bonhomie and conviviality. Yet, "although
so very well known and so well liked by the Club members, most of them
regarded him as a bit of a mystery, for his really intimate friends were few,
and he was very reserved about his personal affairs."

Now glance at the two memoirs, of Buddington and Gilluly. I have
read them once more, with close attention; as I also did, the recollections
of H. S. Washington by those with whom he worked and lived. Reading
James on Buddington, and Nolan on Gilluly, was a joy: besides it being my
good fortune to have known all four personally, the two memoirs convey
a warmth of feeling for an honored and beloved friend; they also tell of
cherished relationships with students and colleagues; of lifelong happy

---

[12] At the time when Dr. Milton wrote this letter, the Cosmos Club's all-male status
was being challenged in the courts. The reference demonstrates Dr. Milton's keen
involvement with the world, despite his advanced years. (The Club subsequently
resolved the matter by voting to admit women members.) *Editor's note.*

marriages, blest with loving children—on all of these, the recordings of those who once knew and worked with Henry S. Washington, are silent. In his lifetime, he loomed, a towering presence, over lesser mortals; and now he is gone, vanished in thin air; with but a few dry bones and dusty scrolls remaining, to tell us that he once lived among us.

You have asked me, and I have agreed, to write a memoir. But what can I do, more than re-arrange and assemble the wording of the records you have given me; as a palaeontologist would assemble scattered bones, hoping at best to construct a plausible skeleton, not an image, of a creature that once lived and died, long, long ago? A biographer should only write what he knows as fact; and he should not moralize over what he does not know.

With such limitations, if you still wish, I shall try to prepare, to the best of my ability, a Henry S. Washington memoir acceptable for the Academy series, by the end of this year; which of course you are free to accept or reject. But should you now feel that this might be in better hands than mine, please don't hesitate to tell me.

No thought of "better hands" could follow such a letter, and I sent Dr. Milton offprints of memoirs on W. H. Bradley (volume 54), Milton N. Bramlette (volume 52), Ernst Cloos (volume 52), and Chester Ray Longwell (volume 53). Later in our correspondence, Dr. Milton offered the following thoughts on the purpose of biography:[13]

These last few weeks I have been thinking about meeting with you to discuss the Henry Stephens Washington Memorial, on which I have been working: and it was a pleasant surprise to find in your letter of October 3, that you had been thinking likewise. So if convenient for you, a day in November after the 10th would also be [good] for me; I shall have returned from a couple of weeks of meetings in Arkansas and California; and will call you to arrange a day and time, perhaps simplest, in the afternoon at your Academy office.

However, before I leave Washington, you will have a rough draft of what I would think would be appropriate in a Henry Stephens Washington Memoir written today, a half century after his death. You may approve it or disapprove it; in either case, it will certainly be an interesting topic to discuss at our meeting.

[13] Letter of October 5, 1989.

However, you should consider, as my study of the matter has led me to believe, that very special circumstances argue against the National Academy now publishing a Memoir of Washington, modeled on the six splendid examples you gave me to follow (on Gilluly by Nolan, Bradley by McKelvey, Longwell by Rodgers, Buddington by James, Cloos by Waters and Stanley, and Bramlette by Gilluly). Because it has been my good fortune to have known personally most of these thirteen men, there is in my mind no question, but that these Memoirs have well served their purpose of ritual memorialization; written timely, they evoke in their readers responsive sentiments, of taking part in grateful tribute to a departed friend.

For Washington such a Memoir, written now, would be incongruous and redundant. Incongruous, because all who once knew and esteemed him, are now long departed with him. Redundant, because many dear friends did write Memoirs, some wonderfully eloquent and revealing; and in them, ancillary services, bibliographies and portraits. There is a time for everything; and in my opinion, worthy Memoirs of Washington have already been duly written, thirty, forty, fifty years ago. One more such, appearing today, would only be perceived as a belated and awkward gesture by the Academy, in discharge of a duty long neglected.

Then what may there be, that should be done? There is a way, that would both honor his memory, and be a service to geologists of this generation, and of those to come. In my reading of all I could find on Washington's life and work, I learned that Henry Stephens Washington was truly a most memorable, indeed almost super-human being. And it is by pondering the lives of great men, that we ourselves become inspired to strive for whatever small measure of achievement we may attain.

As a child, I read Longfellow's

"Lives of great men all remind us
We can make our lives sublime,
And departing, leave behind us
Footprints on the sands of Time."

and now that I am an old man, and perhaps a bit wiser, I will say that this jingle, for all its preachy patter, really has a grain of truth.

Washington's story has been told, and told well; but in scattered, fragmentary articles, often difficult to find. A comprehensive and definitive account of the main events of his life and works, assembled from many sources and retold in the eloquent words of their authors; with an annotated listing of sources of information, and of published bibliographies; portraits; and a critical summary and evaluation, by an outstanding authority in the fields of geochemical and petrological science, of Washington's role in establishing their basic standards—this I think would be a project which the Academy might consider.

I already have the first four of the six biographic notices which you list. The fifth is presumably in Italian, but I would like to see it, and will try to get it translated. The sixth, also by Pelloux (?) may be in French; I have not seen it and will read it. Both are probably in our Geological Survey Library.

. . . Since you have expressed some interest in my style of writing, a few more items are enclosed: the unfortunate Wilhelm Eitel Memoir;[14] something I wrote last year in connection with a Memorial Symposium honoring Hans P. Eugster (1925–1987); and a recent contribution, read in July at the International Geological Congress Symposium on Alkalic Rocks and Carbonatites.[15] You may find them mildly interesting. (Lots of others didn't, though.)

After a trip to Arkansas and California, Dr. Milton sent in a draft of the Washington memoir and promised to come to the Academy for lunch. He also submitted his article to Felix Chayes, Michael Fleischer, and Hatten S. Yoder for review. On December 27, the Academy received a revised version of the Washington memoir forwarded by Dr. Nancy J. Byrd at Dr. Milton's request.[16] She informed us that Dr. Milton had fallen down his steps, fracturing his cheekbone and five ribs. On March 23, 1990, I sent back the edited manuscript and received a reply from Dr. Milton's son, Daniel J. Milton (also a geologist with the U.S. Geological Survey in Reston, Vir-

[14] Dr. Milton had written a biography of Eitel for Scribners' *Dictionary of Scientific Biography*, only to have it "bowdlerized, amputated, gutted" when that publication came under new management. "There was nothing I could do about it," the unhappy author wrote, "not even wipe my name off the mutilated carcass; for they had paid me $50 and it was legally their property."

[15] See n. 9 above.

[16] She also sent several papers Dr. Milton had published, including the "Note on a Drawing by M. C. Escher," *Journal of the Washington Academy of Sciences* 63(1973):91, in which Dr. Milton (citing the contribution of David Fleischer) discusses the philosophical significance of the chess position, "smothered doom," pictured in the Escher drawing, *Metamorphose*.

ginia), who kindly read over the manuscript and answered my queries:

My father is very pleased to see the edited H. S. Washington ms. . . . [He] is much better. Earlier in the winter I would have thought the chance of his reaching his 94th birthday, which is three weeks from tomorrow, was negligible, but he is getting along pretty strongly. He can read, which he couldn't for the first two or three months, and even get out of bed with help and take a few steps with a walker. Most important, his mood is vastly improved, and consequently that of everyone involved with him also. . . .

Charles Milton lived well into his 94th year. His letters reflect a breadth of education, engagement with the world, and enthusiasm rare at any age. It is a pleasure to include his correspondence here, together with his final published work—a tribute to a scientist he so much admired. E. J. Sherman, Editor

Howel Williams

HOWEL WILLIAMS

October 12, 1898-January 12, 1980

BY ALEXANDER R. McBIRNEY

IT IS NOT AN EXAGGERATION to say that Howel Williams, through his own work and that of his students, was largely responsible for the emergence of volcanology as a rigorous branch of modern science. Few have left so pervasive an imprint on their fields; even fewer have inspired wider admiration or deeper affection.

Less interested in the eruptive phenomena of active volcanism than in broad structural and petrographic relations, he had a masterful ability to reconstruct the forms and histories of long-extinct volcanic provinces. It was his uncanny eye for landforms and the regional significance of lithologic relations that enabled him to synthesize the evolution of entire provinces from a few seasons of field reconnaissance and petrographic studies.

EDUCATION AND CAREER

Born in Liverpool, England, Howel Williams was raised along with his identical twin, David, and six other children in a modest middle-class household. He spoke only Welsh until the age of six. His father recognized young Howel's ability early and encouraged his intellectual ambitions. With the help of a series of awards and scholarships, he began the career that soon brought him international repute as one of the foremost igneous geologists of his time.

Williams's academic record was an unbroken series of achievements and scholastic honors. The potential he displayed in secondary school won him a scholarship to the University of Liverpool where, despite an interruption for military duty from 1917 to 1918, he received his bachelor's degree with first class honors before the age of twenty. Though his initial studies were in geography, he soon developed a keen interest in archeology, which in turn, by a singular combination of events, led him to geology.

While engaged in excavations of a Roman camp site in northern Wales, he observed that the floor of the baths was paved with slabs of slate rich in curious fossils. Anxious to learn where the Romans had quarried the slate, he consulted Professor P. G. H. Boswell of Liverpool's Department of Geology. It so happened that Boswell was then studying the Silurian rocks of Denbighshire and immediately recognized the source from the nature of the slate and its distinctive graptolites. Williams was so impressed with this instant solution to his problem that he began to sit in on lectures in geology and, after receiving his M.A. degree in geography, went on to earn an M.S. in geology in 1924.

With his geology degree came another scholarship that enabled him to further his studies at Imperial College. There, working chiefly under Professor W. W. Watts, he completed a detailed study of Snowdon in North Wales. The abundant Ordovician volcanic rocks he encountered there and in the area near Capel Curig aroused his interest in volcanism and led him to the classic volcanic fields of the Eifel district of Germany and the Auvergne in central France. He returned with a firm resolve to make volcanic geology his principal work. Thanks to a fellowship from the Commonwealth Fund he was able to devote the next two years to studies with Professor A. C. Lawson at the University of California at Berkeley. Apart from a single seminar dealing with the geology of California, he took no formal courses while at Berkeley, devoting his time to field studies instead. He concentrated on the ancient volcanoes of the Sutter Buttes in the Sacramento Valley of California and on Lassen Peak, a recently active volcano in the southern part of the Cascade Range. In addition to all this he found time to visit Hawaii and Tahiti.

After two years at Berkeley, Williams returned to Britain to take his D.Sc. in geology at the University of Liverpool in 1928. He then spent two years on the staff of Imperial College before returning to join the faculty at Berkeley in 1930. There he rose to the rank of full professor in just seven years. Between 1945 and 1949 he served as chairman of Berkeley's Department of Geology, doing much to raise the quality of its faculty, teaching, and research. It was largely his influence during these critical postwar years that set the course of the department and helped bring it into the ranks of leading American institutions. He was elected to the National Academy of Sciences in 1950, and two years later was named William Smith Lecturer of the Geological Society of London.

FIELD WORK AND MAJOR PUBLICATIONS

Williams continued his studies of volcanoes in the western United States, particularly at Crater Lake, where his work formed the basis for two of his most important contributions, a monograph on Crater Lake and a general treatise on the origin of calderas. The rapid succession of papers that resulted from this period included many that soon became classics of volcanology. He dealt with volcanic domes, the classification of pyroclastic rocks, the Pliocene volcanic centers of the Navajo-Hopi region, and accounts of several large volcanic centers of the Cascade Range, including Newberry Caldera and The Three Sisters.

Following World War II, during which he worked with the U. S. Geological Survey on the quicksilver deposits of Oregon, his attention began to turn from the Cascades toward Mexico and Central America. When the volcano Parícutin was born in a Mexican cornfield, he joined a group of geologists recording its growth and evolution and completed a reconnaissance study of more than a hundred small cinder cones in the surrounding region.

In Latin America he found opportunities to put to good use his early background in archeology. He used petrographic techniques to trace the origin of stone used in the giant Olmec sculptures of La Venta near the Gulf Coast of Mexico, and in 1950, with the support of the Carnegie Institution of Washington, went to Nicaragua to examine ancient, human footprints near Managua.

While in Nicaragua, Williams was able to delve into the geologic effects and historical records of the great eruption of Coseguina in 1835. This was the beginning of a succession of regional studies which, though less widely known than his work on calderas and domes, was more remarkable, both for its scope and for the extent of its contribution to the previously little-known field of Central American geology.

In 1952 Williams published the first survey of the volcanic geology of central Costa Rica. Three years later, together with Helmut Meyer-Abich, he completed an extensive survey of the volcanoes of El Salvador. This was followed, in 1960, by a study of the great volcanic cones of the Guatemalan Highlands and, in 1964, by a reconnaissance of southeastern Guatemala. (This latter work provided my first occasion to work with Williams in the field and was the beginning of a long and fruitful collaboration.)

In 1965 we completed a survey of the volcanic geology of

Nicaragua and, in 1969, a similar one of Honduras. These last two studies, and one of the Galápagos Archipelago (also completed in 1969) were, in terms of the shear scope of work, the most impressive of Williams's career. All three involved large regional studies where few, if any, geologists had gone before; they allowed us to explore the geology of virtually unknown regions and to work out broad structural and stratigraphic relations of a fascinating volcanic province. Those delightful years of working closely with Williams in the field were, by any measure, the most valuable experience of my career.

In addition to regional field studies, Williams's postwar work produced, in 1954, a popular textbook on petrography and, in 1979, a comprehensive treatise on volcanology. The former was the result of collaboration with Frank Turner and Charles Gilbert at the University of California, the latter a product of the years he spent with me at the University of Oregon following his retirement from Berkeley. Published only two months before his death, *Volcanology* summed up a lifetime's experience and, despite more recent advances, is still widely regarded as the most comprehensive work on the subject.

IN CONCLUSION

All of Williams's published work is characterized by elegant simplicity and clarity, and the same qualities also pervaded his teaching. His courses in petrography and regional geology were illustrated by artistic, hand-drawn diagrams and lucid, colorful, descriptions that left an indelible impression on hundreds of students. His work tended to be more qualitative than quantitative; it emphasized sound descriptions and insightful, deductive reasoning based on observed field relations.

He was at his best pioneering little-known regions, deducing basic geological relations and characterizing petrographic provinces. He was never happier than when travelling by jeep through back regions of Central America, eating tortillas and beans in tiny native villages, joking in Spanish with Indians, and all the while piecing together a new chapter of regional geology.

Though known to most of his friends as "Willie," the title he cherished most was given him by students on the occasion of his retirement: "The Last of the Ordovices" reflected the Welsh background that had dominated Williams's formative years and the undercurrent of classicism that colored his charming joviality and irreverent wit. All who worked with him recognized his penetrating judgment and ability to see through pretense, but few realized that his genial informality masked a deep personal reserve and uncompromising principles of conduct.

Williams's fifty-year career spanned an era of dramatic changes in geology. The classical methods of scholarship, meticulous observations, and elegantly written monographs in which he was trained gave way to complex geochemical and thermodynamic calculations compiled by computers and reported in hastily prepared, multi-authored papers of transient interest. Although he himself contributed to this change and on balance approved of it, Williams was never really part of it. To the end, he was a natural scientist in the classic mode. In that respect, his death was more than a personal loss, for it was also the passing of a style that will never be seen again.

SELECTED BIBLIOGRAPHY

1922

Excavations of bronze-age tumulus near Gorsedd, Flintshire, North Wales. *Archaeol. Cambrensis*, 7th ser., vol. 2:265–89.

Igneous rocks of the Capel Curig district, North Wales. *Proc. Liverpool Geol. Soc.* 13:166–202.

1923

Romano-British site at Rhostryfan, Carnarvonshire, North Wales. *Archaeol. Cambrensis*, 7th ser., vol. 3:335–45.

1926

Notes on the characters and classification of pyroclastic rocks. *Proc. Liverpool Geol. Soc.* 17:223–48.

1927

Geology of Snowdon, North Wales. *Q. J. Geol. Soc. London* 83:346-431.

1928

A recent volcanic eruption near Lassen Peak, California. *Bull. Dept. Geol. Sci. Univ. Calif.* 17:241–63.

1929

Volcanic domes of Lassen Peak and vicinity, California. *Am. J. Sci.* 18:313–30.

Geology of the Marysville Buttes, California. *Bull. Dept. Geol. Sci. Univ. Calif.* 18:103–220.

1930

With E. Greenly. *Methods of Geological Surveying*. London: Thos. Murby & Company. 420 pp.

Notes on the later geological history of Tahiti. *Bull. Dept. Geol. Sci Univ. Calif.* 19:119–35.

The Snowdon district. *Proc. Geol. Assoc. London* 41:190–205.

1931

Dacites of Lassen Peak and vicinity and their basic inclusions. *Am. J. Sci.* 20:313–30.

Geology of the Dolwyddelen syncline, North Wales. *Q. J. Geol. Soc. London* 87:425–58.

1932

Mount Shasta, California. *J. Geol.* 40:417–29.

Geology of Lassen Volcanic National Park, California. *Bull. Dept. Geol. Sci. Univ. Calif.* 21:195–385.

The history and character of volcanic domes. *Bull. Dept. Geol. Sci. Univ. Calif.* 21:51–146.

With C. K. Wentworth. Classification and terminology of the pyroclastic rocks. *Bull. Nat. Res. Coun.* 89:19–53.

1933

Geology of Tahiti, Moorea, and Maiao. *B. P. Bishop Museum Bull.* 105. 89 pp.

Mount Thielsen, a dissected cascade volcano. *Bull. Dept. Geol. Sci. Univ. Calif.* 23:195–214.

1934

Mount Shasta, California. *Z. Vulk.* 15:225–53.

1935

Newberry Volcano of central Oregon. *Bull. Geol. Soc. Am.* 46:253–304.

With R. D. Evans. Radium content of lavas from Lassen Volcanic National Park. *Am. J. Sci.* 29:441–52.

1936

Pliocene volcanoes of the Navajo-Hopi country. *Bull. Geol. Soc. Am.* 47:111–72.

1940

With L. S. Cressman. Early man in south-central Oregon. *Univ. Oregon Monogr., Studies in Anthropology* 3:53–78.

1941

Crater Lake, the story of its origin. Berkeley: University of California Press. 97 pp.

Volcanology, 1888–1938. *50th Anniv. Vol., Geol. Soc. Am.,* pp. 367–90.

Calderas and their origin. *Bull. Dept. Geol. Sci. Univ. Calif.* 25: 239–346.

1942

Geology of Crater Lake National Park, Oregon. Carnegie Inst. Washington, pub. no. 540. 162 pp.

1944

Volcanoes of the Three Sisters Region, Oregon Cascades. *Bull. Dept. Geol. Sci. Univ. Calif.* 27:37–84.

1948

Ancient volcanoes of Oregon. Condon Lecture, Oregon State System Higher Education. 55 pp.

1949

Geology of the Macdoel Quadrangle. *Calif. State Div. Mines Bull.* 151:8–78.

1950

Volcanoes of the Parícutin region, Mexico. *U.S. Geol. Surv. Bull.* 965-B:165–279.

1951

With A. C. Waters. Quicksilver deposits of the Horse Heaven Mining District, Oregon. *U.S. Geol. Surv. Bull.* 969-E:105–49.

Volcanoes. *Sci. Am.* Nov.:3–11.

1952

Volcanic history of the Meseta Central Occidental, Costa Rica. *Bull. Dept. Geol. Sci. Univ. Calif.* 29:145–80.

The Great Eruption of Coseguina in Nicaragua in 1835. *Bull. Dept. Geol. Sci. Univ. Calif.* 29:21–46.

Geological observations on the ancient human footprints near

Managua, Nicaragua. Carnegie Inst. Washington, pub. no. 596. 31 pp.

1953

With R. R. Compton. Quicksilver deposits of Steens and Pueblo Mountains, southeast Oregon. *U.S. Geol. Surv. Bull.* 995-B: 19–77.

1954

Problems and progress in volcanology. *Q. J. Geol. Soc. London* 109:311–332.
With F. J. Turner and C. M. Gilbert. *Petrography.* San Francisco: W. H. Freeman & Co. 406 pp.

1955

With H. Meyer-Abich. Volcanism in the southern part of El Salvador. *Univ. Calif. Pub. Geol. Sci.* 32:1–64.

1957

Geologic maps of the Bend Quadrangle and of the central portion of the High Cascade Mountains. *Oregon Dept. Geol. Min. Ind.*
Glowing avalanche deposits of the Sudbury Basin. *Ontario Dept. Mines* 65:57–89.

1960

Volcanic history of the Guatemalan Highlands. *Univ. Calif. Pub. Geol. Sci.* 38:1–86.

1961

The floor of Crater Lake. *Am. J. Sci.* 259:81–83.

1963

With R. F. Heizer. Geologic notes on the Idolo de Coatlichan. *Am. Antiq.* 29:95–98.

1964

With A. R. McBirney and G. Dengo. Geologic reconnaissance of southeastern Guatemala. *Univ. Calif. Pub. Geol. Sci.* 50:1–56.

1965

With A. R. McBirney. Volcanic history of Nicaragua. *Univ. Calif. Pub. Geol. Sci.* 55:1–73.

1969

With A. R. McBirney. Volcanic history of Honduras. *Univ. Calif. Pub. Geol. Sci.* 85:1–101.

With A. R. McBirney. Geology and petrology of the Galápagos Islands. *Geol. Soc. Am. Mem.* 118. 197 pp.

1977

With G. H. Curtis. The Sutter Buttes of California: a study of Pio-Pleistocene volcanism. *Univ. Calif. Pub. Geol. Sci.* 116:1–56.

1979

With A. R. McBirney. *Volcanology.* San Francisco: Freeman & Cooper. 397 pp.

CUMULATIVE INDEX

A

B

NOTE: An asterisk (*) indicates volumes 17 and 21 of the scientific *Memoir* series, which correspond to volumes 10 and 11, respectively, of the *Biographical Memoirs.*